199 Great Home Businesses
You Can Start (and Succeed In)
for Under $1,000

Other Books by Tyler G. Hicks

How to Start Your Own Business on a Shoestring and Make Up to $500,000 a Year, 4th Revised Edition

203 Home-Based Businesses That Will Make You Rich

101 Great Mail-Order Businesses

Mail-Order Success Secrets, Revised 2nd Edition

199 Great Home Businesses You Can Start (and Succeed In) for Under $1,000

How to Choose the Best
Home Businesses for You
Based on Your Personality Type

Revised 2nd Edition

Tyler G. Hicks

THREE RIVERS PRESS
NEW YORK

Published by Three Rivers Press, New York, New York.
Member of the Crown Publishing Group, a division of Random House, Inc.
www.randomhouse.com

THREE RIVERS PRESS and the Tugboat design are registered trademarks of Random House, Inc.

Originally published by Prima Publishing, Roseville, California, in 1999.

Printed in the United States of America

Library of Congress Cataloging-in-Publication Data
Hicks, Tyler Gregory.
    199 great home businesses you can start (and succeed in) for
under $1,000 : how to choose the best home business for you
based on your personality type / Tyler G. Hicks.—2nd ed.
        p. cm.
    Includes bibliographical references and index.
    1. Home-based businesses. 2. New business enterprises.
I. Title. 11. Title: One hundred ninety-nine great home businesses
you can start (and succeed in) for under $1,000.
HD2333.H53 1999
658. 1'141—dc21   98-50841
                                                     CIP
ISBN 978-0-7615-1743-6

20 19 18 17 16 15 14 13

Second Edition

CONTENTS

CHAPTER 9
50 UNUSUAL HOME BUSINESSES THAT CAN MAKE YOU HAPPY
AND WEALTHY   194

CHAPTER 10
QUICK TIPS FOR STARTING AND PROSPERING IN THE HOME BUSINESS OF YOUR CHOICE 226

RESOURCES: PROFIT-BUILDING TOOLS FROM TYLER HICKS'S INTERNATIONAL WEALTH SUCCESS LIBRARY 255

INDEX 269

Introduction

WHAT THIS BOOK WILL DO FOR YOU

Are you out of work? Strapped for cash? Having trouble making ends meet? Fighting with a complaining spouse who spends faster than you can earn? Do you hate to go to work because your boss is such a pain? Want to stay home to care for someone?

If you answered *Yes* to any of these questions, this book is for *you!* Why? Because this book shows you how to:

- Pick the best business for yourself
- Start your own home business for under $1,000
- Build your fortune in a business *you* like
- Run a business by not leaving your home, or
- Run a business from home while working outside the home
- Profit from unusual business ideas
- Get to know the earnings potentials of hundreds of home businesses
- Finance the business of your choice
- Use the latest technology—personal computer, fax, Internet, e-mail, cell phones, etc.—either in whole or in part in your home business, if you wish to do so, or
- Make use of familiar "low-tech" postal mail, typewriters, and traditional phones to run your home business at a comfortable pace that brings you the income you seek
- Advertise and promote your business
- Comply with the various rules governing home businesses in your area
- Get a merchant credit card account so you can accept credit card charges by your customers

Any home business has many advantages over a business in which you rent space to conduct your profit-making activities. Most home businesses have no, or very little, overhead. This means that more of every sales dollar stays in your pocket because you're not paying money for rent, storage space, or other occupancy needs.

And there are plenty of other savings for you in your own home business. Costs of commuting will be mostly non-existent. And you won't generally have to spend money on expensive go-to-meeting clothes. Nor will you need costly luggage, or plane or train tickets.

More importantly to some people, a home business gives you independence. You can almost always choose your work hours, be they early or late. You don't have to conform to someone else's rigid schedule. *You* make your own schedule. What's more, if you don't like a potential customer you can casually decline to do business with him or her. Try that with a boss when you're working for a salary!

Today, there's even an acronym for small home businesses—*SOHO*—meaning Small Office/Home Office. An entire army of suppliers is ready to serve the SOHO market—office-equipment vendors, phone companies, computer manufacturers, fax-machine sellers, cell-phone dealers, and so forth. And with the Internet providing a worldwide market at your fingertips, the sales potential for your home-based products or services has zoomed far beyond customers in your local area. Truly, a home business is today's ticket to a safe, secure financial future for you and your family.

Since most people are scared at the thought of starting their own home business, this book does the following for *you:*

- Shows you why you should start your own home business, and the many benefits you can derive from such a business
- Helps you choose the *best* home business for yourself, based on your likes and dislikes, skills and experience
- Gives you the 27 easiest home businesses to start anywhere in the world
- Shows you the 32 home businesses that will produce the quickest cash flow into your business checking account

- Details the 26 simplest stay-at-home businesses so you don't have to leave home to earn your fortune
- Outlines the 26 most profitable go-out home businesses, where you work outside your home but still have a home business of your own
- Sketches the 26 most popular "people" home businesses where you work with others to build your fortune
- Shows you the 26 most private "non-people" home businesses where you have little, or no, contact with others
- Explains 50 unusual home businesses that can make you both happy and wealthy

For each of the 199 great home businesses in this book (any of which *you* can start for under $1,000) you're given these key details:

- *Name of the business*—that is, what the business is usually called by its owners.
- *What you do*—the duties you perform to earn the income you get from the home business. The description of the duties will tell you whether the business is for you, or if you should look for another business.
- *How to find clients*—and every business needs clients or customers, and we tell you how, and where, to find them for your business. This is a crucial item for any successful business.
- *Money required to start*—the cash you need to get your business going so you start to earn a profit. Since any of these businesses can be started for less than $1,000, you know in advance that your outlay will be low. (Where special equipment is needed for your business we assume that you'll rent it at the start, rather than buying, to keep your startup costs small.)
- *Earnings potential*—how much you can earn from the business on an annual basis. This is before your direct expenses, but these, in most cases, will be little more than postage, telephone, Internet, and fax costs. A range of earnings is given, from startup income to all-out full-time work income for the experienced home wealth builder. The income range given represents actual numbers achieved

by the some 3 million home workers in business for themselves today.

- *Time for first earnings*—this tells you how long you'll have to work before you receive your first income payment. For folks interested in a fast cash flow, this section of the business description will be important.

- *Equipment needed*—tells you what basic equipment you must have to start your business. In those businesses where a personal computer (PC) is needed, we assume that you already own one, or have access to a PC. The cost of the PC is *not* included in the *Money Required to Start* section because PC costs vary so widely, depending on what you buy and which peripherals you choose. Further, where we suggest a typewriter for your business, we do so because such machines are usually cheaper than a PC, can often be obtained free of charge as a hand-me-down, and still get the job done, even though they're slower and more cumbersome than a PC printer. The world got along on the typewriter for 100 years before the PC and still accepts a neatly typed letter. Many startup home businesses begin with a typewriter as their main machine.

The 199+ businesses recommended for you in this book combine the unusual and the seldom-thought-of activities I've encountered in more than 35 years of advising Beginning Wealth Builders (BWBs). I'm certain that there's at least one business in this book for *you!* If this business isn't exactly the one I recommend, then it's a variant one recommended.

When thinking of a home business, remember that you may find it profitable to run two or more activities from your home. Why? Because this can ensure that you have income in both up and down economies. Your goal in opening your own home business is to have an independent income. Anything you can do to ensure a steady, sufficient, and dependable cash flow is worth the effort!

Since I'm advising BWBs every day of the week, even on weekends, I stand ready to help you get started in your own home business. How? By answering any questions you may have. Call me on the phone, fax me, or mail me your questions about home businesses and I'll be happy to answer them. I'll even consider helping you finance your own home business. (You must have a written business plan if you seek such financing.)

To help you get a flavor of how I work and why I believe in borrowing your way to a great fortune in your own home business, I suggest that you subscribe to my newsletters, described at the back of this book. These newsletters give you hundreds of business ideas each year, along with valuable sources of financing every month. What's more, I have a special affinity for my subscribers. Why? Because they know that I believe in building great wealth from a small start.

So come along with me, good friend, and we'll put you into your own successful home business using the tools you're comfortable with—computers, e-mail, faxes, Internet, cell phones, or traditional postage stamps, mailboxes, typewriters, and telephones. Along the way I'll be as close to you as your phone, ready to answer questions and make suggestions. You *can* get rich in your own home business! All you need do is get started—right here and *now.*

Tyler G. Hicks

CHAPTER 1

WHY START YOUR OWN HOME BUSINESS?

THERE ARE HUNDREDS of reasons for starting your own home business. And *your* reasons may be a lot different from my reasons. But the whole key is this:

> You must know why you want to start your own home business. Knowing why gives your whole business life focus and helps you become more successful, sooner.

But before we show you some of the key reasons for starting your own home business, let's define what we mean by a home business. Then we'll both have an understandable frame of reference.

What Is a Home Business?

A home business is one which you run from some space in your own home. This home could be a single family residence, an apartment, a condo, a mobile home, a boat, etc. The space you use could be your living room, a garage, a basement, an attic, a den, a kitchen, even a bedroom.

Your business might be conducted entirely in the home—you make pies, toys, sculptures, etc. and people come to your home to buy them. Or your business might be partly or wholly outside your home—you travel to other homes or businesses to perform computer programming or maintenance, or lawn care. In such businesses your advertising, sales, and bookkeeping are done in your home, just as they are for a business conducted solely within the home.

In essence, a home business is one in which you do not rent external space to conduct your normal profit-making activities. So you do *not* have any rent to pay for the business because you already own or pay rent for your living accommodations.

Don't scoff at the idea of a home business. Apple Computer and Hewlett-Packard—both billion-dollar enterprises today—started in different garages on the West Coast. The Diebold Group, well-known data processing specialists, started in a bedroom on the East Coast. And the inventor of the ever-popular La-Z-Boy reclining chairs developed them in his Midwest home garage. At this writing, worldwide sales are in the $1-billion range. In the Far West, a young married couple runs a residential mortgage company out of their home. Their mortgage placements are booming!

While your ambitions may not run to starting a billion-dollar business, these brief examples show what can happen when you offer a needed product or service that provides high quality at a competitive price. The world may beat a path to your door!

Now that you know that your home business will be headquartered in your home—with possible outside activities—let's see why you should consider starting your own home business. We'll give you plenty of familiar reasons which will reinforce your resolve to improve yourself! I started my own home business over 30 years ago and it keeps me in a beautiful home with lots of spending money. You, too, can do the same!

And with today's lightning-fast advances in communications—the Internet, e-mail, fax, cell phone, voice mail, pagers, laptop computers—it is easier than ever to succeed big in your own home business. Today you can make it bigger—sooner—with less work!

Why Start One?

Here are 12 good reasons to start your own home business. Among them I'm sure you'll find a number that apply directly to you. Some may even expand on your own thoughts about getting started.

BUILD AN INDEPENDENT INCOME FREE OF BOSSES

When you're on a payroll you almost always have a boss in charge of your life most of the day. What's more, *your* income depends on the success of other people in the organization. You are *not* independent, and neither is your income.

In your own home business your income depends on *your* efforts. So if times are tough you can work longer hours to overcome a falloff in sales. When you work for someone else, you may be "rewarded" in tough times by being laid off, downsized, or otherwise deprived of income.

With an independent income, your earnings come to you *first.* There are *no* deductions for federal income tax withholding, state income tax withholding, medical and dental benefits, union dues, etc. *You* receive *all* the money due you. If $500 is payable to you for work you performed, you receive $500—not $388.82 after all deductions are taken out!

So your home business gives you independence, freedom, and opportunity that no salaried job could ever offer. What's more, your earnings can be much higher than you've ever dreamt they could be.

FREE YOURSELF OF LAYOFF THREATS

When you work for someone else you're at their mercy. You can be fired in an instant. No matter how many years you've put in with a company, you can be called in, told to pack your tool kit, and be out of the building within a few hours.

Or your boss can "suggest" that you take early retirement at a sharply reduced pension payment. You've been fired, even though it sounds like the company gave you a big break by "allowing" you to retire early. The company will generously allow you to spend more time with your family. What's not mentioned is that your income will be reduced so much that everyone in the family will have to try to find work to keep the home together!

In recent years hundreds of thousands of white- and blue-collar workers have been laid off from their jobs. To many of these workers, the layoff was a rude awakening to the real world. For years they gave all to the company, thinking they had a secure job. Not so! Companies don't have a heart, nor does a company have compassion when it comes to cutting expenses by downsizing to reduce the workforce.

In your own home business you're the boss! *You* do the hiring and firing. Knowing what a horror it is to be laid off, you'll never do that to yourself! You'll keep yourself on the payroll for as long as you want.

What's more, in your own home business *you* determine what to do. You don't have a snarling boss telling you to get out by 3 P.M. and never return. Instead, you figure out how you can increase the income in your home business so you end each week with more money in your pocket! So to get away from layoff horrors, start your own home business.

EARN MORE MONEY THAN ON A ROUTINE JOB

No job ever pays you what you're really worth! Companies get rich using your skills, your drive, your know-how, and your enthusiasm. But you're paid only a pittance for what you give to the company and its success.

Why waste your time and energy working for peanuts when you can grow rich in your own home business? Only fools squander their skills for low pay on menial jobs. Ask for a larger income in life and do you know what you'll get? *A larger income!*

As some of my readers know, I publish two monthly newsletters for Beginning Wealth Builders (BWBs, we call them). Almost every day of the week we get one or more letters from our BWB readers saying something like:

"I started my own business in my home. It's going far better than in my wildest dreams. Before I started this business I was working my head off and getting nowhere. Today my time is my own. I work when I feel like working. And my income is four times what it was when I held a job."

Or

"Following your plan, I placed an $8 ad in the local paper and did over $4,000 gross sales in the very beginning. The ad was originally run to see how strong the response would be. After that, it not only merited, but demanded, full-time attention. Without the guidelines you set down, who knows what would have happened?"

Or

"I have engaged in financial brokerage for three years. Most of my work is real-estate related. Last year I closed $873,000 through 28 loans. Several were over $100,000 but most of my applications average $25,000."

Or

"When I started in rental real estate I purchased a total of 33 units the first year with just $10,000 in money borrowed from a bank. Most of these properties are single-family homes. I do have one duplex, one triplex, and one 5-unit apartment building."

Or

"Inspired by your newsletter, I recently began my own mail-order business. Response has been better than expected."

Or

"After reading your book, *How to Borrow Your Way to Real Estate Riches,* I bought my first piece of commercial property. Listed at $675,000, I bought it from the owner for $384,000 with nothing down, a zero-percent interest 20-year loan. I have already been offered a $100,000 profit and assumption of my note with its payments."

Or

"I am getting a very good response to my ad in your newsletter. I had no idea the response was going to be this good."

When you have your own business at home, every dollar you earn is a more powerful one than a dollar you earn on a job. Why? Because a home-income dollar:

• Comes to you free of any withholding or other deductions
• Stays with you for up to three months (one quarter) before any taxes have to be paid on it
• Has certain legitimate no-cash tax deductions included in it, such as depreciation charges for machinery and home space which the business uses and occupies
• Can include allowances for transportation (such as the business use of an automobile)
• Allows you certain expenses for legitimate business costs associated with advertising, publicity, research and development, and entertainment of business associates for the purpose of building taxable sales income

What all of this means is that more of your business dollar stays with you than does a job dollar. The result: *You earn much more for every minute you work in your own home business.* While people will tell you "Money isn't everything," most of us have trouble living without it.

So recognize the facts. You *can*, and *will*, make more in your own home business . . . if you follow my suggestions. I've earned some $10 million in my spare-time home business while serving as the chief executive of two lending organizations. And thousands of my readers throughout the world are right now—today—earning big money in their own home business, using many of my ideas.

HAVE MORE TIME FOR YOURSELF

Today time is more important than money to many people. You'll often hear that "the 64 hours between 5 P.M. Friday and 9 A.M. Monday are the most important hours in the week."

Why do people say this about these 64 hours? Because *free time* away from the job and a surly boss is what they treasure. Work is a bore—just a necessity to pay the bills produced by having fun!

The trouble is that holding a job limits you to your 64-hour weekends and a two- or three-week annual vacation. Your time isn't your own. What's more, your paltry salary limits what you can do with the meager free time you do have!

Start your own home business and you can have endless weekends once you're up and running. Your "weekend" can start at 5 P.M. Thursday and go until 9 A.M. Tuesday. That's the way I've run my life in my own home business for years. And I take "working stiffs" (regular job holders) out on my beautiful new motoryacht on *their* days off, Saturday and Sunday.

Many of these people are big shots on their job. They're puffed-up executives overimpressed with their job title and importance. Yet they don't have two extra dimes to rub together because their salary is spent three months before they get it!

You can have more time for yourself and your loved ones in your own home business than on any job. What's more, you may work at home with your spouse, bringing you closer together.

And once your business is solidly established, you can get part-time workers to run the business for you. This will give you more time to do what you want to do with the rest of your life. You really can't beat a home business for larger income and more free time. What's more, you won't have to put up with threatening and bullying bosses who constantly remind you that a layoff could be just around the corner!

BUILD A TRUE BIG-BUCK RETIREMENT INCOME

In your own business you're entitled to put money away for your retirement, tax-free. The business gets a legitimate deduction for the money it puts away for your retirement.

And the money put away is *not* taxed to you until you start taking it as a pension! Could you ask for a better deal?

In my newsletter publishing business, named International Wealth Success, Inc., which we've run from home for more than 30 years, we have our pension plan with a large insurance company. The money we've put into the plan has been invested by the insurance company. Over the years these tax-deductible dollars have grown by more than ten times!

You can also set up a profit-sharing plan for your home business. It uses tax-deductible dollars also. And the proceeds aren't taxable to members of the plan until they start collecting them.

Older, retired friends of mine who ran their own home businesses live like kings. Their business taxes were lower while they ran their business because they put away tax-deductible dollars for their future retirement. And when they started collecting the pension from their home business, the monthly payment was far larger than they would have received on a job. Their monthly pension check from their own home business is three to ten times the Social Security check.

To set up the pension plan for your own home business you need the advice of a qualified accountant. That person will also help you set up the books for your business, do your tax returns, and help you in other ways. Don't try to do your own accounting—you'll miss out on the many legitimate benefits open to you as the owner of a home business.

So if the idea of retirement "grabs" you, think home business! You can get a larger pension on your own than any employer will ever provide for you. With some 90 percent of the senior citizens at near-poverty level on Social Security, building a strong pension income for yourself is almost a necessity in today's tough economy.

Take Vacations When—and Where—You Want

When you work for a large (or small) company as a paid employee, your vacation options are limited by the amount of time you can take off. Further, you'll often find that your co-workers and boss are envious if you take an exotic vacation (that you may have saved years for) while they can't afford even a rented camper.

In your own home business you're free as a bird to take long or short vacations, on *your* schedule. In my own home business I take a summer vacation on my yacht. Then in the winter I take a Caribbean vacation to get away from the cold weather for a while.

If I were working for a company, I could never afford my yacht. And I'm positive I could never earn enough to pay the cost of two weeks in the Virgin Islands in January or February. Yet with my own home business I can afford both these pleasures, which my family and I enjoy.

When your home business requires travel—as some do, as we'll see later—you can often combine your vacation with business travel. This way you'll save money on air or train fares and lodging. Your accountant can advise you on the rules covering the tax aspects of business travel.

So if you want vacation freedom (and who doesn't?) get your own home business. You'll be as free as a bird to come and go on *your* schedule!

INCREASE YOUR INCOME WITHOUT HAVING TO PLEAD

On a job your income is somewhat fixed. Sure, you may get a 5 percent raise each year. But a raise of this size won't keep you in the luxury items you and your family want. So you're locked into a salary bracket that limits your life choices and experiences. In your own home business you can earn a larger income by:

1. Working longer hours to bring in a bigger amount of money
2. Doing more advertising by mail, Internet, fax, or telephone to increase sales
3. Calling customers to see if they need more of your products to increase your cash flow
4. "Cold canvassing" prospects to make sales where you haven't made them before

The whole key here is that your income can be increased by your own efforts in your home business. On a job you really can't raise your income other than by working overtime. And many jobs don't offer overtime opportunities. Further, some that do won't *pay* for overtime—it's just part of the job! Again, you're locked in.

So if you want income flexibility—especially on the upside—start your own home business. You'll be able to raise your income whenever you want a few extra dollars to do something special!

GET TO MEET NEW PEOPLE (IF YOU WANT TO)

Some people love to meet others with similar interests. If this describes you, then a home business can open a whole new social world for you and your family.

To meet more people through business you must have what I call a "people business." This is a business, run from your home, where you have active contact with your customers. Thus, your home business might be:

- A craft shop where people come to buy what you make, or have others make for you
- A professional service—accountant, attorney, financial planner, insurance agent, etc.
- A computer service business where you do word processing, machine repair, or other work in which people come to you

You'll find that many of your customers can become your friends, if you seek more friendships. This can expand your social life. And at the same time your customer-friends will recommend your business to others who might need your services. Since word-of-mouth advertising is the most effective type for any business, you can expect increased income when you make friends of your customers.

Having friends for customers can also improve your business and the products or services it offers. Why? Because your customer-friends will often:

- Suggest new ideas for your business which can bring in more money
- Recommend ways that you can improve a product or service, based on their use of either
- Offer tips on how you might combine two or more products or services to come up with more attractive offers for your clients

So if you like meeting new people, get into a home business that brings you into contact with your customer. You'll have lots more fun and will probably earn more money than ever before!

WORK IN PRIVACY IF YOU'RE A LONER

Some people dislike meeting their customers. Such people dream of a quiet home office with minimum noise and interruptions. If you're this type (and there's nothing wrong with being a loner), look for a quiet home business where you can be yourself.

For instance, the mail order business is one of the simplest and quietest I know. From the privacy of your home, you can make mailings, take credit-card telephone orders by machine, or download orders from the Internet without ever uttering a word to anyone. You can even watch TV while you're working. This will help you give up any guilt you might have about wasting time watching TV!

Many of my newsletter readers are loners. When they ask me a business question they don't want me to call them with the answer. Why? Because a ringing phone disturbs their work day. So they ask me to have their answer sent by postal mail, e-mail, or fax. This way they're not bothered with a phone call.

It took me a long while to figure out why some people wouldn't call me, even when I gave them my 800 number so they could call free of charge. Finally I realized that these people just don't like the phone. Instead, they enjoy poring over a letter or fax, reading it again and again. So I answer them by postal mail, e-mail, or fax as long as they're readers of my monthly newsletter *International Wealth Success*.

The whole key here is *Know thyself!* There's nothing wrong with being a loner. I'm one myself. Just be sure to pick a business that allows you to be yourself—namely, a loner, if you are one! Then you'll be a happy home business entrepreneur.

MOVE AHEAD WITHOUT HAVING TO QUIT YOUR JOB

Most people want security in life—a steady job with a guaranteed income. Unfortunately, this is almost impossible to achieve in today's corporate life. Companies hire and fire at the drop of a hat. Even the companies known for their long-term job security—telephone companies, electric utilities, and large computer builders—lay off people today. Corporate and employee loyalty are out the window.

So if *you* start a home business, the best way to run it is in your spare time. Continue doing this until the income from the business is large enough to support you in the lifestyle you seek. Then you can quit your job and give 100 percent of your time to your own home business.

While you're starting your home business you'll find that:

- You work longer hours than when you just hold a routine job
- Your life becomes more exciting and interesting because your business brings new challenges and greater variety into your life
- Your mind thrives on the excitement and the accomplishments of your business

In my own home business I find that dealing with customers is great fun. Further, I learn something from every customer I deal with. My day is so full I wonder where the hours go. No sooner do I start answering the phone in the morning than it seems the day is over. And, good friend, I work from 8 A.M. to 10 P.M. because I love what I do—not because I have to work that long!

Being able to hold your regular job while you build your own home business has other advantages for you namely:

- You have enough time to decide if a home business *is* for you
- You can work the kinks out of your home business *before* you decide to eat from the proceeds of it
- Your home business will be stronger when you decide to concentrate on it full-time, as compared with just quitting your job and starting the business from scratch

So you *can* have the "security" your job offers (there are no really secure jobs in the world, but most people choose to ignore this) while getting the advantages of having your own home business. Thus, you really can't lose.

START A PROFITABLE BUSINESS WITHOUT RISKING SAVINGS

It will take some money to start your own home business. But if you follow my ideas you'll be able to get started for under $1,000. I'll even help you finance your home business if you're a subscriber to my newsletter, *International Wealth Success*. See the back of this book for details.

So if you finance your home business you won't have to touch your savings. That should make you feel safe about the whole deal!

My view of a successful home business is one you start for zero cash of your own and build into a profitable cash machine. How can *you* achieve such a business? Follow the tips I give you in this book. Change them where local conditions require a different approach. But the start you get here will, in general, put you on the road to wealth in your own home business without risking any of your savings. Then you can write me a short letter like this one:

> "By way of interest, I've just bought a 2-bedroom condo with—of course—no money down!"

Or you might write a longer letter like the following, which covers multiple ventures started from home:

(1) Business is good—2 taverns left. (This BWB bought 3 taverns with zero cash.) I sold one of the 3. Sale went like this: Paid $80,000, all on borrowed money. Retained it 1 year and 6 months. Paid off all loans—sold business for $165,000. Contract was $35,000 down, $10,000 balloon paid at 1 year with payments to me of $1,345 per month for 10 years with another $80,000 balloon at the end of 10 year contract. They haven't missed a payment.
(2) Other two taverns doing fine; insurance business doing excellent; stock portfolio growing.
(3) Latest venture is 2 coffee shops (franchise), which look good. OPM (Other People's Money) lease for equipment; small amount of capital for startup. Franchisor waived monthly residual if I would open up this state. Franchise is operating in 6 western states.
(4) Just bought new ranch, using old house for rental; it shows a positive cash flow.
(5) Bought 2 racing greyhounds. One dog is racing in Colorado; the other in Florida; cash flow is good. Thanks for everything. Having "big" fun!

Or you might write a letter like this one:

"I am a long-term student of your teachings and a follower of your books. Recently, I started my own mail order business marketing health products to members of my profession. So far, the business is doing well. I am a 26-year-old chiropractic physician. Your methods have helped me succeed in mail order. If not, for my mail order business I would not be able to pay my education bills of $85,000."

Or, a letter such as this:

"Thank you for providing me the motivation to begin my mail-order business. The first few years were questionable but patience and perseverance are two key factors you encourage. If it had not been for your newsletter, we probably would never have either started or become successful in our business. Thanks for your years of encouragement and advertisements (free to IWS subscribers) which continue to produce better results than many of the paid ads we've run in the last 8-and-a-half years!"

The letters above arrived on the day I was at my desk writing this chapter. So they're not from twenty years ago when economic and market conditions were different from today. These letters show you that you *can* get started in your own home business without risking your savings.

As your good friend, and ready listener, I want *you* to succeed in your own home business! And I'm as close to you as your telephone. Just tap my number into your phone and I'll answer your questions on the first ring. You won't have to fight your way through ten secretaries to reach me. And I'll show you ways to get your business started without risking one penny of your own money. Try me and see.

If you don't like talking on the phone, fax me or write me a letter. You'll find my fax number and postal address at the end of this book.

SAVE TIME GETTING STARTED

In running my own home business for years, and in helping others do the same, I've noticed these facts about getting started:

1. The most successful home-business entrepreneurs are those who do what they enjoy.
2. Enthusiasm for your business is more important than details of accounting, organization, etc. Why? Because you can always hire professionals to do the accounting, legal, and other work for your business. And the cost won't be that great. What you cannot buy is enthusiasm, drive, and know-how. Only *you* have these for *your* business!
3. The more you believe in your product or service and the benefits your customers derive from it, the more likely you are to succeed and prosper in your own home business.

You can take your first step this instant to get started in your own home business. "And what's that step," you ask? It's this:

> Sit down with a piece of paper and pen or pencil and finish this sentence: *The home business that would be the most attractive to me is* _____
> *because I have the following skills and interests to bring to the business to make it a success:*_____

Once you've "filled in the blanks" on your piece of paper, put it aside for a day or two. During this time think about the business you listed. See yourself doing the work required in the business. Imagine serving customers, paying bills, receiving payments from customers, going to the bank, paying taxes on your business, settling disputes with suppliers, etc. If you like what you see, go for it!

As readers who've visited me in my New York office in Penn Plaza know, I'm a person who believes in action. You won't get very far just dreaming of the great home business you'll start! Instead, I suggest that you:

- Figure out what you like
- Get help on registration requirements for your state and town
- Start your business

I see some people getting enmeshed in a lot of regulatory mumbo-jumbo and never getting started. That's *not* the way for you! To my way of thinking, and based on my experience in many home businesses:

> Your business idea, your products or services, and your enthusiasm for serving your customers are much more important than the choice of a name, registration of the business, and setting up the books of account.

True, you *must* register your business. And you must set up books that record your income and expenses. But these two steps can be taken in a day, or less, with the help of a competent attorney and accountant. These professionals will advise you on the regulatory aspects of your business. You *must* have their help.

But only *you* can come up with an idea for a unique product or service. Only *you* can figure out how to reach your potential customers with your advertising message.

So save time! Get started fast. Use the services of local professionals who know the laws and rules in your area. The cost of these services should be low—$100 or so. Meanwhile, *you* can concentrate on a home business that can make you and yours wealthy! Start taking your first step—picking a suitable business—this instant. Then perhaps you can call me like this reader did to say:

> I started in the loan finding business a year ago from my home using your *Financial Broker-Finder-Business Broker-Consultant Kit*. In my first year I closed 7 loans, earning an average of $3,000 per loan. My total income of $21,000 in my spare time from home wasn't bad for my first year. And I intend to make my home income larger in the years to come!

Important Points to Remember

- You *can* build an independent income in your own home business, free of snarling bosses.
- Your own home business can free you of the threats of lay-offs, early retirement, downsizings, and staff reductions because *you* control your workforce.
- You can earn more money in your own home business than you might on a routine job because *you* control the income.
- Need more time for yourself or your family? You *can* get it in your own home business, once you get organized.
- You can build a big-buck retirement income in your own home business by carefully setting up a suitable pension plan for yourself.
- You can vacation whenever, and wherever you want. In your own home business, your time is your own; use it the way *you* wish.

- You can work a little more and get any extra funds you seek. Having your own home business allows you to expand and increase your income whenever you choose.
- You can meet new people through your business if you desire social contact. Your home business will often expand your social life, if this is your wish.
- You can work in privacy if people bother you. Be a loner and earn big money in your own home business.
- You can build your own home business while keeping your regular job, moving ahead as much as you wish until you're ready to quit your present job.
- You can start your own profitable home business without risking your savings. Just keep expenses low and finance your purchases of equipment and supplies.
- Save time getting your business started. Use good professional guidance and *you* can concentrate on bringing in the money sooner.

CHAPTER 2

WHAT'S THE IDEAL HOME BUSINESS FOR YOU?

YOU MUST BE HAPPY in your own home business. If you aren't happy with what you're doing, you won't do it as well as you could. So you *must* know what kind of business is for you. This chapter helps you do some soul-searching to come up with the right home business, to make *you* wealthy!

Would You Like to Work with People?

Your home business can be what I call a "people business"—one in which you deal directly with people ever day you work. These people are your customers. So you *must* be sweet to them. You *must* show pleasure and fun working with them.

Why? Because if your customers get a feeling of disinterest on your part they may go elsewhere. Or if you're curt, abrupt, or sarcastic to your customers you'll lose business. And—at the start at least—you'll need every customer you can find. So don't let annoyances show through, even though you're tired, you got some bad news about one of your kids, and you want to take a nap! If you can't control your emotions in front of people, go into a "loner" home business.

Typical examples of people businesses you can run at home include:

- Child care—Parents drop off kids in the morning and pick them up in the evening. All day long you have the "little people" (the kids) to deal with. And at the end of the day you have to face the parent who wants to know if Johnnie or Mary behaved themselves during the day.
- Travel agency—Local people interested in world travel come in to sit down with you to plan their itinerary. And, I guarantee you, they *will.* make what seem like silly changes, which require you to do more work. If dealing with people who can't decide on where they want to go or stay bugs you, then this kind of people business is not for you!

If work forms part, or a lot, of your social life, then a people business will probably make you and your customers happy. Just keep in mind the fact that customers can be a pain. They can drive you up a wall. But they will pay you money! And that, after all, is why you went into your home business in the first place!

In my own home business—newsletter and book publishing—I enjoy talking to my readers. So I'm there when they call me on the phone. And I'm even happy when they come to my office in New York City and I take them out to lunch (for which I *always* pay). These readers give me much valuable information from the "firing line" of their actual home businesses.

Then there are times—when I'm writing a book such as this—that my mind is so preoccupied with what I want to say that I'd rather not see anyone. So I just avoid seeing people for a few days until I feel comfortable with the way the book is progressing. You can arrange your work schedule in a similar way if you're part people person— part loner!

Would You Prefer to Work Alone?

Many home-business people are loners. They enjoy being
by themselves. There's nothing wrong with this. But such
people must:

- Recognize that they enjoy being alone
- Pick a business suited to their desire to be alone
- Carefully prevent the business from being converted to a
  people type, unless they want this to happen

In a loner-type business you communicate with others
by postal mail, fax, e-mail, or phone. Examples of loner-
type businesses include:

- Mail order—You sell any of thousands of products by mail
  to customers all over the world. You never see your customer because the order comes to you in an envelope, by
  phone, by e-mail, or on the Internet and it goes out to
  your customer in an envelope or a box, and you're both
  happy. In our mail order home business we have millions
  of happy customers. And I've never seen more than one-
  tenth of my customers in person. While I'd like to meet
  them all, neither they, nor I, have the time to get together.
  Yet they're happy with what they bought. And if they have
  any questions, they can always call me on the phone or
  send me a fax—day or night—to get answers.
- Writing—whether fiction or nonfiction, writing is another
  loner business. Some authors never want to see or talk to
  outsiders while working on an important writing project.
  They feel that if they talk to someone about their project
  they will reduce their internal drive to get the story, article,
  or book onto paper where it has to be before it can be set
  into type for publication. (It's true, good friend, that some
  authors dictate their work to a machine or human being.
  But the words must almost always be transcribed to paper
  or computer before they can be edited for publication, set
  in type, or checked by the author.) While writing is a lonely
  home business, authors usually enjoy the loneliness almost

as much as they like the payment checks they receive for
their writing in their own home business!

Do You Want a Stay-at-Home Business?

In a stay-at-home business you rarely leave your home for
business purposes. Instead, you conduct essentially all your
business at home. So you're not running out of your home
to jump into a car to deliver an item to a customer. Typical
examples of stay-at-home businesses include:

- Export-import—You handle the paperwork, faxes, and
  phone calls needed to sell, or buy, a product or service,
  which is sent overseas, or brought into your own country for
  resale. In most deals you *never* see or touch the products or
  services you're importing or exporting. So you never have to
  leave home to take care of your business. Your income from
  export-import can easily exceed $100,000 per year. Today
  you can use your home-based personal computer to create
  Letters of Credit (LCs) for your export-import business to
  speed payments through your commercial bank.
- Home computer services—You perform a computer-
  related service for customers who bring, mail, or fax the
  work to you. The work you do is performed on your personal computer (PC) in privacy without your ever having
  to leave home. Such work is ideal for people who are
  shut-ins from one cause or another. They can prosper in
  their own home business without enduring the hardship
  of having to leave home. Likewise this work is ideal for
  people who must remain home because they have to care
  for children or others requiring close attention and care.
  Your income can range from $20,000 to $125,000 a year,
  depending on the services you offer.

Do You Want a Go-Out Home Business?

In a go-out home business you keep your records and do
some work at home. But to earn your income you must

work outside your home. And you're still in your own home business, even though most—or all—of your work is done outside your residence. Typical go-out home businesses include:

- Fund raising—You raise money for worthy causes associated with religious, sporting, charitable, or public needs. You organize personal calling groups that make phone calls, conduct visits door-to-door, send faxes, and make postal mailings to prospective donors. (Some people operate a stay-at-home fund raising business that is conducted solely by postal mail, faxes, e-mail, Internet, and phone. But the business we're talking about here depends on personal calls to the homes of donors.) You meet with these people outside your home and tell them how to get prospects to give until it hurts. Your "troops" do the work—*you* manage their efforts. You receive a percentage of the money raised. While the exact percentage you're paid will vary from one job to another, your typical fee will range from 5 to 10 percent, depending on the deal you can work out. Your income can range from $25,000 to more than $100,000 a year, depending on how many clients you take on.
- Wedding planning—You help brides (and grooms) with the many tasks involved in planning and successfully completing a wedding. You work with your clients in their homes, at the sites of the ceremonies, at the photo settings, and at the reception locations. You will deal with guest lists, invitations, gift acknowledgment, reception seating, band hiring, music selection, reception location, decorations, floral arrangements, etc. Your fee will be a negotiated one, based on the amount of work you do, how much prior experience you've had, etc. Typical fees currently range between 10 and 20 percent of the wedding total cost. This means that the fee you'll receive will range from $2,500 to $20,000 per wedding today. Since May, June, and July are the usual "marrying months" for larger weddings, you may find it wise to combine your wedding planning with another activity that fills in the slack months. Your income can range from $12,000 to $100,000 a year, depending on the size and number of weddings you handle.

Analyze Yourself to Pick Your Home Business!

You *can* make *big* money in a simple home business *you* enjoy! But to be successful you must pick a business you enjoy and which makes you happy. You can find such a business by using the simple analysis chart in Figure 2-1 to learn what really turns you on. Using a separate sheet of paper, answer the questions in the chart and then rate your best type of business. Using this chart will help you avoid false starts in your own home business!

Don't "knock" being happy in business. Why? Because if you *like* what you're doing you'll:

* Do a better job for your customers
* Have more fun from your work
* Earn more because customers who see that you enjoy what you're doing will buy more

Next you'll narrow your choice to a specific business, based on what you like to do, what skills you have, and how large an income you seek. You'll use Figure 2-2 to choose the specific business that would best mesh with your likes and skills.

You now have a better idea of what you'd like as your own home business. To help you pick the best business for yourself, the remaining chapters of this book will give you 199 great home businesses you can start for less than $1,000.

In presenting these businesses to you, we concentrate on:

* Simple businesses which are easy to run
* Low-cost startup businesses
* Every-man and every-woman types of businesses which almost anyone can run successfully
* Direct startups which require little more than pencil and paper

---

Home Business Analysis Chart

	Check	Yes	No

1. I like to work closely with people.   _____ _____

2. I prefer to work alone.   _____ _____

3. I'd like to work in my own home without having to go out.   _____ _____

4. I want my own home business and would not object to going out to work at other locations to make money.   _____ _____

Your *yes* answers will clearly show which type of business would be best for you. Thus if you checked:

1 and 3: You would choose a "people" business in which your customers come to your home.

1 and 4: You would choose a "people" business in which you go out to a job site to work with your customers.

2 and 3: You would choose a business in which you work at home and get your orders by mail or phone with little, or no, face-to-face contact with customers.

2 and 4: You would choose a business where you may have to leave home but your contact with customers on the job would be minimal.

Figure 2-1

Specific Business Analysis Chart

1. The work I most enjoy doing is: _____
2. My greatest skill in working is: _____
3. The annual income I seek is: _____
4. My work situation choice is, from above (1 and 3; 1 and 4; 2 and 3; 2 and 4):   _____

Figure 2-2

So come along, good friend, and we'll put you into your own successful home business. What's more, I'm as close to you as your telephone. If you have a question just give me a ring and I'll be glad to answer it.

And if you need money to start your business, I'll be glad to consider financing it for you. Our interest rates are low and there are *no* points, *no* fees, and *no* retainer of any kind for our borrowers. These loans are available where allowed by local rules. All we suggest is that you be a two-year, or longer, subscriber to our newsletter *International Wealth Success.* Your loan application will be sent to you the same day we receive your subscription order. See the back of this book for full details.

Start Your Home Business As a Spare-Time Second Income

The most successful home-business people I meet (and I meet, and talk to, thousands) start their business in their spare time to earn a second income. Soon the second income booms out, allowing them to work full time at home.

To build a second-income fortune you must follow certain basic rules. These rules have worked for millions of home workers for years. And they'll work for you, too! I call these guides the Ten Rules to Develop Wealth Power. Here they are for *you* to use in *your* home business now:

TEN RULES TO DEVELOP WEALTH POWER

1. *Learn to work with people.* You have little chance of building a real second-income fortune without the help of other people. A few loners—usually inventors and authors—make big money without the help of others. But the biggest spare-time fortunes are made when a man or woman with ideas joins forces with talented people having many skills. For example, Willis H. Carrier, who designed the first practical air-conditioning system, founded Carrier Corporation with the help of six engineers.

Carrier was president and chairman of the firm for 33 years, during which time he had help from many of the six engineers with whom he founded the firm.

So, learn to work with people; you can't expect to be an expert in everything. If your field is electronics you'll probably need the help of accountants, lawyers, sales people, and production managers, if you go into business in your spare time. Learn to forget petty rivalries and get to like everyone. Then, do as the natural wealth builder does—when he or she needs help of any kind, he or she calls on a friend. Remember the friend you make today may help you make your fortune tomorrow. Knowing how to work with people can be one of the most important tools in your wealth-building kit.

2. *Be decisive—learn how to size up situations quickly.* You can't earn substantial spare-time money if you take forever to make up your mind. "He or she who hesitates is lost" is true in most business situations where a large number of people are competing for the same objective.

How do you learn to size up situations quickly? You use all your senses. You look, you feel, you listen; you smell and taste, if necessary. When you encounter a potentially profitable situation, forget everything else, including caution, and concentrate on the facts. Try to absorb as many pertinent facts as quickly as you can. Once you have all the facts in mind, apply your analytical judgment and cautious outlook.

Go over each fact, make a list of pros and cons if you can't evaluate the facts in your mind. If you find one pro equal to one con, cross out each. Should two pros equal, in your judgment, three cons, cross out the five items. After a fast study like this with a pro-and-con balance sheet, you will quickly see which aspect of the situation is strongest because it will have the most factors remaining. Some people perform this type of evaluation mentally and make what appears to be a snap judgment. Actually, they mentally set up a pro-and-con balance sheet and quickly evaluate each of the factors in it.

Try to speed every decision you make. Don't worry about mistakes. If you've been a slow decision maker in the past, you know that slow decisions can be just as

wrong as fast ones. The main advantage of the fast decision is that it often permits you to take advantage of a situation before someone else does.

3. *Learn persistence—it pays off.* If you've been a quitter all
your life, start changing now. Often the difference
between making a spare-time fortune and going broke is a
few more hours, days, or weeks of work. Why give up
when there's still a chance to succeed? Quitting early can
lead you to one failure after another. You get so discour-
aged that you give up completely and the fortune that
might have been, never is.

Do big money-makers give up easily? No. They pursue
their objective until they achieve it. For example, Dr.
Edward H. Land, inventor of the Land Polaroid camera,
tried over three million chemical formulations before he
was satisfied with the pictures produced. Dorothy Parker,
one of the world's great writers, often worked for hours to
perfect one paragraph.

Persistence can make up for many other deficiencies a
man or woman may have. Look around you today. Note
that the people who have the most money often are not
the most intelligent, the most learned, or the most artis-
tic. Instead, the successful person is often a persistent
plodder—a man or woman who knows what he or she
wants and goes after it. His or her "intelligent" friends
may even describe him or her as so stupid that he or she
doesn't know when to give up. Yet he or she often winds
up with a spare-time fortune far exceeding that of all his
or her "smart" friends.

Begin today to finish what you start. Don't start anything unless you are reasonably sure you will finish it.
Begin reinforcing your persistence by finishing simple
things, like reading this book. Then go on to more difficult tasks, completing each one. Every time you finish a
task your confidence will grow. When you begin your
search for wealth you will have more confidence and your
chances for success will be much greater.

4. *Be constantly alert for new wealth ideas.* Wealth won't seek
you out—you must seek after it. Begin today to apply this
wealth-building rule. Resolve to make every task you perform a step toward building spare-time wealth. Read your

newspaper with an eye for second-income wealth opportunities. Study the financial pages for clues to developments that may lead you to wealth. Read the obituaries of wealthy men and women; you will often find helpful hints in the stories of the successes of these men and women. Do your daily job with gusto and with the firm intention of turning out the best work possible.

Keep a notebook handy at all times. Jot down each new spare-time wealth idea you find. Don't try to classify the idea when you first find it. Just enter it on a dated page in your notebook. Continue your notebook entries throughout the year, no matter where you are or how you come across an idea. Be alert for new second-income wealth ideas during all your reading, conversations, business meetings, and other contacts. For once you *resolve* to find new wealth ideas, your mind will be more eager for them. It will be easier for you to trap and make a note of every good second-income idea you encounter.

Evaluate your notebook ideas at your convenience. Pick a quiet spot and review each page of your notebook. When doing this you may find that the ideas you collected are not directly useful to you. However, by combining two or more ideas you may be able to develop a valuable spare-time money-making scheme.

Begin your campaign of wealth-alertness today. Back up your alertness with a good notebook. The combination can lead you to new money that will help build your fortune.

5. *Recognize the rewards of risk-taking.* There is no safe way to build wealth. Recognize this fact today and your road to a second-income fortune will be much easier. You *must* take risks, if you expect to build wealth. If taking risks scares you, makes you jittery or unhappy, you will have to change your outlook. One way to do this is to take some extra money you have—even as little as $100—and invest it in a risky but promising venture. Mentally write off the money before you invest it. This will reduce some of your fear. Should the venture be successful you will be ready to invest more next time, with less apprehension.

The more risks you take to build spare-time wealth, the greater your chances of hitting it big. This doesn't mean, however, that you should take all your savings and invest them in risky enterprises. Look, instead, for a speculative but promising venture. Then invest a portion of your funds in it. The exact amount will depend on your circumstances. But invest enough so you feel that you are really taking a chance. That way, your return will be somewhat larger if the second-income project pays off. Risk-taking is an integral part of building wealth. Recognize this fact today and you'll be way ahead of others who hunger for wealth the "safe" way.

6. *Never be ashamed to borrow money to make money.* Some of the largest spare-time fortunes are built on borrowed money. The natural wealth builder understands and uses credit to the fullest. He or she buys real estate with a minimum investment of personal capital. As a stock market speculator he or she uses margin whenever possible. Certainly, borrowing money costs money. But if you can make money using other people's capital, you can expand your profit potential far beyond that offered by your own resources.

   People (banks, mortgage specialists, loan firms, and many government agencies) are in business to lend money. They *want* you to borrow if you have a good credit standing and you intend to use the money for worthwhile purposes. Understand this fact of life and you'll have fewer problems when you apply for a loan. Also, you'll soon see that to borrow money to earn money is one of the smartest moves you can make as a spare-time fortune builder.

7. *Be time-conscious at all times.* "Time is money" is the famous remark of Ben Franklin. Time consciousness is directly related to spare-time wealth building. There has seldom been a man or woman who built a second-income fortune without first recognizing the importance of time in his or her financial plans. Just think of a few results of being time conscious. You (a) evaluate your efforts in terms of the financial return to you, (b) see each day as a block of time to be devoted to building your spare-time fortune, (c) size up people and the time you spend with them in terms of your financial objectives, and (d) set up time goals for achieving your second-income wealth aims.

   Become time-conscious today. When beginning a new venture you'll often find that, as one spare-time fortune builder said, "... practically your whole life is going to be devoted to its success." In the early days of a new second-income venture, you may work for as little as 50 cents per hour. Later on, when the venture is successful, you may refuse to work for anything less than $500 per hour. In the early efforts to establish the venture, your time-consciousness will tell you that the low hourly rate is worthwhile because you are establishing an equity. At a later date, with business booming, you may feel that your health and golf game are more important than a spare-time income of $500 or more an hour. So don't delay—resolve now to become time-conscious; for delay, as Alex Lewyt so wisely observed "... is responsible for more failures, more lack of success than any other circumstance." His outstandingly successful vacuum cleaner shows the results of avoiding delays.

8. *Be a finisher—finish what you start.* Don't give up; you almost always lose when you abandon your efforts before you finish the task you set out to perform. Spare-time wealth won't run, walk, or crawl to you—you must go after it. If you quit when halfway to your goal, the money you seek will stay where it is and your pockets will be empty. "Great works are performed not by strength but by *perseverance,*" said Samuel Johnson, who knew the secrets of accomplishing great works.

Begin by finishing every small task you start. Go on to larger undertakings, like preparing complex plans for your financial future. Don't give up in the middle of your planning; complete the plans even though you must strain your thinking to do so. Remember—nothing worthwhile is easy. Once you form the habit of finishing your tasks you will gain more self-confidence than you ever thought possible.

9. *Develop your creative powers.* Spare-time wealth comes to the man or woman who can develop new ideas into products or services needed by others. Good ideas can be yours, if you develop your creative powers.

Recognize that you *can* become more creative by using these basic guides to develop creative thinking. First, clearly define what you wish to achieve—for example, a certain sum of money, a home in a given area, or a boat of a certain size. Second, list every possible way you might achieve your objective; don't be afraid if some of the methods seem far-fetched or even silly. Third, when ideas stop coming, forget the problem. Do something completely different—go fishing, tramp through the woods, bowl, swim, read. After this, wait—and be alert for the sudden flash of understanding that solves the problem for you; make an immediate note of the solution. Evaluate your idea at a later time, but be sure to put the idea into action as soon as possible.

10. *Visualize, once every day, what money can do for you and your family.* Try to *see* yourself with the money. Imagine the happiness you and your family will derive from the money you seek. See, in your mind's eye, the bank books, stock certificates, real estate, and other possessions the money will bring you. Feel the money in your hands. Make it real—and you will acquire what you want.

Don't play down the importance of visualizing the effects of wealth in your life. Every man and woman who has accumulated a fortune has a "money dream" that motivated them. This "money dream" kept him or her alert, ready to trap a new idea, method, or process that could be turned into wealth. Begin now to visualize, daily, *your* money dream.

Important Points to Remember

- You must be happy in your own home business if you want to make it a big success.
- You can choose a home business in which you actively work with your customers, if you wish.
- Or, if you prefer to work alone, you can choose a business in which you rarely meet people. Such a business will give you the privacy you prefer.
- And if you prefer to stay at home while you work, you can pick a business that doesn't require you to leave home at all.
- But if you enjoy working outside your home you can choose a business that will get you out to different job sites.
- Many home businesses start as a second-income, spare-time effort. To grow strong and profitable, use the ten rules above to develop the wealth power described for you (and available to you) in this chapter.

CHAPTER 3

THE 27 EASIEST HOME BUSINESSES TO START

*EVERYONE—MYSELF INCLUDED—*is a bit scared when starting a new home business. So if someone tells me, "This the casiest home business you'll ever start," I'm interested. In this chapter we give you 27 of the easiest home businesses to start. And along with the details of the businesses, we've added expanded information for certain chosen businesses. This expanded information will help you get started in your own home business with less fear and more confidence.

The expanded information you receive is based on real-life experiences of many of my readers, my business associates, and my own daily work activities. Using the information you receive here you'll be able to start your own profitable home business quickly and easily. And you won't be too scared! Further, if you ever have a question about any of these businesses, I'm as close to you as your phone. Just pick it up and call me—I'll answer on the first ring and if you're a subscriber of my *International Wealth Success* newsletter I'll answer every question you have. So let's get started making you rich!

AN IDEAL SERVICE BUSINESS

Name of Business. Apartment Finding Service

What You Do. Find apartments for people in crowded cities and in the suburbs for a fee, which can range from $100 to $500, depending on the scarcity of apartments and the rent your client pays. (The higher the rent, the larger your fee.) Most people operate this business on a part-time basis in conjunction with other businesses. Compatible home businesses with which an Apartment Finding Service can be operated include Dating Services, Child Care Services, Reminder Services, Maid Services, Shopping Services, etc.

How to Find Clients. Run classified and small space ads in newspapers and magazines serving people in metro and suburban areas. Crowded cities—Los Angeles, Chicago, New York, Dallas, Miami, Boston—are excellent areas in which to start this business. You can also run the same classified ads on the Internet to appeal nationally to people planning to move from one area to another as part of a job or career change.

Money Required to Start. You'll need $300 to $500 for your initial classified ads in newspapers and magazines in suitable cities. To find the names and addresses of suitable publications look at *Standard Rate & Data* available in almost every large public library.

Earnings Potential. $6,000 to $25,000 per year, part-time.

Time to First Earnings. You can be bringing in income within two weeks after starting your business.

Equipment Needed. Desk, phone, fax, typewriter, or access to a typist. A PC and printer will be a big help to you and will replace your typewriter once your business grows a bit.

A LOW-COST SERVICE BUSINESS FOR ANIMAL LOVERS

Name of Business. Bird, Duck, and Geese Chasing Service

What You Do. Use your dog (or dogs) to chase birds, ducks, geese, and other unwanted creatures from parks, school yards, golf courses, suburban corporate headquarters' lawns, and similar properties. This is an environmentally acceptable way of controlling undesirable winged visitors who make life unpleasant for humans seeking to enjoy the outdoors. Meanwhile, your dog (or dogs) has great fun scaring the undesirables away. And the chased birds, ducks, and geese are not harmed in any way. They're just encouraged to find another place to perch and enjoy themselves. Not even bird lovers and bird watchers object to having an animal, such as a dog, chase their winged friends to another locale. When you provide this service, you bring your dog to the agreed-on location one or more times a day to rid the area of the unwanted winged pests. You are paid a monthly fee for each location you service with your dog or dogs. Using your car, sports utility, or van, you bring your dog to the location and let him/her have oodles of fun chasing the prey. And you'll enjoy watching your dog working for you! You really get your money's worth from a dog who is a natural hunter and wants his/her grassy area free of winged pests.

How to Find Clients. Send letters to local organizations having land areas infested with undesirable flying or waddling creatures, offering your safe, effective service. Run small classified ads in industrial, club, school, university, city, and town publications saying:

> ARE BIRDS, DUCKS, AND GEESE RUINING YOUR LAWN? If they are, contact us for a safe, environmentally acceptable way of getting rid of undesirables. Call (222) 123-4567 now.

Any area of the world having manicured lawns is an excellent candidate for this service. Ads in such areas should pull well for you.

Money Required to Start. If you currently own a dog that's good at bird-chasing, your only investment will be for your direct-mail letters, classified ads in publications, and Internet (on a suitable web site). Such ads will cost you $300 to $500. If you have to get a dog, try your local animal shelter. You'll probably get a good one free of charge. If you can't get a suitable dog immediately, put your name on the shelter's waiting list. A suitable dog will usually show up in a few weeks. And you can rely on shelter personnel to give you lots of free advice about the right dog to adopt for your business use.

Earnings Potential. $15,000 to $50,000 a year part-time; $40,000 to $125,000 per year full-time in heavily grassed areas with golf courses, public parks, numerous schools, and several corporate headquarters with large lawns.

Time to First Earnings. In areas needing this service you can start earning income within two weeks after starting your business to chase birds, ducks, geese, and other pesky winged animals.

Equipment Needed. While your dog is not "equipment," he/she is a key part of your business! You'll also need a desk, phone, typewriter or PC with a printer, and a fax machine.

A BIGGER SERVICE BUSINESS FOR YOU

Name of Business. Building Care Service

What You Do. Operate the mechanical, electrical, and other systems in a building while keeping it open for use by the tenants. Once called a janitor, today's building care operator does much more, is better educated, and has greater responsibility. You can take care of several buildings at once, being a roving manager. And you are paid a monthly fee for your services, based on the size of the building, the number of tenants, and the complexity of the job. Major maintenance work is done by outside firms, which you engage. You hire out this work because it is much cheaper than having a full staff on hand year round. When you manage a residential apartment house you free the superintendent's apartment for rent. This, by itself, ups the owner's income from the building.

How to Find Clients. Contact the local Building or Property Owner's Association and ask to be listed as a qualified Building Care Service operator. Write or call building owners in your area, offering your services. Volunteer to run a building free for a limited time to build your reputation and experience. Run classified ads on the Internet offering your services.

Money Required to Start. You can start this business for $100 to $300, depending on how many mailings and phone calls you make. While advertising can help, you can usually get started just by making local contacts.

Earnings Potential. Your earnings will depend on the number of buildings you accept for management and the size of each building. Larger buildings pay a higher fee. Minimum earnings will be $10,000 a year with a few small buildings. Maximum earnings can range to $100,000 a year with several large buildings under management.

Time to First Earnings. It will take four to six weeks to get your first building under contract. And your first paycheck won't arrive for another four weeks. After that you will have a regular monthly income, working from home.

Equipment Needed. Telephone, fax, desk. A PC will be helpful once you have five buildings under management but you do not need one at the start.

A WIDE-RANGING SERVICE BUSINESS

Name of Business. Finder Service

What You Do. You find things for businesses or people. Thus, you might be asked to find (for an acceptable commission) rare metals, a location for a business requiring a certain traffic pattern (i.e., passage of stipulated number of autos per day), an aircraft having a unique carrying capacity, etc. You do scouting and research work to locate the desired item. Today you may be asked to find foods, oil, or customers for available commodities of many types. Your commission is based on the value your client places on what you find. Thus you might be paid 3 percent of the amount of a sale when you find a customer for a commodity of some kind. You will have a written agreement covering your fee and when it will be paid. Some companies will pay you a retainer when you start your finding work for them so you have a suitable cash flow to sustain your work.

How to Find Clients. Contact local firms with a mailing saying: "We find anything for a fee." Run small classified ads in business magazines and newspapers. Put classified ads on the Internet. Such Internet ads can pay off handsomely for you because finding and the Internet are worldwide in scope.

Money Required to Start. $500 to $999 for mailings, Internet, and classified ads will get you started.

Earnings Potential. You can earn from $25,000 to $100,00 and up per year working as a finder. Much depends on being fortunate enough to bring together a need and availability. Being constantly on the lookout for needs and availabilities increases your chances of earning significant commissions.

Time to First Earnings. It will usually take one to two months for your first earnings from a finder service. The reason for this is that you must do some scouting of needs and availabilities before you can close your first deal.

Equipment Needed. Desk, phone, fax, PC, typewriter. See the back of this book for K-1, which covers the fees and agreements used in the Finder Service business.

Real-Life Home-Business Tips

How Finders Who Are Just Starting Can Make Millions

Many starting finders don't realize that they can make more money if they arrange their deals to get the most from them. To help you get more from your finder deals, here are a few tips which can put big bucks in your pockets soon!

Q.   How can I earn more from finder deals?
A.   Write the agreement you make with your clients in such a way that you get a fee on all deals that are the type you are hired for. For instance, if you are hired to find money for a client, write in the agreement that you will get a fee on all loans the client gets during the next—let's say—five years. This way you will get a fee on loans on which you might not have worked very much.

Q.   But will a client agree to such a deal?
A.   Yes, many clients will agree to such a deal because they need the money when they hire you and they hope that you will continue working for them for a long time. So the use of such a clause in the agreement will usually be acceptable to most of your clients.

Q. Do I need to be in business as a finder to get such a deal?

A. No! You can act as a finder on any type of deal you pick. So your main job might be in any other field. But you can—if you want to—act as a finder on deals you pick because you like them or you feel you can really earn the big money with them. Many of our reader-finders have other jobs or businesses for their regular income and act as finders on deals that appeal to them. This way the client has to work to get the finder to take on the deal. In this type of deal, the finder can often get better terms—like those we mentioned above. *Be hard to get and get more!*

Q. Must finders have a license of any kind?

A. No, you do not need a license of any kind to act as a finder. Nor do you even need a special type of letter paper. Many finders just use their personal letter paper when writing to clients about business finding deals. Some people even say that you should not have the word "finder" on your letter paper. But the people we hear about who've earned the big fees as finders (one states that he earned nearly $2 million on a lead he found in the IWS newsletter) do carry the word *finder* on their letter paper. So pick whichever method you think is best for you!

Q. Finder deals take very long to put together, I've heard. Is this so?

A. Some do—some can be worked out quickly. So the secret to making *big money* as a finder is to have both long—and short-term deals. Then you will have almost constant activity in your finder business. This will keep your name in the minds of people in your area who might need your help on a finding job of some type.

Q. What's the easiest type of finding assignment to get?

A. Finding money is usually the easiest type of finding assignment to get because almost all firms look for money, at some time or another. So if you are a money finder, firms in your area are almost certain to ask you to find money for them—for a fee!

Q. How do big, successful finders get their leads?
A. Many finders do their research and fact finding in reference books that are available in almost any large public library. Other finders do much (or all) of their search work on the Internet. When they are looking for leads, some finders send out 100 or 200 postal letters to the top people in the firms that interest them. Other finders use e-mail to contact their prospects. Thus, the work that is done before a deal gets going does not take a bundle of money— instead it just takes some time and energy, plus some paper and stamps, or Internet on-line time. Finding, you might say, is an ideal "paper"' or electronic-commerce business, needing *no* big money to start.

Q. What is the typical range of fees finders earn?
A. The finders we're talking about here earn 3 percent of the first $3 million in a deal (that is, $90,000 for a $3 million deal), 2 percent on the next $12 million; 1 percent on the remainder. With fees like these, it would be easy for you to earn $250,000 from just one big deal! Thus, finding can make you very rich!

Q. If I went into finding, would I need a big staff?
A. No! Most finders start with just themselves and some paper, stamps, and a typewriter or PC! You do not need a large staff at the start—or ever—if you want to work alone.

Q. Where's the best place for me to start my finding business?
A. There are many "best" places. But most people find that starting close to home is often best. Why? Because you are probably known in your area. Or if you are not known, you probably know of some people or businesses in your area that might use your finder services.

Q. How do I get paid for my finding work?

A. The finders we're talking about here get a fee of $1,000 when the first meeting between the two groups (buyer and seller) is arranged; $500 for a second meeting. This fee is for the time and expense in setting up the meeting and is kept by the finder, even if the deal does not go through. (In general, small fees related to a deal are acceptable to most people for whom the finder is working to close a deal.)

Q. What kind of finding deals are right for me?

A. Some of the finders mentioned above work to bring firms together for a sale or buyout. This is also called mergers and acquisitions. But you might find that other types of deals are the kind that you like better. These deals might be the finding of certain chemicals or products (like oil, coal, cement, etc.), the finding of buyers for equipment (like airplanes, ships, trucks, machines, etc.), the finding of money for a company or client needing it, the finding of cosigners for folks needing loans, etc. The best kind of finding deals for you are those you enjoy working at!

Q. What is the future of the finding business?

A. It is—in our opinion—just great! Why? Because there will be continual shortages of important materials, products, services, money, etc. Hence, the effective finder (one who gets results) will always—in our opinion—be in great demand! So if you learn your finding skills well, we're sure that you will never be looking for work. Instead, work will be looking for you! And when you get to the position where work is looking for you, the fees you can get will make you rich—sooner than you might think! Yes, the life of the finder can be full, interesting, and financially very, very rewarding!

Q. Must a finder be licensed?

A. Finders need *not* be licensed if their only function is to introduce firms or people, with the legal, accounting, real estate, and other functions later handled by licensed specialists in these fields. This is the important aspect of finding—if you just find and introduce, you can earn your fee while others do the necessary paperwork connected with any business deal.

Q. Should a finder agreement be in writing?
A. *Yes!* You *should* have a written agreement with your client, which details what you will do and what you will be paid. Though some finders have been able to collect fees in the hundreds of thousands of dollars based on an oral (spoken) agreement, you're much better off with a written agreement.

Q. Can a finder take fees from both parties?
A. Yes, if the agreement the finder has does not prohibit such fees. But most agreements written today do prevent a finder from taking fees from both parties. And from a business standpoint, it might be best not to take fees from both parties.

Q. What about cofinders?
A. If you have to hire cofinders to put a deal together because you don't have the know-how or contacts, you are responsible for their fees—not your client. So be sure you have a written agreement with your cofinders that covers their fees.

Q. When is the finder's fee paid to you?
A. The fee you get is paid *after* the closing of a deal. This is usually after the transfer of the property or other exchange has been made. To put it another way, you get paid when all the legal and accounting work has been finished and papers are signed.

How to Write Letters of Agreement for Finder Deals

BWBs often ask: "How can I be sure I'll be paid?" What they usually have in mind when they ask this question is being paid for a finder deal. Here are some of the ways successful BWBs have been sure they will be paid. If you want to verify that these arrangements are OK for you, be certain to check with your attorney for more advice.

Most finder-fee deals are based on a "Letter of Agreement." That is, you send a letter to your client which outlines the deal. If your client agrees to the items in the letter he or she signs the letter and returns one copy to you for your files. The other copy of the letter is retained by your client for his or her files. Now here is an example of one such letter. Again, in quoting this letter here we are not offering legal opinions; instead we are just giving an example of a letter which has worked for others and might work for you. *BE CERTAIN TO HAVE A QUALIFIED ATTORNEY PREPARE ANY FINDER LETTER YOU USE IN YOUR BUSINESS!*

Your letter will usually cover: (a) what you are to find, (b) the time limit within which you will find the item, and (c) the fee you will be paid. Here's how such a letter might read:

Dear_____:

In accordance with our recent conversation, I am to find the following items for you by Aug. 1, ____:_____.
For finding the above-named items I will be paid a finder's fee of __% within 30 days after the items have been delivered to you. This fee will be based upon the price you pay for the items found. The price, we agreed, will not exceed _____.

To indicate your acceptance of the above terms, please sign both copies of this letter in the space provided below and return one copy to me for my files; the other copy is for your files.

Very truly yours,

_____

Signed: _____

Date: _____

Agreed: _____

Date: _____

GET YOUR EXERCISE WHILE EARNING

Name of Business. Home Cleaning Service

What You Do. Clean the interiors of homes on a regular basis—weekly, monthly, or some other schedule. Your cleaning can be a "lick-and-promise" type, or it can include every square foot of the home. You arrange the type of cleaning with the owner and charge accordingly. A weekly or monthly payment plan is customary for home cleaners. Since most customers will not be at home when you do the cleaning, you must be careful about the type of personnel you hire to do the cleaning work. It may be wise to bond such employees because this will prevent you from suffering a loss in the event a customer complains about household items disappearing during the cleaning process. At the start you will probably do the first few cleaning jobs yourself. But once you acquire a few customers you will hire cleaners to do the work for you.

How to Find Clients. Use flyers to attract local customers in better areas. Distribute the flyers by hand or by mail to homes and place on autos in shopping mall parking lots (where permitted), clubs, and other areas where the upper middle class gather. As your business grows you will want to take space in your local *Yellow Pages.* You can also advertise at low cost in the *Pennysaver*-type newspaper in your area.

Money Required to Start. You will need $400 to $800 to start this business. But you will have almost instant cash flow. So you can get your startup money from your credit card line of credit and repay the following month out of your earnings.

Earnings Potential. You can earn $12,000 to $75,000 a year cleaning homes. As with similar businesses, your actual income depends on the number of customers you have for your services.

Time to First Earnings. It will take four weeks before you get your first check for cleaning a home. Why? Because you must first find a customer, then negotiate a fee, and then do the work. But once you get a few customers you will have a steady cash flow every week.

Equipment Needed. Desk, telephone, typewriter, auto, and cleaning tools. Most of this equipment can be rented at the start to hold your startup costs low. As your business grows, you'll find a PC extremely helpful for keeping customer records and sending your bills to them.

EARN A GOOD LIVING FROM PAPER

Name of Business. Publication Clipping Service

What You Do. You scan newspapers, magazines, and other publications to find articles, announcements, and other mentions of companies, people, and organizations interested in building a file of all publicity about them. You will be paid either on a monthly fee basis or on a per item-clipped basis. The monthly fee basis is better if there are not too many mentions of a company, person, or organization. Where there are a large number of mentions, the per-item fee is a better basis. Either way, your payment will include the cost of a subscription to the publication or publications you must scan. Once you have several clients, this cost can be spread over these clients, so each one pays less for their part of the subscription. When you find a mention in a publication you cut out the item and mount it on a card containing the name, date, and page number of the publication. You will then make two photocopies of the mention, keeping one for yourself and sending the original and one photocopy to your client. This is an ideal home business because the publications will be delivered to your door by mail and you can work in any area of your home you choose. You will rarely meet your clients because most of your negotiations will be done by telephone, postal mail, e-mail, or fax.

With more news and data appearing on the Internet every day of the year, some clients may ask you to scan the Internet for mentions of them. To do this, you'll need a PC and Internet access via a modem. When you find a mention of your client on the Internet you'll download the item to your computer and print it out. You can print three copies, two for your client and one for your records. Charge for such clips the same way you charge for newspaper and magazine clips.

How to Find Clients. You will advertise in business publications, on the Internet, in entertainment newspapers and magazines, and in industrial magazines using small classified ads. Your ads can be worded as follows:

SUPERB CLIPPING SERVICE. We find every mention of your company and you in the press and on the Internet at low cost. For full information, call (222) 123-4567.

KNOW WHAT IS BEING SAID ABOUT YOU! We search the Internet and every publication you specify and send you every mention of your company and its personnel. For full information, call (222) 123-4567 day or night.

Money Required to Start. You will need $800 to start this business because you will have to run several ads before you find your first client. Once you have a satisfied client you will find that others come to you based on word-of-mouth advertising. Further, you can get an advance on your first month's charges, based on an estimate of the total. A simple letter between you and the client will specify the amount of your monthly or per-item fee. This fee will give you operating cash.

Earnings Potential. You can earn $12,000 to $100,000 per year in this business. The higher earnings come when you have a larger number of clients. If you are unsure what to charge clients in your area, consult your local *Yellow Pages* for other clipping services. Call and ask the typical fees charged for various kinds of work. You can then price your service accordingly. Once you get several clients you will probably need one part-time worker to help you. It is easy to find people to work at minimum wage reading in their own homes.

Time to First Earnings. It will take you four to six weeks to receive your first earnings in this business. Why? Finding clients takes time. Unless there is a strong need for clipping services in your area and no other firm offering to do the work, it will take you awhile to have your firm recognized and hired. Once you have your first client, others will follow soon.

Equipment Needed. Desk, telephone, typewriter, clipping tools, paper, copying machine. Once your business is under way, you'll find a PC helpful. A PC is a necessity if you also offer Internet searches for your clients.

EARN MONEY OUTDOORS IN GOOD WEATHER

Name of Business. Street Sales

What You Do. You offer needed items for sale on streets—often at the corner or in another heavily populated location. In the simplest version of street sales, you use some type of collapsible table and a cardboard box to hold your display and inventory. Items you sell may include neckties, books, maps, belts, jewelry, watches, etc. Sales can be brisk during holiday seasons, vacation time, and special events like conventions. In a more formal version of street selling, you use a specially built cart from which you sell food, such as soft drinks, pretzels, and candy. In most large cities you will need some type of peddler's license to conduct your business. There is a nominal fee for such a license. Street sales give you the opportunity to start a business quickly and be earning cash within hours after you spread your wares on the table. Some cities offer free peddler's licenses to military veterans from any branch of the service.

How to Find Clients. Just stand on the corner and the customers will come to you as soon as your wares are on display. You must be where the people are if you are to make sales!

Money Required to Start. You'll need $250 to $500 to start—mostly for inventory, if you sell from a table. You can borrow or rent a table to keep costs low. If you want to sell food from a cart you can rent one from a local supplier, reducing your startup cost.

Earnings Potential. $300 to $1,000 a day, depending or what you're selling and the density of the population in your sales area. Your prices must be lower than local retailers' if you expect to make big money in street sales.

Time to First Earnings. You can be earning a good income within hours of setting up your table. With a food cart it will take somewhat longer because you will have to negotiate the rental, get the food, etc. Even so, you can be earning within three days of deciding to go into business. All of these time estimates presume you can obtain a temporary peddler's license while waiting for your permanent license to be approved. Contact your County Clerk (given in your local phone book) for data on the licensing agency you must contact. There is no examination—just an application and a fee.

Equipment Needed. Table or cart, handheld calculator, money bag.

GET UP EARLY AND EARN MORE MONEY

Name of Business. Wake-up and Reminder Service

What You Do. You call people in the morning (or other pre-arranged times) to wake them up. And you keep calling them until you're sure they're up and about. You can also include a reminder service in which you remind your clients of important birthdays, anniversaries, meetings, etc. You do wake-ups by phone; birthdays and meetings can be done by phone, e-mail, or fax; anniversaries are best done by phone so your client is forcefully reminded of the importance of the date. If you wish, you can include any other personal or business reminder-type service that can be done by phone, e-mail, or fax. And you'll find that satisfied clients will suggest other ways in which you can help them remember.

How to Find Clients. Run classified and small space ads in large-city magazines and newspapers, and *Yellow Pages*. For national coverage, use Internet ads.

Money Required to Start. $500 to $700 for space and classified ads in magazines, newspapers, and *Yellow Pages*.

Earnings Potential. Your monthly fee will range between $25 and $100 per client, depending on how much service you provide. Annual earnings for you will range from $12,000 to $75,000, depending on the number of clients, and your monthly fees for each client.

Time to First Earnings. You can start depositing earning checks within four weeks after you open your business.

Equipment Needed. Desk, phone, fax, typewriter, or access to a typist. A PC can help you get your dates and calls better organized, once you have a number of clients.

A GREAT USE-YOUR-HEAD BUSINESS

Name of Business. Develop Ideas for New Franchises

What You Do. You develop ideas for new franchise businesses. These new businesses could be in the areas of fast foods, auto services, tool rental, child care, etc. You come up with the idea based on a need you see for a product or service, develop the idea in the form of a business plan, and then offer it to people seeking to go into business for themselves. Once you have some interested Beginning Wealth Builders (BWBs), you offer them your plan at a suitable price. The price—called the franchise fee—can range from a low of $50 to a high of $50,000 or more. You earn this fee for supplying the basic idea for the franchise, the business plan, and advice on how to run the business successfully. By using your head and finding ideas for needed businesses, you can earn a significant income. And what's best of all, you can do this in the privacy of your home with little more than paper, a PC with printer, and a typewriter!

How to Find Clients. Run small classified ads in opportunity-type magazines, national newspapers, local papers, and on the Internet. Your ads might read:

> GREAT BUSINESS OPPORTUNITY for you; secure income, short hours. For full data, call (222) 123-4567 day or night.

> WANT YOUR OWN BUSINESS? We show you how to get started on small cash. Earn big money soon. Call (222) 123-4567 for full data.

Money Required to Start. You can start this business with $300 capital. All you need is enough money to run a few small ads to bring in some prospects. Once you've sold your first franchise you'll have enough cash to start a nationwide ad campaign to bring in many more hot prospects.

Earnings Potential. You can earn as much as $250,000 a year in this business, with a higher-priced offer ($5,000 and up) and active seeking of new franchisees. With low-priced franchises, you might earn $25,000 to $50,000 a year.

Time to First Earnings. It will take two to three weeks for your first earnings from a low-priced franchise. Higher-priced franchises will take six to eight weeks before you develop your first sale.

Equipment Needed. Desk, telephone, typewriter, PC, and fax will be helpful in your business.

Real-Life Home-Business Tips

HOW TO EARN ENORMOUS FEES FROM YOUR BUSINESS DEALS

What's the fastest way to build a big sum of money ($50,000 to $1 million) that doesn't have to be paid back? There are really just two ways: (1) Franchise your ideas, methods, or techniques, or (2) sell stock to the public. Of the two, we think that franchising can be the better route to wealth for new, untried firms. Why? Here are *your* answers.

Franchising brings in big chunks of money ($1,000 to $50,000, or more) from each franchise sale. So you can build up more capital, faster, with fewer sales. Next, franchising your ideas builds word-of-mouth advertising. A happy franchisee (your customer who pays you) tells his or her friends, who come to you, wanting to get in on the deal. And franchising helps people—so your business grows as more people use the products or services of your franchise.

"What can I franchise?" you ask. There are plenty of ideas, methods, techniques, or products which you can franchise. Certainly, we all know the more common franchises such as:

- Fast foods (ice cream, hamburgers, etc.)
- Auto services (mufflers, transmissions, etc.)
- Business help (accounting and bookkeeping, taxes)
- Employment agencies (temps, permanents, etc.)
- Mail order
- Export-import
- Tool rental
- Financial adviser
- Boat rental
- Real estate deals
- Auto rental, etc.
- Internet site design and usage

But there are less common franchises you might want to consider, such as:

- Consulting services for business
- Financing sources for business, real estate
- Schools for different money-making skills
- Computer-skills courses and training
- Licensing of products and services

You can get started in franchising for $300, or less if you plan your moves carefully. Thus, all you have to do is sell one franchise, say for $1,000, and you have the money to start advertising to sell the second, third, fourth, etc. And don't forget that 100 franchises sold at $1,000 each will give you $100,000. And the same number sold at $5,000 each will give you $500,000.

For the world's best help (we think) on franchising, we suggest that you use the IWS K-3 *Franchise Riches Program* listed at the back of this book. It tells you the What, How, Why, and When of franchising. Become a franchisor where people pay you money—and learn how you can become a millionaire quickly!

A NEEDED MONEY BUSINESS

Name of Business. Financial Brokerage

What You Do. You find loans for people and businesses for a fee. Your fee typically starts at 5 percent of the loan amount for the first million dollars (that's $50,000 for you) and declines by 1 percent for each additional million dollars. To protect your fee you will have to sign a written agreement between yourself and the borrower covering the amount of the fee you will be paid and when it will be paid (when the borrower receives the loan money). If you work with lenders who say "Brokers Protected" or "Brokers Welcome" you will be paid the fee by the lender when the borrower receives the loan money. Since almost every business and every individual needs money at some time or other, you have an enormous potential market for your financial brokerage service. While it is permissible to charge a nominal fee for out-of-pocket expenses associated with finding a loan—telephone, postage, fax messages, e-mail, etc.—you must not charge advance fees or front-money fees in the thousand of dollars. Such fees can produce unhappy clients and legal investigations when a loan is not found for the potential borrower. So do not charge front money—it only leads to trouble! A nominal processing fee for actual expenses, based on a written agreement, is usually acceptable.

How to Find Clients. Classified ads in business newspapers, local newspapers, on the Internet, and in magazines can produce hundreds of potential clients in just days.

Money Required to Start. $350 to $500 for space and classified ads will get you started. You should also have the K-1 *Financial Broker/Finder/Business Broker/Consultant Success Kit,* listed at the back of this book to get started in the right way. Using the Kit will help you quote acceptable commissions, use suitable agreements, and find interested lenders.

Earnings Potential. You can earn from $50,000 to $100,000, or more, per year from your own home in this great business if you have suitable lenders and qualified borrowers. The main key to large fees is willing lenders; the second key is qualified borrowers. You earn your fee for bringing the two together. In the few states where a license is required, you can easily qualify by working with a local attorney interested in this type of business.

Time to First Earnings. You can receive fees within one week after starting your business if you're in an area where people are seeking money. This is almost every area in the world!

Equipment Needed. Desk, phone, fax, copying machine, typewriter. Once your business grows you'll need a PC for the various records you'll want to keep and to access the Internet.

Real-Life Home-Business Tips

WHY MONEY FINDING IS A GREAT CAREER FOR YOU

Today we were reading a long-range forecast of the U.S. ranging from this year through the year 2010. And one very interesting fact struck us. This report says, in brief:

Between now and the year 2010 there will be few, if any, shortages of minerals, fuels, energy, or other items that will hurt the growth of the U.S. or the world! But the report says, there will be a shortage of capital—that is, money for business.

Now what favorable facts can you draw from such a report? A number—such as these for you:

- Money finding will be more in demand than ever before
- Finder's fees will probably start to go up very soon. You can have more business than you can handle
- Finders will be sought by all kinds of firms
- Most finders will be able to pick their work
- New finders will be able to start faster
- Experienced finders will be in demand almost everywhere
- Good finders will be able to make enormous fees

Do you need any special licenses to be a finder? No—you can operate as a finder even though you can't drive a car because you don't have a license! What we're trying to say is that the finder is "as free as a bird—if he or she can find money for others."

Is there any secret to hitting it big in finding money? There really aren't any secrets. But there are certain traits that will almost always pay off for the finder, such as:

- Keep looking until "your eyes fall out"—*looking pays off!*
- Never give up—*the loan you want may be at the next door!*
- Push ahead—*pushing pays profits to finders*
- Develop a good list of lenders—*lists make money for finders*
- Find as many clients as you can—*clients pay profits!*
- Get your name spread around—*this is easy*
- Learn your business well—*know-how pays off!*
- Know that you are in command—*the person with money controls*
- Never start working without a written agreement!

Some of the top business people in the world act as finders when they have a chance to put a deal together for their business associates. And these top people gladly take the fee that they deserve. So keep these other finder rules in mind also.

- Never work free—*always charge a fee*
- Be professional in all your work at *all* times
- Make finding an honorable career—even if you're a beginner
- Get good advice from legal and accounting specialists
- Treat your clients in a businesslike way
- Don't fight with clients—keep them happy
- *Always* have a written agreement covering your fee!

To start as a finder, get some know-how. You can read up on the finding profession in libraries, talk to other finders, or study the IWS K-1 *Financial Broker/Finder/Business Broker/Consultant Success Kit,* described at the back of this book. Once you know a little about the field, you can start looking for clients or customers. This, too, is easy!

With your clients under your wing and with a written agreement covering your fee, you are ready to start finding money sources. Here this book can help you, and you can help yourself by making a list of every money source you come across. Look, look, look!

And don't overlook the Internet as a source of clients and lenders. Your PC can help you earn more, once you know how to run your business. The Kit, K-1, mentioned above, will give you the needed know-how.

ONE OF THE MOST NEEDED SERVICE BUSINESSES TODAY

Name of Business. Employment Contact Group for Young Mothers Seeking Part-Time Work

What You Do. Find part-time employment for mothers with young (and not so young) children. These mothers may range from unskilled workers to the most advanced professionals—PhD's in science and engineering, lawyers, accountants, computer programmers, system managers, website designers, etc. You assemble data on your employment candidates. Once you have key information on 12 candidates with a variety of skills, you contact local firms by postal mail, e-mail, phone, or fax and offer the services of your candidates. For each candidate hired by a firm you contact, you will be paid a fee by the hiring company or organization based on the expected total earnings of the candidate. There is no charge of any kind to any of your candidates. All any candidate need do is submit to you a resume covering her skills, previous experience, the type of part-time position being sought, and the days and hours during which each wishes to work. You make copies of these resumes for submission to target firms. Or you can ask each candidate to supply you with 12 copies of her resume. This reduces your copying costs.

How to Find Clients. Just tell your female friends (or your spouse's friends if you're a male) that you have a service for finding part-time work for mothers seeking a spare-time income. If you don't have many female friends and acquaintances, you can: (1) put 3 × 5-inch-card notices on free bulletin boards in shopping malls, drug stores, convenience stores, and similar outlets; (2) run small classified ads in weekly newspapers in your area; (3) run small classified ads (usually free of charge) in religious bulletins published by various houses of worship; (4) use word-of-mouth ads to tell a few mothers about your service and ask them to "spread the word" about the free opportunities you offer them to find part-time work in a local firm on the days and during the hours that are convenient to their child-rearing schedules. If you're in an area of young families, the word will spread fast and you'll soon have a full list of qualified candidates.

The ads you run on free bulletin boards or as classifieds in various newspapers and religious bulletins can read thus:

MOTHERS: Do you seek a part-time job in your local area? Are you a skilled worker in a special field? Call (222) 123-4567 for a unique opportunity to work your chosen hours and days at excellent wages.

To find employers for mothers who want to work part-time, write local firms and organizations and offer your services. Your letter can read thus:

ABC Company
Attn. Director of Human Resources
123 Main Street
Anytown, State USA 12345

Dear Director _____:

Do you need the services of highly skilled part-time professionals who are dedicated, competent, and loyal employees? Workers who will serve your needs with no benefit costs to your company?

If you do—and almost every firm has such needs today— we have a unique answer for you. That answer? It is "Mothers

Seeking Part-Time Work." These mothers are exclusively listed in our "Part-Time Availability List," which we will send to you free of charge. The only cost to you is a nominal fee of _____ percent of our candidate's annual earnings, payable one week after hiring. This fee is not deductible from the candidate's earnings.

If this proposal interests you, please contact us by mail, phone, or fax, and we will send our exclusive list to you.

Very truly yours,

Your Name

When you send your list of candidates to potential clients, do not include the name and address of any candidate. Just identify each candidate by using a Code Number for specific applicants. Thus, for accounting professionals, you can use the Code Number of A-1, A-2, A-3, etc. For banking professionals, use the Code Number B-1, B-2, B-3, etc. Computer professionals will be identified as C-1, C-2, C-3, etc.

You can find the names of local companies in your nearby Public Library. The Library will have directories of local companies, along with the names and job titles of key personnel. Send your letter to the Director of Human Resources.

Money Required to Start. This is really a low-cost-startup business. You can get by with just $300 to $500. Some people start for even less, just $50 to $100. Why? Because your only cost is for paper, stamps, and envelopes.

Earnings Potential. $25,000 to $75,000 per year can be earned in this business in areas where you have a large supply of mothers seeking part-time work and a goodly number of local firms needing part-timers. In remote areas your earnings will be lower because you will have fewer mothers looking for part-time work.

Time to First Earnings. It will take you four to six weeks before you place your first candidate. Then you'll have a two to four week wait for your first payment check. However, once you begin placing people you'll have a fairly steady flow of checks into your bank account. Your typical fee will range from 15 to 25 percent of your candidate's annual salary, depending on what kind of a deal you can negotiate.

Equipment Needed. Desk, phone, typewriter, PC with printer, and fax.

Sixteen More Easy-Start Businesses

Here are 16 more of the easiest-to-start home businesses you might want to consider. While none of these businesses may be an exact fit for you, any of them can suggest an easy-start business, which you'll like. The main points to keep in mind while looking over this list are:

1. Be ready to have one business suggest another, closely related business.
2. Don't turn off a business until you've thought about it. The businesses listed here *do* work, *can* earn money for you, and *will* take care of you if you take care of them!
3. Pick a business *you* like. You'll have more fun and you'll earn more money when customers see you enjoy what you're doing. Everyone likes enthusiasm!
4. If you need help picking a business, financing the business, or with any other aspect of your future home business, call me and I'll try to help. I'm as near as your telephone, if you're a subscriber to my monthly newsletter on home businesses *International Wealth Success*. See the back of this book for details.

Business	What You Do	How to Find Clients	Money Required to Start	Earnings Potential	Time to First Earnings	Equipment Needed
Apartment rental agency	Find tenants for local apartments	Classified ads in local papers	$500 to $600	$15,000 to $30,000	4 to 6 weeks	Desk, phone, typewriter
Art and craft sales	Sell art and crafts locally and by mail	Ads in local papers and magazines	$800 to $900	$12,000 to $60,000	2 to 3 weeks	Display area, desk, phone, typewriter
Auto driving instruction	Teach people how to drive	Ads in local papers, *Yellow Pages*, magazines	$750 to $900	$10,000 to $50,000	6 to 8 weeks	Auto, desk, phone, typewriter
Auto washing and polishing	Clean, polish autos for local customers	Ads in local papers, at gas stations	$300 to $500	$8,000 to $25,000	1 to 2 weeks	Desk, phone, typewriter, cleaning supplies
Autograph collection sales	Find famous autographs, sell them	Ads in autograph publications	$500 to $700	$5,000 to $75,000	4 to 6 weeks	Desk, phone, typewriter
Baton twirling lessons	Teach young people how to use a baton	Ads in local school twirling lessons	$400 to $600	$5,000 to $12,000	4 to 6 weeks	Desk, phone, typewriter
Beauty consultation and guidance	Teach others how to accent their beauty	Ads in local papers, magazines	$500 to $800	$6,000 to $24,000	2 to 3 weeks	Desk, phone, typewriter
Bird watchers' tours	Conduct tours to local bird nesting areas	Ads in bird watchers' publications	$600 to $800	$12,000 to $20,000	4 to 8 weeks	Desk, phone, typewriter
Cake baking and decoration	Bake and/or decorate cakes for special events	Ads in local papers	$500 to $600	$4,000 to $8,000	2 to 4 weeks	Desk, phone, typewriter, oven, supplies
Chauffeur service	Drive people to requested destinations	Ads in local *Yellow Pages*	$600 to $900	$12,000 to $60,000	8 to 12 weeks	Desk, phone, typewriter, auto, chauffeur's license
Maid and housekeeper service	Find jobs for maids and housekeepers	Ads in local papers and magazines	$500 to $800	$10,000 to $50,000	6 to 8 weeks	Desk, phone, typewriter

Business	What You Do	How to Find Clients	Money Required to Start	Earnings Potential	Time to First Earnings	Equipment Needed
Party sales	Sell a product or service to gatherings of people in a home	Word-of-mouth, local classified ads	$500 to $800	$12,000 to $60,000	2 to 3 weeks	Desk, phone, typewriter
Small animal boarding	Care for small animals in your home	Ads in pet shops and local papers	$400 to $600	$5,000 to $12,000	3 to 4 weeks	Desk, phone, typewriter, kennel license in some areas
Street parking shuffler	Move cars around on a street to avoid parking tickets	Ads in heavily peopled areas— hospitals, offices, apartment houses	$200 to $500	$8,000 to $50,000	2 to 3 weeks	Desk, phone, typewriter
Summer camp information service	Supply data and prices on summer camps to parents	Classified ads in newspapers and magazines	$700 to $900	$6,000 to $24,000	4 to 6 weeks	Desk, phone, typewriter
Used book sales	Find and sell used books of all types by mail	Classified ads in local papers, national magazines	$600 to $900	$10,000 to $250,000	4 to 6 weeks	Desk, phone, typewriter, fax, PC

CHAPTER 4

THE 32 FASTEST CASH PRODUCING HOME BUSINESSES

PEOPLE CALL AND FAX ME day and night for business ideas and advice. If they're subscribers to my *International Wealth Success* newsletter (see the back of this book) I'm glad to spend hours (if necessary) giving them ideas and advice.

Probably the most frequently asked question during these phone and fax communications is: *What business can I go into in my own home that will produce the fastest cash flow for me?*

This chapter answers that question with 25 of the fastest cash producing home businesses for you. Go into any of these businesses and you can have a positive cash flow in just days or weeks. And the beautiful feature of many of these businesses is that you can start them quickly. There is no need to wait weeks and weeks to get started! What's more, most of these home businesses don't require years and years of experience to run right.

So let's get you started earning a big home income quickly. Even if none of these businesses turn you on, I'm sure they'll suggest plenty of other businesses that *do* turn you on!

MIX WITH THE BEST PEOPLE

Name of Business. Professional Practice Marketing

What You Do. You find additional clients for professionals of all types—doctors, dentists, engineers, accountants, attorneys, etc. The biggest market for this business is health professionals, who always seem to be looking for more clients. What you do is get the name of the health professional (or any other professional) in front of large groups of people who might want to use his or her services. You do this by sending flyers about the professional's services to large groups, getting the professional to run a Question and Answer column in papers or on the Internet, which serves large groups of people, having the professional offer a free first visit exam of some kind, etc. You are paid a monthly retainer for the work you do—there is no fee splitting or other sharing in the revenues you produce for the professional. You can, however, work for a number of professionals at the same time provided they do not offer competing services.

How to Find Clients. Run small classified ads in professional magazines, journals, on the Internet, and in newspapers. These ad might say:

> INCREASE YOUR PATIENT FLOW by helping them recognize symptoms earlier. Call (222) 123-4567.

> ENGINEERS CAN GET MORE CLIENTS when their work is known. Call (222) 123-4567 for details.

Money Required to Start. You'll need $400 to $500 to pay for your initial ads, phone calls, Internet ads, and your letterhead. Once you have a steady monthly cash flow you can expand your ads.

Earnings Potential. You can earn from $10,000 to as much as $100,000 a year in this home business. To earn the higher levels of income you must have a larger number of clients under contract. See the K-14 *Professional Practice Builders Kit* described at the back of this book for full details on how to earn the most from this interesting and rewarding business.

Time to First Earnings. You can have your first advance income check within one week after you start your business—if you do a planned marketing program to professionals in your area. Once you get a number of professionals in your program, you will have a steady cash flow, which you can arrange to be received on either a weekly or monthly basis depending on your wishes.

Equipment Needed. Desk, telephone, fax, typewriter, PC (after you have a number of clients), plus an Internet modem.

Real-Life Examples

Here is an example of flyer ad material prepared for health professionals by a professional practice marketer. As you can see, the ad promotes the benefits of dealing with a particular health professional who is a client of one home worker. The ad is shown in Figures 4-1 and 4-2.

These ads are easy to prepare because the health professional gives you the data he or she wants to emphasize. You can lay the ad out on your computer screen and adjust your layout until it looks attractive enough to get results. Next, print out the ad on your printer. You then show your ad to the health professional for approval. Once you have approval, you either print out enough copies on your computer printer or take the approved layout to a printer with the go-ahead to print a large enough quantity for distribution to interested people. (If you do not have a PC, you can have a friend who has a PC do the work for you. Without such a friend, try a quick-copy shop which does offer PC services at a modest fee. Or you can prepare the ad layout by hand and have the printer make the final layout and print the number of copies needed.)

A BUSINESS NEEDED EVERYWHERE

Name of Business. Mail Order Loan Finder

What You Do. You help people get loans by applying through the mail. While this is slower than applying in person or by telephone, many borrowers prefer using the mail to apply

UNIVERSAL PSYCHO-THERAPY SERVICE

Easy to get to the Service.

We're conveniently located between Main and Front Streets. By bus or by train take the Main Street line.

Hours suited to your needs.

Appointments are conveniently arranged to suit your own schedule.

UNIVERSAL PSYCHOTHERAPY SERVICE

123 Main St.
Anytown, State 00000-0000
(123) 456-7890

Figure 4-1

Living in a pressure cooker.

Today's stressful world takes its toll. It affects people's health, their careers, and their relationships with family and friends.

It's these all-important "people" relationships that concern our therapists.

The therapists here know the problems and strains produced by everyday living. They know the strengths people must develop in order to cope with modern life. They're experienced in helping you develop the insights you need in order to overcome the stress of today's world.

You no longer have to face the problems of "the pressure cooker" alone.

We're interested in the whole you.

At our Service, we are especially sensitive to you as a distinctive human being. While our therapists are, naturally, concerned with the specific problems you present, we are also concerned with the whole person. We want all of you to flourish.

Here's how our Service works for you.

We modify our therapeutic approach to suit your one-of-a-kind needs. Such a tailor-made therapy makes for a more pertinent therapeutic experience, and therefore a more successful one. We are expert at choosing the right approach for the right person.

Our concerned professionalism.

We combine deep human concern with the highest standards of professionalism in every phase of our Service. For instance, you will meet our therapist in a setting designed to emphasize our acceptance of you as a person. The setting is also designed for concerned listening.

During your first meeting, you will discuss the problems that brought you to us, you will talk over your needs with your therapist, and together work out a suitable treatment plan.

What we offer.

INDIVIDUAL AND GROUP PSYCHOTHERAPY.
STRESS MANAGEMENT.
HYPNOSIS THERAPY AND SELF-HYPNOSIS.
CRISIS INTERVENTION.
BIOFEEDBACK.
ASSERTIVENESS TRAINING.
MARITAL AND FAMILY THERAPY.
SINGLE PARENT COUNSELING.

We can help with these life situations.

ANXIETY STRESS AND TENSION.
OVERWEIGHT.
SMOKING.
PHOBIAS.
GAMBLING.
SELF-IMAGE AND SELF-ESTEEM.
OVERCOMING BLOCKS TO SUCCESS.
BEREAVEMENT.
MID-LIFE CRISIS.
DIVORCE COUNSELING.
TRAUMA OF A PHYSICAL DISABILITY.

123 Main St.
Anytown, State 00000-0000
(123) 456-7890

UNIVERSAL PSYCHOTHERAPY SERVICE

Figure 4-2

for a loan because it allows them to remain anonymous. What you do is to connect the lender and borrower, helping the borrower fill out the loan application, if necessary. You also help the borrower select a suitable lender, depending upon the type of loan the borrower seeks. So you might say you are a "paper shuffler." For this work you are paid a fee by the borrower. Typically this fee is 5 percent of the amount borrowed. Where the loan is small, say $10,000, the fee will rise to 8 percent. Why? Because you have to do just as much work on a small loan as on a larger loan. So your percentage fee is higher on smaller loans to repay you for the time you put in on the paperwork for your clients. The most popular type of mail-order loan is debt consolidation. You could keep busy for the rest of your life handling debt consolidation loans because so many people are in over their heads on credit card debt. You should give some consideration to specializing in debt consolidation loans because your clients will keep you busy day and night! And if you offer your services on the Internet, you can work seven days a week, if you wish!

How to Find Clients. You run small classified ads in local papers and magazines (and on the Internet if you want to work nationally) giving details of your service. Here are two typical ads:

GET OUT OF DEBT. We show you how. Call (222) 123-4567 day or night.

NEED A LOAN? We can help you get it for any personal use. Call (222) 123-4567 day or night.

You can also advertise in local *Pennysaver*-type newspapers, religious publications, and real estate papers and get good results.

Money Required to Start. You can start this business with $500 for ads and stationery. And, if you wish, you can charge your clients a nominal fee—say $25 to $50 for an initial consultation and analysis of their credit situation. This income will help pay for ads and will also pay for the time you invest for the prospective borrower.

Earnings Potential. You can earn from $25,000 to $75,000 a year in this business. If you specialize in debt consolidation you could have more customers than you have time for. Other types of mail-order loans you can help people get include auto financing, vacation, medical or dental, education, home equity, and home refinance. But none of these loans will give you as many clients as debt consolidation.

Time to First Earnings. You can have earnings one week after you start this business. Why? Because the consultation fees you receive will be the start of your income. With so many people trying to consolidate their debts, you will find that they will keep your telephone busy day and night when they learn that you may be able to help them get out of their debts.

Equipment Needed. Desk, telephone, typewriter. Once your business begins to boom, you will find a PC and fax helpful. A PC is a must if you plan to run ads on the Internet.

Real-Life Home-Business Tips

The many advantages of being a Mail-Order Loan Finder are shown in Figure 4-3. The ad gives you—in concise form—the many benefits you'll have when you work as a Mail-Order Loan Finder. The kit mentioned in the ad is designed to get you started earning money quickly. You will also be pleased with the many advantages such a home business gives you.

A BUSINESS THAT'S NEEDED EVERYWHERE

Name of Business. Child Care Referral Agency

What You Do. You find people interested in caring for children while the child's mother or father works, the parents

How to Get Rich in
MAIL ORDER
CASH

LOAN
DOLLARS.

- <u>Overcome</u> BAD CREDIT for yourself and others!
- <u>Get CASH</u> in a flash—maybe one day, or less!
- Find an "Angel" for your cash needs!
- Develop signature-loan MONEY POWER!
- Rate <u>YOUR</u> loan chances in minutes!
- Wipe out <u>ALL DEBTS</u> with just one loan!
- Deal by mail—<u>NO</u> interviews; <u>NO</u> pain!
- Get liquid assets for any personal need!

- Get <u>DOZENS</u> of different kinds of loans!
- Be a <u>MAIL-ORDER UNSECURED SIGNATURE LOAN</u> <u>wheeler, dealer!</u>
- Make friends with money lenders forever!
- Get <u>MAIL-ORDER LOAN</u> convenience, speed, efficiency, confidentiality!
- Earn <u>BIG FEES</u> helping others get quick unsecured signature loans!
- Know who's lending for what use!
- Laugh "all the way to the bank" <u>NOW</u>!

Figure 4-3

- Get INTEREST ONLY mail-order loans!

- Be the "fastest loan broker" around!

- Deal by mail and avoid face-to-face hassles and arguments!

GET UNSECURED PERSONAL SIGNATURE LOANS FOR YOUR CLIENTS OR YOURSELF using the IWS MAIL-ORDER LOAN SUCCESS SYSTEM—the fastest way to get a signature loan today! Learn how to deal with lenders—prepare winning loan applications—help yourself or others to the BILLIONS available for unsecured loans! Build your own, or your client's loan rating fast! It's ALL here—plus much, much more in this NEW powerful SYSTEM!

Written by Ty Hicks, a man who has supervised the lending of some $50-million in all types of unsecured signature loans, this SYSTEM is just what's needed to get people the money they seek! And YOU can use the SYSTEM for your clients, or for yourself. It works, works, works for YOU! And it works for anyone you're helping get a loan. The SYSTEM gives you thousands of lenders to contact—shows YOU how to build your own list of willing and interested lenders! Send your check or money order for your SYSTEM today! Get loans SOON!

THIS IS THE ORDER BLANK

$$
$ Here's $100. Send me my MAIL-ORDER LOAN SUCCESS SYSTEM. If you wish, you can call Ty Hicks with your $
$ credit-card (Master or Visa) order at 516-766-5850 9am to 10pm. Have your credit card ready? Ask Ty any $
$ questions you may have! $
$ NAME _____ Apt/Suite # _____ $
$ ADDRESS _____ CITY _____ STATE _____ ZIP _____ $
$ $
$ Send check or money order to: IWS, Inc., 24 Canterbury Rd, Rockville Centre, NY 11570 $
$$

Figure 4-3 (continued)

travel, or the child needs watching for any other non-medical reason. Your work is *not* baby-sitting! Instead, you find baby-sitters, check out their qualifications, and then refer them to people needing dependable child-care service. For this work you are paid a fee by the person seeking the childcare services. With the large increase in working mothers throughout the world, the child-care referral service business is booming. Yet you'll never see the children for whom your service provides sitters and home-care personnel. Instead, you function as a locator of qualified people and bring the need and solution together. Normally, you do not need a license of any kind to perform this work because you are not functioning as an employment agency or other licensed business.

How to Find Clients. Run ads in local papers, in religious publications, on the Internet, and in mall bulletin boards. Your ad can say:

NEED A RELIABLE BABY-SITTER? We can provide the person you seek, at low cost. Call (222) 123-4567 day or night.

SAFE, RELIABLE CHILD CARE AT LOW COST. Full information call (222) 123-4567, day or night.

You'll get a good response to such ads because reliable childcare providers are needed everywhere.

Money Required to Start. You can start this business for $500 because you can run ads at no cost or very low cost in a number of local outlets. These ads will get you started in just days.

Earnings Potential. This business can bring you $12,000 to $100,000 a year from finding child-care providers and the people who need them. The more child-care providers you can recommend, the larger your income will be. There's profit in volume in the business!

Time to First Earnings. You can start earning within the first week you're in this business if you have some ready applicants. Once your ads start running you can be swamped by applicants needing baby-sitters of some kind.

Equipment Needed. Desk, telephone, typewriter, PC, fax. You will find much helpful information in IWS-35 *How to Run a Profitable Child-Care Referral Service* by William Frederick, described at the back of this book.

If you'd prefer to consider other types of child-care businesses, look at those in Table 4-1, This table lists six other child-care type businesses from which you can earn money at home. The table shows you that there are many exciting and rewarding opportunities in the field of child-care—which is probably one of the most important fields in the development of the world today. Why? Because if the children of the world aren't properly cared for, there is little future for any of us!

WORK IN THE HEALTHY OUTDOORS

Name of Business. Pleasure Boat Maintenance Service

What You Do. Clean, wax, paint, and otherwise service pleasure boats in your area. You will work at yacht clubs, marinas, and docking facilities in your area. Your customers will be boat owners who don't have the time or the desire to clean, wax, or paint their vessels. This includes most of the owners of boats 35 feet long or longer. You will clean their boat on a weekly basis and be paid weekly. Once you establish a group of satisfied customers you can get young people to do the actual cleaning work. This will free you up to look for new customers. If desired, you can follow the sun in this business, working in the North during the summer and moving South during the winter. Most of your work will be done outdoors in the sun. Few boats are stored indoors. And those that are get little cleaning while inside.

How to Find Clients. Leaflets distributed to marinas, yacht clubs, and dockside shops, Figure 4-4, are cheap to produce and get good results. Such ads can also be mailed to local boat owners to publicize your service. You can also post your notice on the bulletin boards of local yacht clubs free of charge.

Business	What You Do	How to Find Clients	Money Required to Start	Earnings Potential	Time to First Income	Equipment Needed
Company child-care facility listings	Compile lists of what firms offer employees in terms of child-care benefits	Ads in local papers, parents' newsletters, magazines	$500 to $1,000	$7,500 to $60,000	4 to 8 weeks	Desk, phone, PC, fax typewriter
Child-care referral service	Find and check out baby-sitters for parents	Ads in local papers, religious publications, mall bulletin boards	$500	$12,000 to $48,000	2 to 4 weeks	Desk, phone, PC, fax, typewriter
Summer camp for kids	Provide a summer camp for kids in your home	Ads in local papers, religious publications	$500 to $800	$6,000 to $48,000	8 to 12 weeks	Desk, phone, PC, fax, typewriter
Baby-sitting	Care for children in your home	Ads in papers, mall bulletin boards	$250 to $600	$30,000 to $90,000	4 to 6 weeks	Desk, phone, typewriter
Children's tours	Take kids to interesting places in your area	Ads in school papers, mall bulletin boards	$300 to $600	$8,000 to $40,000	6 to 8 weeks	Desk, phone, PC, fax, typewriter
Special courses for kids	Teach kids specialized subjects	Ads in local papers, religious publications, mall bulletin boards	$600 to $1,000	$12,000 to $75,000	6 to 8 weeks	Desk, phone, PC, fax, typewriter

YACHT CLUB SPECIAL

Professional Waxing
Weekly Washings
Teak Restorations

Complete Waxing—Including:

1–Waxing Hull and Topsides

2–Bright Work Polished

3–Fenders and Power Cords Cleaned

4–Dock Box Waxed

5–Curtains Cleaned

6–Final Wash Included

Complete Weekly Washing—Includes:

a–Wax One Quarter of Topsides

b–Wash Entire Boat (Including Hull)

c–Curtains Cleaned

d–Boat Left in Sparkling Condition (No Water Spots)

e–Basic Wash

CLUB SPECIAL

CALL: 123-4567 ANY TIME

FREE ESTIMATES!!

• Fully Insured

• Over 5 Years Experience

COUPON FOR

10% Off

COMPLETE WAXING
BY

CLUB SPECIAL

Figure 4-4

Money Required to Start. You can get started with $25 worth of equipment and flyers. Once you do a good job on a boat, word-of-mouth advertising—the best kind—will bring more owners seeking your service. Do what owners call a "Palm Beach Job" and you'll have customers begging for your services—and paying for them!

Earnings Potential. $30 to $100 per boat per week depending on boat size. Special work, like varnishing and painting, is negotiated; the price will vary with the size of the job, who supplies the materials, and any time limits placed on you by the owner. Such work is not included as part of your weekly cleaning fee.

Time to First Earnings. You can have a cash income within one week after getting your leaflets or flyers around to clubs, marinas, and boats. It will probably take you four weeks to reach your full capacity because owners may take time to decide on using your cleaning services.

Equipment Needed. Desk, phone, PC for records and ad preparation, mops, brushes, cloths, soap, wax.

A Fast Cash Income Business

Name of Business. Publishing Special-Interest Newsletters

What You Do. Publish one or more newsletters—on a regular or irregular basis—to serve special-interest groups. These groups can be in any field from ants to zoology and everyone in between. Thus, your author has been publishing a business opportunity newsletter for more than 30 years. During this time the monthly newsletter has put many millions into my waiting bank account! Yet this is a highly specialized newsletter. As such it follows the tradition of almost all newsletters—that is, a close look at a specialized subject. One newsletter, for example, just won an annual prize for overall excellence. Its subject? Ships and shipwrecks! This is an ideal example of a specialty. Another good example is E. Jane Mall, author of *How to Become Wealthy Publishing a Newsletter,* described at the back of this book. She successfully publishes a newsletter for church secretaries! So if you have a specialized interest or can find one needing a newsletter, jump on the wealth train now!

How to Find Subscribers. Newsletters are primarily promoted by direct mail, on the Internet, and by telemarketing. While there are a few newsletters that do well selling their subscriptions through space ads—such as *Vacation Hideaways*—most newsletters do best with promotion by mail, Internet, and phone. To promote by mail you can buy specialized mailing lists, exchange names for free if you have a mailing list you developed for another business, or use lists of seminar attendees. You mail a strong advertising piece to prospects to get them to subscribe to your newsletter.

When you promote on the Internet, you will probably start on a mall—which is an Internet service advertising a variety of products. It's called a *mall* because it resembles a shopping mall with lots of shops in it. You will probably start on an Internet mall because you can often arrange to be "put up" (run ads) on a mall free of charge. You'll pay the service provider a fee for each order you get—usually 25 percent of the order amount. Meanwhile, you'll get lots of free advertising on the mall.

Telemarketing promotion of your newsletter can be handled by an agency working on a commission basis. The agency calls prospects and asks them to subscribe, using the sales message you give them. Good results (i.e., a large number of subscribers) are often possible with telemarketing.

Money Required to Start. You'll need $750 to start your newsletter because you'll have to prepare your first issue and do a mailing or Internet promotion to get subscribers. But once the money starts rolling in you can use it to fund future issues, mailings, and Internet promotions. So your business becomes self-financing. And all this can be done from one small room or part of a larger room at home. So you have no overhead in this business when you run it from home.

Earnings Potential. You'll earn from $25,000 to $1,000,000 a year per newsletter with just a nominal amount of advertising. As you get one newsletter established you can then think about starting another. When you do this, your income jumps because there's little expense for the second, third, fourth newsletters.

Time to First Earnings. You can bring in money within two weeks after you start mailing subscription solicitations or go on the Internet. Some of this money can be used to make more mailings and other direct-marketing presentations. You can even delay your first issue until you have enough subscribers—usually 100—to make the business a success.

Equipment Needed. Desk, telephone, typewriter, PC (paid for by your newsletter after you have a strong cash flow), fax, e-mail address.

Real-Life Sample

To get your newsletter income started, you'll need a mailing piece that describes your publication and the benefits readers will get from it. While you may think that it's best to have such a mailing piece written by a professional copywriter, you'll find that:

1. You can usually write a better piece than anyone else because you know best what will be in your newsletter
2. You'll save lots of time when you write your own mailing piece because professional copywriters are often too busy to give you immediate attention
3. Writing your own copy allows you to say what you want to—not what someone else thinks should be said

Figure 4-5 shows four pages of an eight-page flyer your author wrote for his newsletter, *International Wealth Success.* This flyer rakes in sales every week of the year, and has been doing so for more than 30 years!

Copywriters can criticize it. Yet the flyer has sold several million dollars' worth of subscriptions all over the world. While it may be true that a professionally written flyer would sell more, I've yet to find one that did. And I've tried a number of them.

So save yourself some time and money. *Your* copy will probably be as good as—or better than—more professionally written flyers.

If you don't agree with this advice, write your own copy. Then have it reviewed by a professional. You'll feel better and your copy may be sharpened somewhat. Figure 4-5 was gone over by several copywriters. None changed a word!

Further, you can use your direct-mail letter on the Internet. As a general guide you can say: *What works well in direct mail will work well on the Internet!* So you can get double mileage out of the promotion copy you write. This is another good reason for writing your own ad copy!

THE WORLD'S BEST BUSINESS

Name of Business. Mail Order, Direct Mail, and Direct Marketing

What You Do. You sell products or services to a variety of people or firms using small space ads (or large ones, if you can afford them) in suitable publications, on the Internet, with radio or TV spots, and by telemarketing. You might also try to sell the same products or services mailing ads directly (called direct mail) to potential customers. Direct mail is often included in the overall term mail order. And almost all mail order companies, do some direct mail. Likewise, most direct mail firms do some mail order. You'll find all of this explained in K-4 *Mail-Order Riches Success Kit,* listed at the back of this book. Mail order is the world's best business for the home-based entrepreneur because it is easy to start, can produce enormous profit quickly, and does not require any previous experience. Some home-based BWBs earn $500,000 their first year in mail order. Others are almost driven out of their homes by the pile of mail the post office delivers to their door!

And the Internet, along with radio and TV spots combined with some telemarketing, can zoom your income beyond your wildest dreams. Why? As someone once said: *It pays to advertise!*

How to Find Customers. Space and classified ads in suitable publications, along with an Internet presence and telemarketing will bring customers to you. Direct mail to a carefully chosen list can give you instant sales, especially if you have a merchant account and can accept credit card orders from potential customers.

INTERNATIONAL WEALTH SUCCESS, Inc.

P.O. Box 186, Merrick, NY 11566

516-766-5850

Dear Wealth Builder:

What kind of a wealth builder are *You*—a BWB (Beginning Wealth Builder), or an EWB (Experienced Wealth Builder)? Be *You* a BWB or an EWB, I have *good* news for *You!*

Do *You* want to get rich in your own successful business? Have Independence, security, vacations, and *all* the good things *You* see (beautiful home, impressive car, a boat or airplane)? If *You* do, I think we can help *You* find great success!

To make *You* the success *You* should be in your own independent business we have a number of powerful helps. These are:

➤ Our monthly Newsletter, *INTERNATIONAL WEALTH SUCCESS*— The Newsletter of Business Success Methods which gives *You* many wealth-building ideas and money sources every month

➤ Practical *SUCCESS KITS* and books which may give *You* a new view and new ideas while putting *Big Money* into *Your* Life

➤ Loan sources sought out for our subscribers who need funds to buy, start, expand, or take over a business of their own

➤ Personal consultations to help *You* get ahead faster in *Your* own successful small business which can grow into a big one

➤ Free ads which *You*, as a subscriber, can run in our monthly newsletter to get the help *You* need to grow wealthy soon

Figure 4-5 page 1

Please read every page of this 8-page flyer. It gives *You* a full view of our many services—like books, Success Kits, our Newsletter, hotline phone number, etc. We are specialists in WEALTH AND FORTUNE BUILDING! We want to help you get rich!

We Hope *You* join our group of SWBs—Successful Wealth Builders! Be sure to read page 8 of the flyer to get the flavor of what we do for BWBs throughout the world. *You* should—we believe—start doing—instead of dreaming. And we'll help!

Don't waste another moment! Get started *Now* by sending for our Newsletter, one or more Success Kits, and books! Put the methods we give *You* to work and they'll work for *You*—bringing in money, freedom, independence, and comfort soon.

I'm here to help *You* when *You* need me—seven days and nights a week. So let me help *You*. Send for the items *You* think will help—and I'll help *YOU!*

Cordially yours in great success,

INTERNATIONAL WEALTH SUCCESS, INC

Tyler G. Hicks, President.

P.S. If *You* have already subscribed to IWS, please pass this along to a friend!
P.P.S. We've helped thousands. We want to help *YOU. Subscribe NOW!*

Credit Reference: The Bank of New York, New York, NY 10019. Member: Better Business Bureau (This is not an endorsement). Founded 1967: In business continuously since that date.

over

Figure 4-5 page 1 (continued)

INTERNATIONAL WEALTH SUCCESS, Inc.

THE WORLD-WIDE MONTHLY NEWSLETTER OF UNUSUAL BUSINESS OPPORTUNITIES FOR WEALTH BUILDERS

Twelve BIG issues each year bring you profitable money-making ideas you can use anywhere any time. Here are a few ways you are shown to help you on your path to GREAT riches:

☞ 100%, 110%, 115% FINANCING (MONEY) SOURCES
☞ COMPENSATING BALANCE loan sources
☞ NEW WEALTH IDEAS EVERY MONTH
☞ MANY, many sources of BUSINESS LOANS
☞ Part-time MONEY-MAKING IDEAS
☞ MAIL-ORDER RICHES opportunities
☞ FINDER FEE listings of many types
☞ WORLDWIDE money-making ideas for YOU.
☞ FAST-FORTUNE money-making wealth deals
☞ FRANCHISE RICHES ideas and METHODS
☞ CAPITAL AVAILABLE pages in each issue
☞ Monthly TY HICKS PAGE where Ty talks to you
☞ FINANCIAL BROKER OPPORTUNITIES
☞ COSIGNER LISTINGS for YOU and others
☞ Ways to Get Money you need for business
☞ UNUSUAL TECHNIQUES you can use to grow
☞ SECRETS that can put cash in your pocket
☞ Hundreds of Wealth Ideas each year

See a sample page
from a recent issue
of the IWS Newsletter

***

16 or more pages
each month!

SUBSCRIBE TODAY — only $24 per year brings you this up-to-date NEWSLETTER.
ONE IDEA FROM ONE ISSUE COULD MAKE YOU WEALTHY FOREVER.

Figure 4-5 page 2

FILL IN THE COUPON BELOW: ENCLOSE YOUR CHECK OR MONEY ORDER NOW!

YOU'LL BE GLAD YOU DID. MAIL TODAY!

☎ Credit Card Orders only: 1-516-766-5850 Operators cannot answer questions. ☎

INTERNATIONAL WEALTH SUCCESS, INC. P.O. BOX 186 MERRICK, NY 11566

Here's my $24 for a one-year subscription to the
INTERNATIONAL WEALTH SUCCESS Newsletter.
Begin my subscription with the CURRENT ISSUE!

NAME _____

STREET _____

CITY _____ STATE _____ ZIP _____

To order by credit card please give the following information:

CARD NO. _____ Expiration date _____

Home Phone # _____ Signature _____

*WHEN YOU SEND US YOUR $24.00 FOR YOUR FIRST YEAR'S
SUBSCRIPTION TO THE IWS NEWSLETTER, YOU can also send us 1 or
more ads to run FREE in the first issue in which space is available! Send
us a different ad for each month and we'll run one after the other! Do NOT
run the same ad every month! It won't pull as well! Overseas subscribers add $18 U.S. for Air Mail delivery. NO extra charge for
surface mail.*

**BONUS ITEMS FOR
YOU WHEN YOU
SUBSCRIBE TO THE
IWS NEWSLETTER:**

***MAIL ORDER
LENDERS LIST** shows
many sources of mail-
order loans for people
in business!*

***HOW TO BORROW
YOUR WAY TO GREAT
RICHES**—a 24 pg
booklet by Ty Hicks
showing the how,
where and why!*

***HELP YOU CAN GET
FROM IWS AT NO
EXTRA COST** when
You subscribe:*

***Talks with Ty Hicks,
either in person or via
phone.*

***Review of Loan
Packages for
suggestions as to how
package may be
improved.*

***Review of Mail Order
promotion to see what
can be done to make it
pull better.*

Figure 4-5 page 2 (continued)

EVERY MONTH YOU GET 16 OR MORE PAGES OF ADS AND SPECIFIC HOW-TO DATA LIKE THIS! SOME ISSUES CONTAIN UP TO 200 BIG-MONEY LEADS — ENOUGH TO KEEP YOU BUSY FOR WEEKS—SUBSCRIBE NOW AND PROFIT!

<u>WEALTH NEWS FLASHES</u>

COMPENSATING-BALANCE LOANS. Unlimited funds available for compensating-balance loans and/or for releasing your compensating balances. Write or call: LENDER'S NAME, lender's address, lender's phone number.

100% FINANCING AVAILABLE for going businesses, start-ups, new ventures, other worthwhile xxx data to: LENDER'S NAME, lender's address, lender's phone number.

EARN BIG FINDER'S FEES (xxxxxxxxx for lathes, drill presses, planers, etc.). FINDER'S FEE FOR EACH machine you find us. IMMEDIATE ACTION. Write or call for finder's fees of $xxxx more. FIRM NAME, firm address, firm phone number.

PERMANENT FINANCING AVAILABLE, Apartments, motels, hotels, nursing homes, inventory, and receivables. We give 3-day service. No large deposits. Triple-A company. Write or call: LENDER'S NAME, lender's address, lender's phone number.

$25-MILLION AVAILABLE start-ups, certificates of deposit, business loans, construction loans, and real estate loans. LENDER'S NAME, lender's address, lender's phone number.

SAMPLE PAGE

SAMPLE

(SMI of eussi hcae ni nevig era noitomorp siht morf deteled)

If YOU are a regular one-year, or longer, their ads pay off in loans, capital and start on YOUR way to profits!

Figure 4-5 page 3

(NOTE: The lender's names were piece. The full name and ad-dress

EXECUTIVE MAIL-ORDER LOAN. $__,__0 with NO collateral, NO cosigners, NO bank credit check. Up to 5 yrs to pay. INSECURED loan. Call COLLECT or write. LENDER'S NAME, lender's address, lender's phone number.

BORROW THE MONEY YOU NEED! Get the financing YOU need quickly, easily, without long interviews, extensive investigations, etc. How? By going where the money is! Call or write for information. LENDER'S NAME, lender's address, lender's phone number.

24-HOUR ANSWER (YES OR NO) ON YOUR REAL-ESTATE LOAN! Minimum amount is $100,000; maximum amount _____ fat, fast, fully funded, and friendly! LENDER'S NAME, _____ phone number.

INSTANT CASH—IN A FLASH—_____ able for any honest, worthwhile, profitable business _____ NOW and see how helpful we can be to you! LENDER'S NAME, lender's address, lender's phone number.

CASH FOR BUSINESS NEEDS of all kinds. Get a loan NOW to build your new business to a high profit in no time! We have the cash—if YOU are ready to put it to use in your own business—start-ups, real estate, new ventures, expansion of present plant, etc. Call or write: LENDER'S NAME, lender's address, lender's phone number.

SAMPLE PAGE

GET LUCKY! READ IWS EVERY MONTH!

You can run YOUR own ads free of charge subscriber! A number of readers find that sources, finder fees, etc! Subscribe Now

Figure 4-5 page #3 (continued)

OTHER VALUABLE WAYS TO USE AND GUIDE TO MAKE YOU GETTING RICHER—FASTER FROM NOW!

BORROW WITH US—yes, that's right! IWSC WILL BE A SOURCE FOR LOAN LENDER FOR YOU—if YOU need money for BUSINESS USE. Here's how this works for YOU.

* HELP! YOU EVER SUBSCRIBE TO THE NEWSLETTER can be high to apply on a business loan application to the IWS BUSINESS LOAN SERVICE PLAN! Ask what does IWS LOAN plan?

Result:

☐ Send YOU a loan application which we a general type—meets most business needs might probably accept. While YOU may have to fill out a larger application a later date, these are supply MUST get YOU started in getting YOUR business loan by THIS BADT SERVICE.

● We send YOU—with YOUR application—a selected list of possible lenders between YOU can send loan request an application after YOU have filled out one-by-one and ready (this important—we have—that YOU type YOUR loan application request or hand-typed by someone).

❸ Then we will call YOU free of charge in the evening (if YOU request him in order to try to answer any business questions YOU may are about your loan application.

* IN SENDING YOU THIS BUSINESS LOAN APPLICATION, we want to point out that THERE IS NO GUARANTEE THAT YOUR APPLICATION WILL BE APPROVED. The reason is no guarantee can be made, because business conditions and people vary so much, that any loan guarantee is impossible to make.

* WE DO GUARANTEE THAT NO QUALIFIED LENDERS NAMES WILL BE SENT TO YOU, and that you send your loan application to each of these lenders if YOU want to try to get YOUR business loan. SO WHILE YOU CAN...

Fig. # 45 Page 1

Here's my $48 for a 2-year (24-issue) subscription to the monthly newsletter, *INTERNATIONAL WEALTH SUCCESS:* Send my loan application and lender list NOW! I understand that no guarantee can be made that a loan will be granted.

Type of loan wanted, please check one　☐ Real Estate　☐ Business

NAME

ADDRESS

CITY　　　　　　　STATE　　　　　　　ZIP

Note: To order any IWS item by credit card please include the following: Signature

Credit Card #　　　　　　Expiration Date

Phone Number　　　　　　Best time to call

(Note: If Ty can't call you, he will send YOU his "HOT-LINE" phone number and the secret password YOU can use to call him COLLECT—FREE OF ANY PHONE CHARGE. Just ask for the Ty Hicks "Hot Line" phone number when YOU send your payment above).

HOW TO FIND COSIGNERS FOR THE BUSINESS LOANS AND REAL ESTATE LOANS YOU NEED.

How? By advertising for cosigners in the pages of the IWS newsletter and in the special inserts we send to people and firms seeking to earn cosigner fees. Join the GLOBAL COSIGNER AND MONEY FINDERS ASSOCIATION GCMFA) by sending $50 today for an individual membership, or $100 for a company or corporate membership. We'll send you your papers which tell your potential cosigners 1) WHAT you need in terms of the amount of money 2) WHAT you offer the cosigner for helping you get the money you need for your business or real estate deal. So send your check or money order today and we'll get you started by circulating your need to people who might be able to help you. Your need gets wide distribution around the world in our many mailings.

While we cannot, do not and will not guarantee that you'll find a cosigner, we DO guarantee that your need will be circulated in a number of our mailings around the world. Your chances of finding a cosigner are—we believe—better than if you do nothing & just sit at home and dream away. So send your check or money order NOW and we'll work hard for you—starting right NOW!

NAME

ADDRESS

CITY　　　　　　　PHONE #

STATE　　　　　　ZIP

Credit card#　　　Expiration Date

Signature

GLOBAL COSIGNER AND MONEY FINDERS ASSOCIATION

Figure 4-5 page 4 (continued)

Money Required to Start. You'll need at least $500 to start running ads for a mail order/direct-marketing business. But once you start selling products or services your income will support future ads and an Internet presence. If you go the direct mail route, you can start with $400 for printing, postage, and mailing. With strong sales you can easily support future mailings to bring in more business.

Earnings Potential. With a dynamite product or service you can make $1 million your first year in the world's greatest business. But less exciting products can still generate an income of anywhere from $12,000 to $100,000 a year for you. It will take work on your part, running ads, making mailings, and shipping products or ordering service. But the financial freedom you'll enjoy will make every bit of work worthwhile!

Time to First Earnings. If you go the direct mail route you can have earnings within two weeks of your startup. With space ads your first earnings will take longer. Especially if you choose to run your ads in monthly publications where the time lag for ads can be as much as 90 days. Internet ads can be placed for running within 2 days and can bring in money in 3 to 5 days after first placed. Telemarketing can produce overnight sales!

Equipment Needed. Desk, telephone, typewriter. As your business expands you will need a PC to keep your mailing lists up to date, access the Internet, receive e-mail, and to track your sales and advertising results.

Real-Life Home-Business Tips

WHY MAIL ORDER DIRECT MAIL IS WHERE FORTUNES ARE STILL BEING MADE BY BEGINNERS

Many times BWBs don't know exactly why they pick a business to go into. But many times they do pick the right business! Take for example those BWBs who want to go into mail order/direct mail (MO/DM). They're picking the right business as the following Department of Commerce quote indicates.

MAIL ORDER AND DIRECT SELLING:
Direct and mail order sales will continue to expand rapidly. A more affluent and older population, with limited time for shopping at a retail store, will prefer to make purchases in the home. Ease of entry into direct selling should continue to offer enterprising people and companies an opportunity to provide a viable service. The field is expected to remain dominated by large firms using modern sales management and production techniques.

The big secret of hitting the big money in mail order/direct marketing is having a unique product that not many other people have for sale. The unique or different product or service can make you millions in MO/DM—if you can buy the product at a suitable price.

Or, if you can't get products at a suitable price, can you get your supplier to do more work for you at a slightly higher price? Work, like drop-shipping, wrapping, or the packing of an order, special services to your customers, etc., can save you money while giving better service to your customers. This will reflect favorably on you!

Another key secret to big money in mail order/direct-marketing is finding the right customers for your offer. What you want are prospects, not suspects! And prospects come in many sizes, colors of skin, views of life, etc. The main thought here is this: Find people who want your product or service and you may be able to sell them!

When you think about mail order/direct mail, give some thought to doing things differently while doing the same! "And what do you mean by that?" you ask. Doing things in many different ways while doing the same, we mean this:

- Advertise differently from your competition—use different magazines, newspapers, the Internet, and unique kinds of ads
- Try new ideas—the world is ready for new ideas that can help save time, money, energy, tempers, etc.

- Don't try to sell items you "love" because you might find that your loving of the item makes you see the facts less clearly
- Be sure to cover the same fields as your competition does so you get a "free ride" from the promotional effort of your competitor. While competition can help a field grow by calling more attention to it and making folks more aware of you, stay away from nasty name calling, etc.
- Try other forms of ads, such as "stand-up inserts" in the Sunday papers; insertions with the billing statements of other firms, the Internet, telemarketing, etc.

Yes, there are all sorts of ways for people with new ideas on how to hit the big money in MO/DM. Do you have a new idea that you think can really sell big in the MO/DM field? If you do, then your best chance usually lies in testing the idea to see if it goes. To test, you can:

- Run ads in papers, magazines, on the Internet, etc.
- Get free publicity for your item
- Make a mailing to prospects (not suspects)
- Show the item to mail order houses

Each of these tests will tell you something. If your ads pull strongly, you know you have a hot item; the same goes for your test mailing. If publicity and mail-order houses order, then you know that your idea is a winner. Recently a BWB introduced a new item that sold $176,000 worth of product in its first four months. It took off so fast he couldn't keep up with the orders! His tests were so good he stopped testing and launched a full ad campaign on the basis of his early results. Money poured in!

Gross a Million Dollars in Mail Order/Direct Mail from Your Own Home!

Can you borrow your way to mail order riches? Some folks do—using many different and unusual ways. What are these? Well, here are a few: (1) Get free advertising in local newspapers that don't charge you for your ad until after you have sold the item to a customer from the newspaper ad; (2) Get free "co-op" ads in magazines and newspapers which take a commission—usually 33 percent on every sale that is made; (3) Get free TV and radio time on a "PI" (Per Inquiry) basis where you pay for each inquiry the station gets for your product or service from the ad run on the station; (4) Find an Internet mall that will put your ads up free of charge on the mall pages; you pay the mall a commission on each sale after it is made.

With some business activity from these free sources, you can then go to a lender—such as a bank, finance company, a state or federal government agency—and ask for a business loan to help you expand your mail-order, direct-mail business. Some starting MO operators have been able to borrow all they needed to get their business started once they had a strong flow of inquiries or orders, which they got free of charge! So they started by borrowing!

You must be very careful, though, to be certain that you have a strong, steady, and reliable flow of orders or inquiries showing interest in your product or service! If you start with only a few orders you may find that the interest you thought people had in your product or service really wasn't there. Then, if you had borrowed the money, you might have trouble paying it back! So always be sure of your market *before* you spend borrowed money on more advertising! Wait and see—don't rush ahead!

Mail-order/direct-mail fortunes have been made on borrowed money! But the people who made their fortunes this way carefully tested their offers before spending borrowed money! Be sure you do the same, so you are not disappointed by the results. There are fortunes to be made in mail order and you can make yours—if you are careful and think!

HOW TO MAKE MONEY FAST IN MAIL ORDER/ DIRECT MAIL TODAY

Do you want to make money fast? If you do, then you might want to consider selling items you can buy at huge discounts from merchandise suppliers who specialize in supplying the items needed by mail-order operators, chain stores, specialty stores, etc.

But the big question that comes up is: Where do you find these high-discount bargains? There are plenty of places including:

- Active importers who work good deals
- Merchandise specialists having valuable items
- Overseas suppliers who sell directly to you
- Other types of high-discount houses

The secret to making money in this business is finding the houses that will sell you good items at low prices. Why do we say this? Because if you have a good product at a low price, finding buyers is easy. You don't even have to sell hard!

But, you say, I don't like selling. Probably what you mean is that you don't like face-to-face selling. What you do like is selling that does not take a meeting with the customer to get the money. And that type of selling, of course, is best known as mail order, or direct mail. To get started selling high-discount items by mail:

- Decide what types of items you'd like to sell
- Make a list, naming the items you plan to sell
- Find out who can supply these to you
- Contact "your" sellers and get catalogs
- Pick the items you think you can sell
- Ask your seller for price quotations
- Figure your selling costs per item
- Decide what price you will have to charge
- Compute your profit per unit

For best results in mail order/direct mail, your selling cost (ads, postage, etc.) should be less than 30 cents on each sales $1. Thus, if you sell a $100 item, your sales costs should be less than $30 per item if you are to show a good profit.

Your product or item cost can go higher as your sales cost goes lower. But if you have a high (also called a *long*) discount on the product, you will make a larger profit as your selling cost goes down.

So it is important that you get a large discount on the items you buy for resale. Millions are made each year selling—by mail—items having a large discount. Thus with an item you sell for $10 you may pay only (let's say) $3. This gives you $7 (= $10 − $3) for selling expenses, overhead, and profit. But you will not get this high a discount on all items you sell. If this happens, then to make money:

- Reduce your selling costs
- Sell a number of items at the same time
- Get your supplier to ship the item for you
- Don't spend money for an expensive office or help
- Run as many free ads as possible

There *are* ways to make money from high-discount items. And we think you can make some of this money, by using the hints above. Why not start trying—right now. Move ahead! For a directory of high-discount items, see the back of this book (IWS-13 *Directory of High-Discount Merchandise Sources*).

MAKE YOUR FORTUNE SELLING HOW-TO VIDEOS

Name of Business. How-to Video Sales to Individuals and Firms

What You Do. This is the age of learning. People are eager to learn new skills, become more proficient at their jobs, play a better game of golf, etc. Result? Many people and organizations turn to how-to videos that teach much of what they want to learn. To service these learning needs, you can assemble a list of how-to videos in a specific field such as sports (golf, tennis, swimming, etc.) and promote this list to people interested in becoming proficient at the topic covered. Your first promotional "catalog" can be a single typewritten sheet listing the video titles, their prices, and running times. When you sell a how-to video it's a final sale—you are not renting the video to someone for a few dollars. How-to videos are rarely rented—they are sold!

Your videos can cover a wide variety of topics ranging from sports to business, computers, electrical wiring, plumbing, home construction, boating, kitchen renovation, etc. At the start, specialize in one field. As your business sales increase, you can expand your coverage. Thus, a distributor of boating-skills videos expanded his line to fishing, cruising, travel to exotic locations, and various other water skills.

How to Find Clients. Run classified ads in publications serving the field you'll be covering with your videos. Thus, videos on electric wiring are advertised in electrician's publications, golfing videos are advertised in golf magazines, etc. Internet ads are placed on web sites serving the field covered. Direct mail letters are sent to prospects interested in the video topic. Radio and TV commercials can also be run late at night when the air time costs much less.

Money Required to Start. You can start this business with a simple typed or computer-printed list of videos as mentioned above. This list plus some small classified ads will run you $300 to $600. You can advertise free on some Internet sites. This will save you money as you get going.

Earnings Potential. Your earnings in this business can range from a low of $10,000 to a high of $70,000 per year part-time. If you spend full-time on the business you can earn from $100,000 to $250,000 per year out of your home. But at these higher earnings levels, you'll need a warehouse to store your video inventory. This usually cannot be your home because most homes don't have enough room. Also, to achieve the higher earnings level you must have a four-color catalog that illustrates and describes your videos.

Time to First Earnings. You can start bringing in money within four weeks after you make your first mailing of your video listing. Once your cash flow starts, you can expand your listing to a black-and-white catalog to increase your sales.

Equipment Needed. Telephone and desk at the start. A fax and personal computer (PC) will be needed as your business expands.

A REAL FUN BUSINESS FOR COMPUTER BUFFS

Name of Business. Personal Computer Business Service

What You Do. Though it may seem impossible, there are still many businesses that either do not have PCs or do not want to be bothered with inputting business data into a PC. This is where you come in! You receive key information from the business—such as inquiries on products, sales data, returns information, etc.—and input it in suitable form. Thus, you will prepare mailing lists from their inquiries using a data base program: the names can be sorted by type of product inquired about, section of country in which the inquirer is located, etc. You will use a spreadsheet program to plot sales by the day, week, month, etc. Your output will be supplied in hard copy form, if requested. Or you can be on a local area network to supply your information over suitable wire lines. You are paid a monthly fee for doing this work, which some business owners are too busy to do themselves. Your PC and you can have long quiet hours together while you input information, print it out, and send it to your clients—all without having to interface with another human!

How to Find Clients. Classified ads in local business publications can get you plenty of clients. Ads that work say:

> BURIED IN DATA? Let us clear up your problems quickly and economically! Call (222) 123-4567.

> DATA CRUNCH GOT YOU SNARLED? Let us get you unsnarled quickly, economically. Call (222) 123-4567 now!

You can also try local newspapers, using the business section. And don't overlook the Internet. You may find lots of prospects on it!

Money Required to Start. If you already own a PC, you can get started for $500 or less for ads. If you do not own a PC, you can still get started by leasing one until you have a strong enough cash flow to buy your own.

Earnings Potential. You can earn from $12,000 to $100,000 a year in this business, depending on the number of clients you amass. Once your income goes over $50,000 you'll probably need help with data input. You can hire college kids or retired people to do this at an hourly rate somewhat above the minimum wage and they'll be glad to get the work.

Time to First Earnings. It will take at least two weeks to get your first check for your PC work. Once you get a few happy clients, the word will spread about your work and new clients will come to you to do their work.

Equipment Needed. Desk, telephone, fax, typewriter, PC.

WORK WITH BUSINESSES EVERYWHERE

Name of Business. Venture Capital Agent

What You Do. You find venture capital for companies seeking money to start or expand a business. In your function as a venture capital agent you can provide a variety of other services, such as: (1) preparing an Executive Summary of the firm's business proposal. If you are a user of the K-15 *Venture Capital Millions Kit* (see the back of this book) we write such one page summaries for you free of charge; you can charge your client company up to $250 for the service and keep all the money; (2) prepare a Business Plan for the firm by having members of the firm write it for you using the outline you provide, which comes from the Kit mentioned earlier. Some users of the Kit have earned fees as high as $13,000 within two weeks after they started offering their services to local firms. In this unique home business, you visit the firms needing money; they never come to your home. So it is an ideal go-out people business, which can pay high rewards. Some venture capital agents do not take all of their fees in current payments. Instead they accept part ownership of the company in the form of stocks or bonds. If the company prospers, the rewards can be enormous—in the millions of dollars.

How to Find Clients. Use small classified ads in local business publications. One good ad is:

> GET THE VENTURE CAPITAL YOU NEED—QUICKLY.
> Full information free. Call (222) 123-4567.

Such ads can pull well and steadily for you.

Money Required to Start. You can get started for $500, or less. Your main cost will be the classified ads run to attract clients.

Earnings Potential. You can earn from $12,000 a year to $150,000 a year, depending on the number and type of deals you get from your ads. The higher income level will be earned by agents in areas where there is strong high tech industrial activity, such as in California, Massachusetts, Texas, etc.

Time to First Earnings. You can be receiving venture capital agent retainers within one week after you start promoting your service. In high technology areas there is a constant and intense search for venture capital every day of the week. If you can answer this need, you'll have more clients than you can handle!

Equipment Needed. Desk, telephone, fax, typewriter, PC (after you have several clients). See the K-15 *Venture Capital Millions Kit* at the back of this book for full details on organizing your business.

Seventeen More Fastest Cash Producing Businesses

Here are 17 more businesses that can produce fast cash for you. And these great cash cows can suggest other, related home businesses that might turn you on. When choosing a home business, be sure to keep these important guidelines in mind:

1. You must enjoy the business. If you don't, your chances of success are much reduced.
2. For the fastest cash start, get your customers to pay you a retainer at the beginning. Then you'll have a cash income before you start the actual work.
3. Work at getting more than just one customer. There's comfort in numbers and your income will be steadier and more reliable.
4. Be good to your customers and they'll be good to you!
5. Take care of your business and it will take care of you.

Business	What You Do	How to Find Clients	Money Required to Start	Annual Earnings Potential	Time to First Earnings	Equipment Needed
Addressing Service	Address items for ads and other mailings	Contact local firms by mail and phone; offer your service	$300 to $500	$25,000 to $50,000	1 to 2 weeks	Desk, phone, typewriter, fax
Animal walking and exercise	Walk animals for busy owners	Classified ads in local high-income newspapers and magazines	$400 to $600	$12,000 to $40,000	1 to 2 weeks	Desk, phone, typewriter, fax
Answer telephones for selected customers	Give special answering service to companies	Contact local small- and medium-size companies by phone and mail	$300 to $500	$10,000 to $25,000	1 to 2 weeks	Desk, phone, typewriter, fax
Baby-sitting in your own home	Care for children in your home during the day	Ads in local family and religious papers and magazines	$250 to $600	$30,000 to $90,000	4 to 6 weeks	Desk, phone, typewriter, fax
Children's clothing made to order	Design and make children's clothing to special order	Ads in local family and religious papers and magazines	$400 to $800	$12,000 to $35,000	1 to 2 weeks	Desk, phone, typewriter
Dance instruction	Teach people ballroom and/or classic dance	Advertise in local papers, club publications, Yellow Pages	$300 to $600	$5,000 to $20,000	1 to 2 weeks	Desk, phone, typewriter
Local delivery service for businesses	Deliver small, lightweight items in your area	Contact local businesses by mail and phone	$400 to $900	$6,000 to $24,000	1 to 2 weeks	Desk, phone, typewriter, fax
Executive search service	Find people suitable for executive jobs	Contact local companies by mail and phone	$300 to $800	$12,000 to $90,000	1 to 2 weeks (for first retainer)	Desk, phone, typewriter, fax, PC
Floor cleaning, polishing	Clean, polish floors in homes and businesses	Ads in local papers and Yellow Pages	$300 to $900	$6,000 to $36,000	1 to 2 weeks	Desk, phone, typewriter, fax

Business	What You Do	How to Find Clients	Money Required to Start	Annual Earnings Potential	Time to First Earnings	Equipment Needed
Foreign language translation service	Translate letters and documents from one language to another	Contact local companies by mail and phone; ads in *Yellow Pages*	$300 to $900	$5,000 to $20,000	1 to 2 weeks	Desk, phone, typewriter, fax, PC
Garage or tag sale management	Run garage or tag sales for people in your area	Advertise in local papers and religious publications	$300 to $600	$4,000 to $18,000	1 to 2 weeks	Desk, phone, typewriter
Health food sales and/or preparation	Sell and/or prepare selected health foods in your area	Ads in local papers and in religious publications	$300 to $600	$8,000 to $24,000	1 to 2 weeks	Desk, phone, typewriter
Information service for businesses	Supply specialized information to businesses	Contact local firms by mail and phone	$300 to $700	$12,000 to $60,000	1 to 2 weeks	Desk, phone, typewriter, fax, PC
Jelly, jams, and sauce making	Prepare homemade jellies, jams, sauces	Ads in local papers; sell at local fairs	$200 to $500	$3,000 to $18,000	1 to 2 weeks	Desk, phone, typewriter
Matching service for single people	Arrange meetings after matching two people	Ads in local papers and in religious publications	$300 to $500	$6,000 to $48,000	1 to 2 weeks	Desk, phone, typewriter
Painting interiors and exteriors of homes	Paint the insides and outsides of homes in your area	Ads in local papers and in *Yellow Pages*	$200 to $500	$8,000 to $25,000	1 to 2 weeks	Desk, phone, typewriter
Shopping service for busy people	Shop for items busy people want and need	Ads in upscale publications	$300 to $600	$4,000 to $20,000	1 to 2 weeks	Desk, phone, typewriter, fax, PC

CHAPTER 5

THE 26 SIMPLEST STAY-AT-HOME BUSINESSES

MANY BEGINNING WEALTH BUILDERS (BWBs) want to stay at home to make their fortune. There are many reasons why some BWBs prefer to stay at home rather than go out to earn their money. Reasons I hear in my daily talks with BWBs around the world include:

- Need, or desire, to care for children at home while earning money
- Reluctance to go outside the home because of bad experiences in the past
- Unwillingness to meet people in a work situation
- Preference to be a loner and to work without interruptions or communication with other people
- A physical handicap of some kind that prevents the BWB from either leaving his/her home or from functioning freely in a business outside the home

Most writers I know prefer to stay at home to do their work. Why? Because they can get an enormous amount of work done at home. My friend, Isaac Asimov, the famous author of more than 500 full-length books, preferred to work at home. Sunday, he said, was his best work day. Why? Because there was no mail and almost no phone calls. So he could get more writing done at home on Sunday than on any other day!

Interestingly, Isaac didn't use a literary agent. He opened all his mail himself and answered his own phone. A true home worker who earned enormous royalties—all his hundreds of best-selling books were written at home!

In a stay-at-home business you rarely leave for business purposes. Sure, you may make a trip to the bank or office. But you need not do this. Why? Because:

- You can bank by mail, if you wish. People even send cash deposits by mail, having the local postal delivery clerk pick up the mail at their door. (We do not recommend sending cash through the mail.)
- You can buy postage stamps by mail or phone, eliminating the need to visit the post office.

When you stay at home you may work alone, as a writer does. Or you may have customers come to your house to use your services. If people come to your home for business purposes you should:

1. Check your local zoning laws to see if there are any restrictions on people visiting your home for business purposes.
2. Review the parking situation if people will drive to your home. Neighbors may object to large numbers of cars parked in the street or outside your home.

The best stay-at-home businesses are those in which you rarely have people come to your home for business purposes. So you'll find that mail-order/direct-marketing businesses are good for stay-at-homers. This chapter gives you many ideas for a variety of such businesses.

AN IDEAL BUSINESS FOR STAY-AT-HOMERS

Name of Business. Selling Books by Mail, Internet, or Phone

What You Do. You sell specialized books by mail, Internet, or phone. The books can cover a full range of topics within the specialties you choose. For example, if your specialty is fishing, the books you sell by mail, Internet, or phone can range from the basics of fishing to detailed studies of certain classes of fish, such as tuna, bluefish, etc. At the start it is best to specialize when you sell books by mail, Internet, or phone because it is easier to find customers than if you are selling a general line of books. So if you have a special interest, or detect a need for books in a special interest area, get started *now!* When you sell specialized interest books by mail, Internet, or phone you do not need as large an inventory as when you sell general books by mail or other methods. Further, you can charge a higher price for a specialized book than you can for most general books. Selling specialized books by mail, Internet, or phone can give you a comfortable, steady, and dependable income while you deal with interesting and pleasant people.

How to Find Customers. Specialized book buyers read certain magazines, newspapers, and other publications, and often go on the Internet to find the books they seek. So you reach them by advertising in such publications and on the Internet. Friends of mine run very small (one-half inch) classified ads in specialized publications and on the Internet and get excellent results. A small ad of this type is very reasonable in price and can produce superb sales results. Most users of small classified ads request that a person interested in a line of specialized books pay a nominal fee—$2 to $4 for a copy of the specialized book catalog. The income from the sale of the catalog offsets the cost of the classified or space ad. Be sure before you start a business selling specialized books by any of these methods that you know what publications and other outlets you will advertise in once you start your business. If there aren't a few publications in the field it may be difficult to start your business. While renting mailing lists can help with your sales, you should look to see if there are at least two publications in a field before starting your book business. There should also be one or more chat rooms on the Internet in which you can mention your books as helpful to readers.

Money Required to Start. You will need at least $600 to start this business. Why? Because you will have to either run ads, rent mailing lists, get a site on the Internet, or do some selling on the phone. This will cost money. But once you have made a few sales the income from these sales will support additional ads. You buy your books on credit (called *consignment*) and pay after you sell.

Earnings Potential. $10,000 to $150,000 per year.

Time to First Earnings. It will take three to four weeks before you get your first earnings from a mailing to specialized book buyers. Advertising in monthly publications will delay your first earnings. But such ads produce excellent results over the years. To accelerate your sales you can advertise on the Internet. Your ad will appear sooner than in most publications and will probably be seen by more potential buyers. And the fastest way to get on the Internet is to put your offerings up on an Internet mall. You'll find malls discussed throughout this book because they're so helpful and so readily available to BWBs in every business.

Equipment Needed. Desk, phone, typewriter, and PC.

Business Source. You can sell the books, kits, and newsletters published by my firm, IWS, Inc., and be paid a 40 percent commission for your first $2,000 in sales and a 50 percent commission for life thereafter. And we drop-ship to your customer at no cost to you or the customer. The Executive Rep dealership is open immediately to people who subscribe for 5 years or longer to the IWS newsletter, *International Wealth Success*. See the back of this book for details. The books, kits, and newsletters you sell can all be marketed by mail, the Internet, or telemarketing from the comfort of your own home!

Real-Life Success Story

A friend of mine in the Midwest is grossing more than $235,000 a year selling books out of his home and books by mail, the Internet, telemarketing, and direct contact with his customers. He sells both used and new books and his sales grow every year. Customers all over the United States buy books by mail, Internet, and phone from him. Quick service and a wide choice of specialized titles allows him to satisfy almost any book want or need a customer may have. To keep his business growing, he recently added a line of remainder titles—big, beautiful books that publishers have in excess quantities. Loyal customers love these books and have been ordering them by the bushel!

IDEAL BUSINESS FOR THE TECHNICALLY INCLINED

Name of Business. Licensing Agent

What You Do. You bring together businesses having an item to license—such as a design, a patent, a copyright, etc.—and businesses handling sale or distribution of such items. Thus, one firm might have a patent on an electronic product that another company would like to make and sell. A license agreement is worked out after you bring the two firms together. You receive a commission or fee on every one of the units sold by the firm seeking the license.

Or the item being sold might be the right to use a famous name on a company's products. Such names might be those of sports figures, entertainers, authors, etc. Again, you receive a fee every time the name is used. You find firms wanting to license their design, patent, or copyright and put them in touch with other firms seeking the right to use the available offer. Your commission fee will depend on the price of the licensed item sold, the number of units sold, and the value of the name. Thus, the higher the price, the larger the number of units sold, the lower the per-unit commission. With popular names your earnings can be enormous, even when the per-unit commission is small. When thinking of licensing, you can divide it into two main categories—(1) industrial-product and patent licensing, (2) entertainment and sports licensing where you deal with popular individuals or characters. Take your pick—depending on your interests and previous experience.

How to Find Clients. Decide on what types of products you want to work with. Contact companies in the field. Offer to find licensees for the firm for a percentage fee on each unit sold. Base your fee on the guidelines above.

Money Required to Start. $500 to $750 for letters and calls to firms whose items you want to license. Small classified ads in selected industry magazines will run another $200. Internet ads can run $100 to $250, depending on the type of page you use.

Earnings Potential. You can earn anywhere from $12,000 to $250,000 a year, depending on the number of licensing deals you close and the size of each deal. It is usually easier to sign smaller deals with lesser known products or names. But your income will be smaller from such signings. So the way to build your income is to sign more deals or deals with products or people who rate higher fees.

Time to First Earnings. It will take one to three months before your first licensing commission check arrives. These deals take time to put together because at least two firms are involved. But your income can flow into your bank for years without you having to take one more step in the process.

Equipment Needed. Desk, phone, fax, personal computer, typewriter.

Why Licensing Is a Good Business for Many Beginning Wealth Builders

Is licensing a *good* business for you? We think so! Why? Because in a recent year United States firms received more than $6 billion in fees and royalties from overseas users of license information. And how can you get in on this billion-dollar market? By becoming a licensing agent for one or more U.S. or overseas firms! It's easy to get started and you need only a few dollars to set up your own "shop." And best of all, it's a "paper" business—using either letter paper, fax paper, or computer printer paper, and stamps! You can speed up your results and income cash flow by using e-mail, fax, and the Internet. Electronic exchange of licensing information speeds agreements and cash flow, helping you get results sooner.

As a licensing agent all you do is arrange to exchange information (usually technical data) between a United States firm (or a firm in the country in which you reside) and an overseas firm which wants to use it. Sometimes a firm will also supply data on manufacturing a product, or permit using a trade name or trademark. You also get paid for arranging such deals! And the way you do this is by a license agreement.

Once the agreement is signed, "your" firm begins to collect license fees on the sales made by the overseas firm. Typical fees will be 2 to 5 percent of sales. Thus, if the overseas firm sells $100,000 worth of product which you licensed, the United States firm gets $2,000 to $5,000, depending on the percentage. You, as the licensing agent will get 10 percent of this, or $200 or $500. While this may seem like a small amount, it can go on forever. And your work ends with the signing of the agreement! And on a sale of $1 million, your fee would be between $2,000 and $5,000. And a $1 million sale isn't that big!

Do I need a special license or degree to start? The answer is no! You can start now, if you want! But we suggest that you get some basic information—such as that given in a good book, *How to Make a Big Fortune as a Licensing Agent,* available from IWS, Inc., PO Box 186, Merrick NY 11566-0186 for $15 plus $3 for postage and handling. With this book you receive a copy of a Master Licensing Agreement which gives you many ideas on what such an agreement should include. Becoming a Licensing Agent is one way for you to get started in your own business without a big factory, office, payroll, or the other items needed by some businesses.

TEN STEPS TO STARTING A SUCCESSFUL LICENSING BUSINESS IN YOUR HOME

- Decide what field you'd like to work in—such as electronics, computers, software, autos, boats, etc.
- Look in IWS and other publications for leads on the page titled "Licensing Opportunities"

- Find local firms that make the item the overseas firm wants (see following for information)
- Contact the local firm and tell them you want to help them license an item
- Use the phone, postal mail, e-mail, or the Internet when you contact a local firm you want to help
- Get your local firm to give you a signed letter stating what they'll pay you
- Send data on the cost of the license, including any royalties, to the overseas firm so they can include this expense in their cost estimate. (Do not reveal the commission you'll earn on the deal.)
- Have the overseas firm sign an agreement stating what they'll pay and for how long
- Close the deal by having the local firm sign the agreement; send a copy to your overseas client for their records
- Collect the commission money due you as sales are made; go on to the next license deal!

Now there are two areas in licensing that usually cause questions to be asked. They are: (1) How do I find local firms to contact? (2) How do I live while I'm doing this work if I don't have any income from any other source? Here are your answers to these two questions.

Local firms are often listed in a book called *Industrial Directory for the State of . . . or . . . State Name Industrial Directory.* Such directories are available for all 50 states, but some of the small states are covered in one volume devoted to three states. But the big states have just one volume devoted entirely to them. In some of the large state volumes as many as 2,500 local firms are listed. These volumes are often available from, or through, your local Chamber of Commerce or public library.

To live while you are getting started in licensing, you might want to have the local firms you are working with give you an advance on your future commission earnings. Such an advance might be in the range of $1,000 to $5,000 per firm. So, if you are working with four firms, and each advances $5,000, you will have $20,000 to keep yourself going while you are getting deals started. A number of our readers have set up highly successful licensing deals.

And to learn how to get started in this great business get a copy of *How to Make a Big Fortune as a Licensing Agent* listed earlier in this section. It tells you much of what you need to know to get going in this business. And you need not travel—you can do all your business by mail. Or, some can be done by mail and some by phone, fax, e-mail, and PC, our readers who've tried this business tell us. You—we believe—can do the same.

You *can* get started in licensing on zero cash. You will spend a few weeks in getting started, but once the money starts to roll in, you will have a great zero-cash "paper" business, which can go on and on for years paying you a big income!

ONE OF THE MOST PROFITABLE HOME BUSINESSES

Name of Business. Exporting from Your Own Country

What You Do. You find overseas firms seeking the products and services of your country. This is easy to do because most countries and states have publications listing Products Wanted by other countries around the world. You contact the overseas firm seeking the product or service and tell them you can supply it once you know the quantity and specifications for the item. Then you contact a domestic supplier and tell them you have a potential order from an overseas firm or government and need a price quotation. Once you have the quote you send it to the overseas buyer, after adding a suitable commission for yourself. Your typical commission will be in the 10 percent range for small orders. As the dollar amount of the order rises, your commission percentage will decrease. If the overseas buyer agrees to the quote you give him or her, you are sent a Letter of Credit covering the amount of the sale. Using this, you arrange with a freight forward to have the order shipped. Your commission comes directly from the Letter of Credit. So there are *no* bounced checks, no chasing after people for payment!

How to Find Clients. Use government and state export services; refer to IWS-3 Vol. I and IWS-4 Vol. 2 of *Worldwide Riches Opportunities* listed at the back of this book. The references give you the name, address, fax number, and other data about overseas firms seeking specific products or services. Using the Department of Commerce STAT-US service, you can download daily from the Internet to your computer printer new Products Wanted listings. And you can pick products in any of the many SIC (Standard Industrial Classification) categories to download to your computer for export consideration. Call 1-800-STAT-USA or 202-482-1986 for more data on this helpful service.

Money Required to Start. $300 to $600 will get you started because the sources of information you'll use are relatively low cost and no advertising is required.

Earnings Potential. You can easily earn $25,000 per year exporting. And if you devote full time to it, your earnings can exceed $250,000 per year.

Time to First Earnings. Some of our readers receive orders on their first overseas contact. But this is somewhat unusual. It generally takes about three months to obtain your first order and receive income from it. But once the orders start they can continue for years without you having to do much more than respond to a faxed or e-mail request.

Equipment Needed. Desk, phone, fax, personal computer, the training kit, K-17 *Export-Import Riches Kit,* listed at the back of this book.

Real-Life Home-Business Tips

BECOME AN EXPORT MANAGEMENT AGENT (EMA) TO MAKE BIG MONEY TODAY

Exports are booming! Are you getting some of the big money that others are earning from exports—using little more than a few envelopes, stamps, a telephone, fax, e-mail, or the Internet. If you aren't, then now is the time to start, we think. And here's how.

Let's say you live in a small city, or a small town (though what we're about to say works just as well in a large city, town, or country). And let's say you would like to get into exporting, that wonderful paper business which:

- Needs hardly any money to start—usually less than $600
- Can be run from your home—be it an apartment, bungalow, house, etc.
- Is easy to start in just a matter of days—usually less than a week
- Does not require you to travel—but you can if you want to
- Is easily combined with mail order/direct mail—if you want to
- Can be operated with or without a computer, with or without e-mail or the Internet

Yes, exporting is a great business—in our opinion! Exporting will always be a good business because people always want the products of other nations to improve their lifestyle, give them a taste of the foreign, etc. So if you start in exporting today, you will have a lifetime business which can put you into the big money sooner than you might now realize. Here's how.

Look around your city or town. Make a list of the manufacturing firms there. Then go to a city or town directory and look up the names and addresses of other firms that you may have overlooked. Go to your local library for the directory you need. You'll find that your librarian is most helpful and can show you the books you need to get names of local businesses that might have products you can export.

Next, write, fax, or e-mail a letter to these firms, telling them that you are a local Export Management Agent (EMA) and that you would like to help the firm export some of its product overseas. (Of course, you must use a printed letterhead when you contact these firms. If you don't, it is likely that your letter, fax, or e-mail will be ignored. So start right! Get a letterhead printed and use it! Be sure to register your business, if you use a name different from your own, or if your state requires such registration.)

Some creative BWBs charge a small fee ($100 per month) for acting as an EMA for any firm—even before the EMA gets business for the firm. This fee is later (in some cases) deducted from the commissions the EMA earns by exporting products. In other cases the fee is charge over and above any commissions. But if you can get the firms to pay you a $100 per month retainer fee for acting as their EMA, your fee income will be $5,000 per month or $60,000 per year! Add to this commissions of $40,000 a year by the end of your second year and you will be earning $100,000 per year before your small expenses! Not bad for a paper business that can be started in just a few days!

But suppose there are no manufacturing firms in your town? What then? Just go to the nearest town having such firms. Again, use your local library for the names of these firms. Keep writing until you get a few firms to agree to allow you to represent them as their EMA—either for a monthly fee plus commission or on a straight commission basis. (If you meet resistance to the idea of a monthly fee then agree to work on the basis of commission only.) The main point is to get started as soon as possible!

Once a firm makes you its EMA, get copies of the catalogs of products and study them. Learn what "your" firm makes, what its advantages are (such as low cost, long life, greater efficiency, etc.). Next, study the pages of the IWS newsletter, looking for overseas firms that want the products that "your" firm makes. As soon as you find such overseas firms (and there are thousands seeking products of many kinds), send an airmail letter or fax telling the overseas firm that you can supply the items that are needed. Ask for details of how many items are wanted, when they are wanted, etc. As soon as you get this info, compare it with the information in your catalogs. If you have any questions go back to "your" firm and ask for answers on price shipping, specifications, etc. Then send this to your overseas customer and wait for your first order. It could happen to you soon!

QUICK STEPS TO MAKING YOUR FORTUNE IN EXPORTING USING BORROWED MONEY

In this book we keep urging you to think of getting into exporting. "Why?" you ask. Because the export market is growing faster than most parts of the U.S. market. So there's a bigger chance for you to hit the big money in exporting than in many parts of the domestic market.

Under 15 percent of the U.S. gross national products comes from exports. So there's a big world out there for you to take over for making your fortune! And you—we believe—can do it if you start with fortune-building information like the following facts:

- Banks can help you with export information free
- Financing is available to you in the form of loans for exports
- Your customer can often get credit to buy from you
- Some banks will answer your export loan request in 24 hours
- Letters of Credit can be set up in 48 hours or less
- Revolving credit is also available to you as an exporter
- The Internet, e-mail, and the fax machine are cutting many hours out of the export process, making it easier and faster for you to get started earning big money

How can you start as an exporter? That's easy! Look at the "Products Wanted" page of your IWS newsletter and similar publications. Access STAT-US mentioned earlier in this chapter. Pick the type of product you know something about or which interests you from a business angle. Then write, fax, or e-mail a few firms in the United States that make the item, asking for prices to sell the item to you. Next:

- Contact the overseas firm seeking the item
- Supply price quotes and delivery dates
- Go to your bank when the order arrives; show the order
- Ask for a loan, if you need one to get and ship the item
- Get help for your customer if financing is needed
- Have the item shipped once the funding is arranged

Exporting is really a form of mail order/direct mail/direct marketing. But instead of selling items in small quantities, you will usually be selling them in the hundreds or thousands. And there are other neat features about exporting:

- Each successive sale is usually for more money
- You spend little for ads, promotion, postage, fax, e-mail
- Your customers stay with you longer, because they need you
- Firms pay with checks or Letters of Credit that don't bounce—your money is good
- It's easier to build wealth with firms than individuals
- As an exporter with products to sell, you will be sought out. You do not have to plead to see people, beg for loans, or crawl for an order! Why? Because you have what people want to buy because the items they buy will make money for them! So they pay—and fast!

HOW TO FINANCE EXPORT SALES TO MAKE BIG MONEY TODAY

Some BWBs ask: "Is 100 percent financing still possible?" It sure is! And one of the best areas in which you can use 100 percent financing is in exporting. For years we've pushed the idea of exporting as a great way for you to build your fast fortune. Here's some useful information.

You can get a full guarantee of your money from the U.S. government, as we shall explain. This means that you will not be stuck with bad checks, people changing their minds over the goods they ordered, etc. And, as shown below, this guarantee goes up to 100 percent of the loan the borrower takes out to buy your exports! Most people start as an EMA (Export Management Agent), exporting products for others for a fee. When will you start/act?

The Export-Import Bank of the United States (Eximbank) is an independent agency of the U.S. government which works directly with American suppliers and private financial institutions to finance U.S. export sales. Eximbank has over 20 financing programs to assist U.S. firms. These include direct loans, bank guarantees, discount facilities, leasing guarantees, and other programs to cover overseas design and engineering studies, construction operation, licensing technology, and agricultural export financing.

Financing packages for major industrial projects and exports of high-value products are normally supported under Participation Financing, a combination of the Direct Loan and Financial Guarantee programs.

Direct Loans are dollar credits extended by Eximbank to borrowers outside of the United States for purchases of U.S. goods and services. Disbursements under the local agreement are made in the United States to the suppliers of the goods and services, and the loans, plus interest, are repaid in dollars by the borrowers.

For additional information on these, and many other loans, contact the Export-Import Bank of the United States, 811 Vermont Avenue, N.W., Washington, DC 20571; Toll-free: 1-800-565-3946; Fax: 1-202-565-3380.

Also be certain to check the Small Business Administration (SBA) for its export loans and loan guarantees. A number of new programs have recently been introduced for exporters. Call your local SBA office for free details.

For full directions on how to start and succeed in your own export-import business, see the K-17 *Import-Export Riches Kit* listed at the back of this book.

GET IN ON THE COMPUTER BOOM WITH THIS BUSINESS

Name of Business. Software Sales by Mail Order/Direct Marketing

What You Do. The biggest business boom in recent years is in computers. Hundreds of millionaires (and some billionaires) have been created by the computer business. You can get into this great business by selling computer software—for games, personal organization, business, education, etc.—to individuals and companies using mail order/direct mail marketing, and the Internet to reach your prospects. Each software program you sell is a final sale (except for a defective program) because programs can be copied and returned for a refund. You don't want to be in the business of supplying programs people copy and return for credit! Since every computer needs software, your market is almost unlimited. Why? Because computer usage is expanding like wildfire worldwide. You—too—can be in on this great change in the way the computer is changing all of our lives— including that of your author whose books are now all written on computer!

How to Find Clients. Run classified ads in publications serving the field you want to sell to. Thus, with games software, you'll advertise in games magazines; with business software you'll advertise in business magazines. Classified ads on the Internet on suitable web pages will also produce sales results that can show a profit for you. And computer clubs can generate lots of sales for you if you give their members discounts on the software they buy from you.

Prepare a catalog of your software offerings as soon as you can. Your prospects will keep your catalog on hand and will turn to it as soon as they need more software. As your sales increase you can produce a larger catalog and mail it several times a year. Eventually, you will print a 4-color catalog because such catalogs sell better than black-and-white catalogs.

Money Required to Start. Work out deals with software houses to drop-ship the software to your customers and you won't need to stock any inventory at the start. Nor will you have to spend money to stock a warehouse. This strategy can reduce your startup costs to no more than $500 to $800, depending on how much initial advertising you do. And if you run free classified ads on the Internet, you can get started for even less.

Earnings Potential. Part-time you can earn $10,000 to $50,000 a year in this business. Full-time earnings can range up to $500,000 a year with a group of corporate and individual customers. Your greatest income will come from serving corporate customers. Why? Because corporations buy software in large quantities, pay on time, and don't change their mind about what they ordered, as individuals may be prone to do.

Time to First Earnings. It will take 4 to 6 weeks for you to get your first sale in this business. But once your sales start, they should continue to grow as you do more advertising in publications and on the Internet. At the start, it's best to concentrate your sales efforts in one area—say games. You can then expand to other areas after your sales build strongly in the first subject area. Just be patient and keep selling!

Equipment Needed. Phone, desk, fax, PC, modem, and printer. At the start, a typewriter will be handy for typing bills.

A PROFITABLE MONEY BUSINESS

Name of Business. Credit and Collection Agency

What You Do. You collect overdue bills for companies and individuals. And since there are "slow pays" in good times and bad times, you will always have a source of income. Also, you can combine your collection-agency work with ten other related services. Your income will rise because you offer comprehensive and full services to your clients. What's more, people can use all, or any one, of your services and you'll still be earning money in your own home business! The additional ten services you can offer your clients are discussed separately at the end of this listing. Here we concentrate on collecting overdue bills for a fee. Your fee can range from a low of 20 percent of the amount collected to a high of 50 percent of the amount you bring in. The average fee is 33 percent of the amount you collect.

How to Find Clients. Contact local companies by mail, phone, or fax, telling them that you have a superior bill collecting service. Offer to take on a few test collections for a lower than normal fee—say 10 percent of the amount collected—to show how capable you are. You can also run small ads in local papers to attract companies and individuals who have bills to be collected.

Money Required to Start. Figure on $300 to $600 to get started. You needn't do too much advertising because there are lots of companies seeking a good collection agency. Or they want to try another agency when they're not satisfied with the results of their current agency.

Earnings Potential. You can earn from $12,000 to $150,000 a year in this business, depending on how many clients you take on.

Time to First Earnings. It will take at least one month to start earning money in this business because you must first get a client, then make your first collection. But once you start making collections your income can accelerate.

Equipment Needed. Desk, phone, fax, PC at a later stage, typewriter, or access to a typist. IWS-9 *The Credits and Collection Kit* described at the back of this book is helpful for getting you started in this excellent home business.

Ten Additional Services to Offer

1. Personal call service on overdue bills
2. Process service for summons
3. Bad check service to collect on returned checks
4. Repossession service to recover unpaid-for goods
5. Credit card pickup service from delinquent card holders
6. Special credit investigations
7. Employee background check service
8. Motor vehicle research service (who owns what vehicle[s])
9. Skip-tracing service (finding people who skip out of town)
10. Consumer credit counseling (helping people cope with their many bills)

THE WORLD'S BEST PAPER HOME BUSINESS

Name of Business. Loan Portfolio Broker

What You Do. You find collections of loans (called portfolios) and bring them to the attention of investors who will buy the portfolio. Another name for the business is Financial Portfolio Specialist. You are paid a fee for finding the portfolio and bringing it to the attention of investors. The loan portfolios you find can be from financial institutions (banks, S&Ls, etc.), retail and service businesses of many types, automobile and boat dealerships, and medical receivables. No selling is involved in this business! You just find suitable portfolios and call them to the attention of investors who buy them. The fee you receive can be large with amounts of $160,000 being reported for just one transaction.

How to Find Clients. Contact by phone or mail organizations that might have portfolios of loans they've made that they want to sell to get cash in their hands for more lending. You can also run small classified ads in financial and trade papers saying:

> LOAN PORTFOLIOS BOUGHT. Fast action, good
> price. Call (222) 123-4567 day or night.

> NEED CASH? Sell your loan portfolios; fast action;
> good price. Call (222) 123-4567 day or night.

Money Required to Start. You can get this business going for $600, or less. If you don't know this business, you should have a copy of the *Portfolio Brokering Kit,* listed at the back of this book. It shows you exactly how to get started.

Earnings Potential. You can earn from $50,000 to $175,000 a year in this business if you actively seek large portfolios. The key to large earnings is active promotion of your services to a variety of holders of loan portfolios.

Time to First Earnings. It will take one month to produce your first earnings in this business. Why? Because you must do some prospecting among lenders in your area. This takes time and will produce a lag between the time you start and the date of your first check. But your check can be extremely large—sometimes large enough for a year's income from one sale!

Equipment Needed. Desk, telephone, typewriter; at a later date a PC and fax will be helpful. Figure 5-1 gives information on a helpful source of data on this excellent business.

To conclude this chapter, we give you 20 more simplest stay-at-home businesses. You may like one or more of them. Or the businesses listed may suggest others you might like better!

"FINANCIAL PORTFOLIO SPECIALIST" NETS $160,000 ON A SINGLE TRANSACTION... so might you!

Like the $160,000 Portfolio Financial Specialist whose case study is documented in the 180 page—4 Volume Portfolio Network Training Library, you can also have the opportunity to realize tremendous profits. Now is the time to *CASH IN* and take advantage of the tremendous opportunities created by the banking debacle of the 80's. This program will teach you, step by step, all the ways you can make MEGA-BUCKS from the bank screw-ups!

You will also plug into an existing Network of investors all eager to do business with you. This program has been put together by Kevin S. Clark, a financial specialist with over 10 years in this industry. He has come up with a truly unique, truly different approach on what we commonly refer to as the "paper business."

He has developed a network of investors who invest in hundreds, even thousands of "loan portfolios" and "receivable portfolios" in a single transaction. The Training Library will show you how to locate the "deals" and bring them to the Network. For doing this, you are paid a very large, very handsome commission. You invest the same time and effort as you do for a single transaction; but, your financial return is in *MULTIPLES!* This is the beauty of the portfolio/receivables business!

Order the Training Library, read it. NO...study it! Put the techniques and strategies to work for you. We will refund your full cost of the Training Library from the proceeds of the first completed and fully funded transaction you close using the information in this great Training Library!

DOUBLE BONUS! Just for purchasing the complete Training Library and becoming a member (included in your purchase) of the Portfolio Network, you will receive two special reports absolutely FREE! You can literally make thousands of dollars with just this information alone, and even if you decide to return your Training Library, you can keep these reports as our way of saying *Thank You.*

The first bonus report is "HOW TO PURCHASE REAL ESTATE FROM THE RESOLUTION TRUST CORPORATION." This report will show you how to profit (or even buy your own home) from the mess created by the collapse of so many S & L's. You'll learn how to be in the driver's seat when it comes to putting deals together with the RTC, how to get the RTC to finance your purchase, and you'll learn the seven ways to obtain information from the RTC to find the right property for you.

Figure 5-1

You do not have to have any previous experience in this field. You receive complete training. All you need is the genuine desire to want to make a ton of money. You will receive *FOUR VOLUMES* of complete, no nonsense, factual information (not theory) on how to make money in the Portfolio Paper Business; Vol. 1) Financial Institutions, Vol. 2) Retail and Service Businesses; Vol. 3) Automobile Dealerships, and Vol. 4) Medical Receivables.

You will learn from real world experience with numerous examples and case studies to teach you. Each volume includes all the forms, sample agreements...all the paperwork necessary to operate your business.

<u>NO RISK—Try it For As Long As You Want</u>

"HOW TO PURCHASE LOAN PORTFOLIOS FROM THE RESOLUTION TRUST CORPORATION" is the second bonus report you will receive absolutely free! Learn how to effectively bid on these portfolios and sometimes acquire them for pennies on the dollar. You'll learn whom to contact and how to submit a bid.

<u>NO WAY YOU CAN LOSE</u>

The complete Portfolio Training Library is being marketed nationally for $395... however, readers of this newsletter are being offered a $100 discount. You pay only $295—a small fraction of the thousands and thousands of dollars this information can earn for you. Just having access to the Network of investors is worth many times this cost.

YES! I want to become a Financial Portfolio Specialist! Please send me the Portfolio Network Training Library. Here's my $295

Send check or money order to

IWS, Inc., 24 Canterbury Rd., Rockville Centre, NY 11570

or to order by credit card include the information below or call 516-766-5850 day or night.

NAME _____

ADDRESS _____

CITY _____ STATE _____ ZIP _____

CREDIT CARD # _____

PHONE # _____ SIGNATURE _____ EXPIRATION DATE _____

Figure 5-1 (continued)

Business	What You Do	How to Find Clients	Money Required to Start	Annual Earnings Potential	Time to First Earnings	Equipment Needed
Resume preparation service	Write, type resumes for job seekers	Ads in local and national papers, magazines	$400 to $600	$12,000 to $30,000	2 weeks	Desk, phone, fax, PC, typewriter
Selling by telephone	Sell products or services by phone	Contact local and national firms by mail/phone	$300 to $700	$10,000 to $60,000	4 to 6 weeks	Desk, phone, fax, typewriter
Vitamin advice and sales by mail and phone	Offer advice on and sell vitamins by mail	Direct mail, ads in health publications	$400 to $900	$12,000 to $100,000	5 to 10 weeks	Desk, phone, fax, PC, typewriter
Writing articles and books for publication	Write articles and books on useful topics	Contact magazine and book publishers with your ideas	$100 to $500	$5,000 to $150,000	6 to 8 weeks	Desk, phone, fax, PC, typewriter
Reviewing new and revised books	Write reviews of new books for magazines, newspapers, and publishers	Contact publishers of magazines, newspapers, books	$200 to $600	$6,000 to $24,000	8 to 10 weeks	Desk, phone, fax, typewriter
Travel agency	Sell travel and lodging tickets	Ads in local papers and magazines	$300 to $900	$5,000 to $36,000	4 to 6 weeks	Desk, phone, fax, PC, typewriter
Home tutoring for students and/or adults	Teach people special subjects in your home	Ads in local papers and magazines	$300 to $600	$5,000 to $15,000	2 to 4 weeks	Desk, phone, fax, PC, typewriter
Quilt-making, repair, and sales	Make, repair, and sell quilts from home	Ads in local papers and magazines	$200 to $400	$4,000 to $18,000	3 to 6 weeks	Desk, phone, typewriter
Sports cards sales and collection	Sell sports cards (such as baseball cards) from home	Ads in national and local sports papers and magazines	$300 to $800	$6,000 to $24,000	4 to 6 weeks	Desk, phone, fax, PC, typewriter
Medical claims processing	Do the paperwork processing for medical claims	Contact firms by mail and phone	$300 to $800	$6,000 to $24,000	4 to 6 weeks	Desk, phone, fax, PC, typewriter
Postage stamp sales and collection	Sell stamps to collectors by mail and phone	Ads in national stamp magazines	$300 to $900	$6,000 to $45,000	8 to 10 weeks	Desk, phone, fax, PC, typewriter

Business	What You Do	How to Find Clients	Money Required to Start	Annual Earnings Potential	Time to First Needed	Equipment
Magazine and journal binding	Make a book out of back issues of magazines and journals	Ads in local and national magazines	$400 to $900	$5,000 to $50,000	10 to 12 weeks	Desk, phone, fax, PC, typewriter
Sitting and registry service	Care for people's valued items—pets, plants, fish, etc. Supply lists of people who do this	Ads in local papers and magazines	$200 to $600	$12,000 to $35,000	2 to 4 weeks	Desk, phone, typewriter, fax
Political appointee search service	Find political appointees for local and distant governments	Contact local and national political parties by phone and mail	$300 to $900	$10,000 to $100,000	4 to 8 weeks	Desk, phone, typewriter, fax, PC
Printing brokerage service	Find printing work for local and distant printers	Phone and mail contacts with printers	$200 to $800	$8,000 to $75,000	6 to 10 weeks	Desk, phone, typewriter, fax
Registry service for specialists (nurses, baby-sitters, housekeepers, etc.)	Provide info on who's available for special work	Ads in local and national papers and magazines	$300 to $900	$12,000 to $48,000	8 to 12 weeks	Desk, phone, typewriter, fax, PC
Dental claims processing	Fill out the paperwork for dental claims	Contact large companies handling claims	$200 to $400	$8,000 to $45,000	8 to 12 weeks	Desk, phone, typewriter, fax
Supply imprinted items from home	Sell imprinted pens, mugs, cups, pencils, etc.	Contact local firms by phone and mail	$400 to $900	$10,000 to $100,000	8 to 12 weeks	Desk, phone, typewriter, fax, PC
Preparation of special foods for home events	Bake, or cook, special items that are unique and not available elsewhere	Ads in local business and religious publications	$300 to $600	$5,000 to $20,000	4 to 6 weeks	Desk, phone, typewriter, fax
Copyediting service for book and magazine publishers	Edit manuscripts for book and magazine publishers	Contact publishers by mail and phone, offering your services	$200 to $500	$6,000 to $24,000	10 to 12 weeks	Passing score on a competency examination; desk, phone, type writer, fax, PC

CHAPTER 6

THE 26 MOST PROFITABLE
GO-OUT HOME BUSINESSES

IN A GO-OUT HOME BUSINESS you do much of your work outside your home. The work you do inside your home is
mostly "book work"—that is, keeping accounts, making up
bank deposit tickets, etc. Your real income is made away
from your home. Yet your business is an honest business!

Go-outers are typically people who like to mix with
others. They may detest staying at home all day. Why?
Because they like to talk with others, see the sights of the
city or town, and so on.

A typical go-outer may even work in someone else's
office or building. But the go-outer is still in business for
himself or herself. The fact that the go-outer works on
someone else's premises doesn't mean he or she has given
up independence. It just shows that the go-outer is flexible
and will work anywhere outside the home.

Working Outside Your Home Has Advantages

When you work in your own home you have some added
costs—electricity, heat (possibly), telephone, fax line,
Internet connection, etc. Outside your home these costs
are paid by the organization for whom you're working—if
you work indoors.

Obviously, you'll meet more people outside your home than if you work inside your home 100 percent of the time. And the people you meet can bring you more work increasing your income. What's more, the people you meet will "ventilate your schedule"—that is, give you new ideas, new enthusiasms, new sources of larger income.

Getting out of the house will keep you interested in dressing better, especially if your business requires a jacket and tie for men or a business suit outfit for women. Dressing properly is—in my view—good for your mind. Why? You think better when you know you look good because you're dressed properly. Having a sharp mind will impress your customers and can get you more work for your business.

And even if you're shy with strangers, meeting new people is good for business. You never know what a new friend has to offer in the way of added work or expand opportunities for your business!

If you're an exercise buff, getting out of the house gives you some of the body movement you seek. For example, when I travel to my New York City office, I must climb 111 steps out of the railroad station, into the subway, and onto the street. Then I must walk several blocks to get to the office. All this exercise is great for physical conditioning. And traveling by yourself gives you time to think, time to plan new business moves, time to sort out what's important to you and your loved ones!

In this chapter, we give you a number of go-out businesses you can run from home that will give *you* high profit. And since profits are what you bank or use to expand your business, the ideas you get here could have a major impact on your life today and tomorrow. Even if none of the businesses turn you on, they may give you ideas for a related business that *will* turn you on!

If I can put *you* into a profitable home business today, my job is done!

ONE OF THE MOST PROFITABLE BUSINESSES

Name of Business. Seminars on Business Subjects

What You Do. Present seminars on business subjects to other business people. These seminars can run for one day, two days, three days, even a week. Topics you present must be related to making money in a business. Typical subjects are advertising, purchasing, research and development, engineering design, office efficiency, computer applications, etc. Attendees pay you, through their company, to learn methods and techniques that can increase profits in their business. Since this information is valuable to every company, the fee you charge attendees can be large. Thus, one friend of mine who teaches an advertising seminar charges $7,500 per attendee for a four-day seminar on advertising. If two people from the same company attend the seminar, the second person gets in free. This makes the effective charge per attendee, when both are from the same firm, $3,750. With ten attendees from different firms, your income from your seminar would be $75,000. If you have 20 attendees your gross income would be $150,000. Conduct two such seminars a year and your gross income will be $300,000. And since expenses rarely exceed 25 percent of the gross, or 0.25 × $300,000 $75,000, your net profit for the year could be $300,000 − $75,000 − $225,000! But to earn this level of profit you must go out of your home—you can't stay in and give a seminar.

How to Find Clients. Direct mail to companies needing the information you'll present in your seminar. It won't pay to mail to individuals; they can't afford to pay seminar fees that may range from $2,500 to $10,000 per attendee. Your mailing should be large-size format and high quality. Why? Because you want to impress prospects with the excellent quality of your seminar. If your mailing is high quality, you provide a subconscious message that so, too, is your seminar! Today, seminars are being advertised on the Internet. Such ads can reach potential seminar attendees who are difficult to reach by direct mail.

Money Required to Start. You can start this business with $300 to $900, depending on how close you are to sources of names of people in large firms to whom you'll make your mailings. You can also sell by phone, but you must provide printed registration forms by mail or fax.

Earnings Potential. You can earn from $25,000 to $500,000 a year in this business, depending on how many seminars you wish to present. If you want to shoot for the higher income, you'll have to be able to present seminars on a number of different topics. Why? Because the market for any given topic is restricted. So you can give a seminar only once or twice a year; after that you can't attract a large enough audience to make it profitable for you. Thus, your author has given seminars for years and can keep up with the demand. Why? The topics ran from engineering to book publishing to real estate, and the audiences never get tired because the topics are rarely repeated in a given year.

Another feature of your author's seminars is that I give them in Europe twice a year. European audiences are different—of course—from audiences in the United States. One of the ultimate compliments I've had from European seminar attendees is that many have returned for their fourth, and fifth, seminar with me. For an American, that's a real show of appreciation!

Time to First Earnings. It will take three months for you to get your first seminar on the road and bringing in money. This is because it takes time to get your message into the hands of firms and for them to decide to send one or more people to your seminar.

Equipment Needed. Desk, phone, typewriter, fax, PC, Internet connection.

Real-Life Success Story

A retired businessman decided that his earlier experiences in advertising and publishing would be valuable to today's firms if presented at a seminar. I developed a mailing piece and sent it to firms who were prospects for successful ad techniques. Pricing his seminar at $7,500 per attendee, he was delighted to get 30 attendees at his first seminar. This gave him a gross income of $225,000 for four days' work on his part at the seminar. The seminar was so well received he now runs it twice a year in a hotel near his retirement home, with highly successful results. While it is a go-out home business, it certainly is one of the most profitable around!

HIGH EARNINGS ON LITTLE CASH OUTLAY

Name of Business. Income Property Ownership

What You Do. You own and rent out real estate of some type. What you rent can range from conventional apartments to trailer park space to mini-warehouse cubicles. Your income comes from the monthly rental, less the expenses associated with the property. When operating this business from your home you may actually live in one of the units on the property. Since a capital investment is required to take over property, you must look for a situation in which you can acquire the income producer for zero cash down. While this may seem difficult, we have hundreds of readers who have found such property after searches of varying lengths. Some people find zero-down property the first day they look. Others require three to six months before they find suitable property. But the key message here is that you can find zero-down property if you look long enough. And the property must have a positive cash flow after all expenses, including the payoff of all mortgages.

How to Find Properties. Look in your local papers on Sunday. Concentrate on the Real Estate for Sale columns. If you look long enough you're almost certain to find a suitable property.

Money Required to Start. If you invest in zero-cash property your only startup costs will be for publications and phone calls, plus some mileage to look at the properties. So your expenses will range from $200 to $500, at the most.

Earnings Potential. You can earn from $5,000 to $100,000 and more per year, depending on the number of rental units you own. The more units, the larger your income!

Time to First Earnings. It will take at least three months to get an income flow in real estate. Why? Because you will spend about six weeks finding and buying a property. Then you must allow another six weeks before you have money you can put into *your* bank. While some deals may go through faster, you should figure on the three months mentioned above. Then you won't be disappointed when it takes longer than you hoped!

Equipment Needed. Desk, phone, typewriter; a personal computer could be helpful to you but it is not needed at the start.

How to Make Your Real Estate Fortune from Single-Family Repossessions

How can a BWB who likes real estate as a business get around the problems, which may be met when he or she takes over zero-cash down (also called repossessed) property? Here's a great solution used by a number of millionaire BWBs. It works this way:

- You take over a single-family house (we'll say) for no (or very little) cash down
- You rent out the house (for let's say $500 a month) to a nice family
- Your mortgage payment on the house is $295 a month, leaving you $205 a month
- You soon find that your "nice" family neglects the house and it looks run down

Now what can you do? The family won't move out because they're getting a bargain on the rent. Yet your house is getting dirtier, needs paint, has a few leaks here at there, etc. Your property is going downhill and you may never be able to sell it because the cost of fixing it would be (or might be) more than you could get for the house. Here's what to do:

You talk to your "nice" family and learn that they always wanted to own their own home. But they never had a big enough income to get a loan from the bank. You think about this for a few days and decide that you:

- Will sell the house to your tenant
- Using a "land" or conditional sales contract
- Allowing the buyer to make your mortgage payment
- While paying you $150 a month interest and principal on a second mortgage loan you made to the buyer

Let's take a closer look at this to see it more clearly. Then you will see how you can start building your real estate fortune quickly and easily. Here are the facts:

- The tenant likes your house and wants to own that house
- But the tenant cannot get a mortgage loan to buy the house and pay you off
- You do have a mortgage loan on the house, which you got when you took it over
- So you decide to leave your loan on the house because this costs you nothing in closing costs
- But instead of you paying the bank, the buyer of the house pays for you
- Immediately there's $295 a month you do not have to pay the bank
- You sell the house for $5,000 more than you "paid" for it
- But the buyer does not have $5,000 to pay you for the house
- So you "lend" the buyer the $5,000 in the form of a second mortgage
- You use a "land" or conditional sales contract for the "sale"
- The house stays in your name until a certain amount is paid off to you

Now what has happened to this house which was going downhill because the tenants were not keeping it up? And what has happened to you—the person worried about this house?

THE HOUSE YOU "SOLD"

- The tenants have owner pride, so
- The house looks great, spotless

- All spruced up and clean, no leaks
- If you had to sell because the new owner left, it would be easy to do so
- The neighbors like the new look

YOUR FINANCIAL CONDITION

- You don't make any more mortgage payments
- You have more income than before
- Your house is in great condition
- You don't get any more calls about leaks, etc.
- You are protected if the tenant does not pay because you will get the house back

Let's take this a step further and see how you will do in your fortune building. We'll say that you start with this one house and then take over a number of houses which give you the same amount each month from the second mortgage. Your income will then be:

Number of Houses	Your Income, $ per Month and per Year	
5	$750	9,000
10	$1,500	18,000
15	$2,250	27,000
20	$3,000	36,000
50	$7,500	90,000
150	$22,500	270,000

i.e., 5 houses x $150/mo./house for the 2nd mortgage = $750/mo.

Seven Lucky Fast Financing Methods for Your Future Real Estate Riches

You can make big money in real estate today—just the way millions have been made in the past by thousands of people. And we think that you can make money faster in real estate if you use fast financing methods! Here are seven fast financing methods for you:

1. *Get 100 percent financing* by taking over repossessions from banks, insurance companies, savings and loan associations, mortgage lenders, etc. How? Just by asking if they have any homes, buildings, or other property they've taken back because the owner wasn't paying the bills. This method is quick, easy, efficient.
2. *Get second mortgage "advance financing"* by arranging—long before you take over a property—the loan you'll need. How? By contacting second mortgage lenders before you need the money and getting most of the paperwork done. Today many people use cash from their credit card line of credit as the source of their second mortgage money. You don't have to fill out an application nor give any reason for needing the money. And the interest you pay is provable and tax-deductible because it is being paid for business purposes.
3. *Set up a "blind pool" limited partnership* or Real Estate Investment Trust (REIT) before you find the income property you seek. The "blind pool" feature allows you to invest in any type of income property you think will build wealth for the partners. (Be sure to have an attorney to help you.)
4. *Sell stock in your own real estate corporation.* As an officer of your corporation you are usually allowed to sell stock without being a registered representative. This means you can build a nice cash balance in your corporation for investment in property when you find the kind of income buildings you think will earn big money. (Be sure to have an attorney help you.)
5. *Borrow from private or specialty lenders* you search out using your own ingenuity or the help of this handbook.
6. *Become a financial broker/finder/business broker* and learn where the money is. While you'll be paid for finding money for your clients, you'll also be educating yourself as to where the money is and what kinds of loans are being made. This will save you time!
7. *Borrow or rent collateral for your loans.* Borrow stock, bonds, or other paper collateral to help you get the loans you need for your real estate wealth building. Arrange for such borrowing in advance and you will be able to get your real estate loan faster.

So there you have seven fast financing methods. Try a few—or combine a few to come up with your own method! Using methods like these, some young—and not-so young—BWBs expect to have gross incomes of $150,000 a year from their real estate, starting with no—or very little— cash! We think you might be able to do the same starting today. How? By taking your first step now turning to the real estate section of your local large-city newspaper, and looking for the offerings available to you! Then act quickly.

And a beautiful aspect of real estate is this: Once you "own" a property—that is, have taken it over for no cash down—you can then borrow on it for improvement purposes. Thus, it is usually very easy to get a $5,000 or $10,000 property improvement loan, once you have property that gives you an income. This money can be used to spruce up the property so you can raise the rent to increase your income from the property!

Also, you can repeat the financing method you use and go from one property to the next! This means that if you work at it, you can build holdings of $1 million in real estate in just a few years. With these holdings working for you, you can sit back and enjoy life, or you can go on to larger holdings with more and more income. You're the boss and you can do as you please when you're in charge of your own destiny!

Making Big Money from Small Single-Family Houses

Today I find many BWBs buying real estate appreciation— that is, its rise in value over a period time. Here's what some do:

1. Pay about $5,000 down for a single-family house (the $5,000 is borrowed)
2. Rent out the house for a $50-per-month (or better) profit
3. Hold the house for 12 to 14 months
4. Sell the house for $10,000 to $20,000 more than they paid for it

5. Show a profit of $20,000 + $1,200 – $400 legal costs = $20,800 in 2 years
6. Do this with 20 houses over 2 years to earn a total profit of $416,000, or $208,000 a year, while
7. They hold another job or run a business of their own

Of course, items 6 and 7 will depend on the continued rise in value of real estate as time goes by. But even if the rise isn't as great as predicted, profits will still be made!

You, too, I believe, can do something like this in your area when values are rising. And you can—if you have a good credit rating—borrow the money you need for the down payment on your first house. And you can work this method with other properties you buy later on.

But you want to have a rental income instead of appreciation? Then go the "no real estate real estate route." How? Let's get some words straight.

Real estate is made up of "real property," which is land. So if you own real estate, you own land, with the possibility of something on the land—such as building a stadium, an airport, etc.

But if you own a movable house such as a mobile home or trailer, you have a chattel—even though you can rent it out just like an apartment or a home. Let us take a closer look at this "no real estate real estate."

A reader in the Southwest can buy an 8-year-old mobile home for $5,000. To finance the purchase, the reader can borrow $5,000 for 60 months with a monthly payment of $110. A mobile home will serve as collateral; so he won't have any trouble getting the loan.

Once he or she has the mobile home, he or she can put it on a rented pad for $100 a month. And he or she can then rent the mobile home for $450/month. Let's see how he or she does:

    Rental income = $450 per month
    Pad Rent = $100
    Loan = $110
    Insurance = $30
    Total cost = $240

Net income = $450 - $240 = $210/month or $2,520 per year per mobile home

With a number of mobile homes, this can really get interesting. Thus, the profits with different numbers of homes will be:

10 homes	$25,200	per year profit
20 homes	$50,400	per year profit
50 homes	$126,000	per year profit
100 homes	$252,000	per year profit

And for the first five years the income will be nearly tax-free because you can take a deduction for:

• Mobile home depreciation
• Interest on the loan for buying the home
• Insurance on the mobile home
• Maintenance (fixing up) of the mobile home

You can get rich in "no real estate real estate" which you take over using borrowed money. All you need is some creative money thinking plus some other things like:

• Action on your part
• Pushes toward success by yourself
• A steady drive for money income

CATERING TO THE NEEDS OF HOBBYISTS

Name of Business. Antique and Rare Auto Finding Service

What You Do. You locate antique and/or rare automobiles for collectors, restorers, and museums. A fee is paid to you by the buyer (5 to 10 percent of the price paid for the car). In dollar amounts your fee can run from $250 for a routine find to as much as $5,000 for a rare jewel of a car. You may also be paid a fee from the seller of the car for finding a buyer. If such a fee is paid, you should inform the buyer that you were also paid by the seller. Then there is little chance of the buyer being annoyed by the double fee. Most people operate this business on a part-time basis in conjunction with another business related to the auto field.

How to Find Clients. Run classified ads in upscale magazines appealing to the wealthy saying: *We'll find any antique or rare car for you. Call (222) 123-4567.* When you get responses, as you surely will, send interested buyers a simple flyer describing your services and fees. Charge a minimum fee of $250 for any search, $5,000 for a rare gem of a car. Read the antique car journal to get a quick idea of which cars are scarce and which are easy to find.

Money Required to Start. $200 to $400 for your initial classified ad space to bring in interested buyers and sellers. Note: You have two potential sources of fees—buyers and sellers!

Earnings Potential. $12,000 to $75,000 per year, part time. If you are lucky and find eight rare cars in a year, your earnings could rocket to $100,000!

Time to First Earnings. It will take up to three months before you receive your first earnings from this business because you must locate both the potential customer and the car meeting the customer's needs. Once you have a list of potential customers and car suppliers, your business will begin to earn steady profits.

Equipment Needed. Desk, phone, typewriter, fax, PC.

HELPING LOCAL FIRMS BE MORE PROFITABLE

Name of Business. Computer Consulting

What You Do. You advise companies and individuals on what type of system to buy, how to best handle specific data problems, where to find needed personnel and any other computer-related problems they may have. Your background should be either in the PC field or in the large-systems field. Today you'll find that many consultants have experience in both fields. But the successful consultant will specialize in one field or the other. Why? Because the firms hiring you think that way. As time passes, though, they will expect a consultant to be proficient in both fields, unless the only equipment is PCs. The best opportunities today are for PC specialists because that's where small and medium-size firms need the greatest help. You can earn an excellent living from your home giving advice to PC-heavy firms in your area. And these are usually the companies who need the most help because they don't have PC experts on staff.

How to Find Clients. Classified ads in business publications can get you started. Giving papers at technical conferences can get your name in front of companies needing computer consulting. Putting flyers in local computer stores catering to companies and individuals will also keep your phone ringing.

Money Required to Start. You'll need $700 to get classified ads running and to have 500 flyers printed advertising your consulting services. Once you get your first client it will be easier to find others because you can casually "drop names"— which will impress your prospects.

Earnings Potential. You will be able to earn $25,000 to $100,000 a year as a computer consultant. Aim for large firms and your fees will be higher. But if you want a lot of clients, aim for the small- and medium-size firm. The larger the number of clients you have, the higher your fee earnings.

Time to First Earnings. Allow at least four weeks for your first consulting check to arrive. Why? Because you must first find a client, next negotiate a fee, then complete the work, and finally, be paid. But once your fee flow starts, it should continue strong for years!

Equipment Needed. Desk, phone, fax, typewriter, PC.

Real-Life Success Story

A home-based BWB had an idea for a high-tech computer magazine. Approaching several magazine publishers with his idea, the BWB was quickly turned down. But he refused to give up on his idea. Using $1,500 of his savings and working out of his large-city apartment, this BWB started his high-tech magazine for computer specialists. Within four years, his home-based company reached $3.5 million in sales. Its products include the magazine, two newsletters, three other magazines, a directory, and six conferences held in various cities all over the world. Turned down by other publishers, this BWB decided to go it alone. Today he's glad he did because his income is much higher than if other firms were publishing and selling his items. And it all started in a rented apartment!

TRANSPORTATION AT GOOD RATES

Name of Business. Car Service for Local Customers

What You Do. You find drivers to take people to local destinations—such as an airport, stores, railroad, sporting events, meetings, etc. Your maximum distance might be 50 miles or less. You are not driving people cross-country! Instead, you provide local transportation, making numerous short trips instead of a few long trips. Your drivers are paid a flat fee which you base on mileage and time (and a percentage comes to you). Thus, a 15-mile trip to the local airport might be priced at $25 for two people, each with no more than two bags. But a 10-mile trip to a local sporting event might be priced at $22 because it might take almost as long as the airport trip since there can be heavy traffic at a sporting event. Some of your driving can be of the contract type where you transport several people to the same destination (usually their jobs) five days a week. And you pick them up in the evening to bring them home.

How to Find Clients. Advertise your services in local papers and the *Yellow Pages.* Distribute flyers at travel agencies, airports, rail lines, and other places where people need transportation.

Money Required to Start. You can work with drivers who own their own cars. When you do this there is no outlay for vehicles. But your income from each will be lower than if you own your own car. Starting without a car can hold your startup cost to just advertising. An investment of $250 to $750 will get you started, especially if you use flyers placed at strategic locations where people need transportation. Be sure your drivers have their own insurance coverage so you do not have this expense.

Earnings Potential. In populated areas near airports and sport arenas, you can earn $15,000 to $75,000 a year from a car service. Where there is intense competition you must offer unique services so you stand out from the crowd. This might include services such as automatic pickup at the airport on return flights, uniformed driver, etc.

Time to First Earnings. It will take four to six weeks to get your first cash flow from this business because you must wait for your ads to be seen. But once you get a group of customers you will benefit from word-of-mouth advertising. This will provide you with a steady flow of customers if you offer on-time and courteous service.

Equipment Needed. Desk, phone, fax, typewriter, PC.

A SERVICE THAT'S NEEDED IN EVERY AREA

Name of Business. Credit Card Merchant Account Service Organization

What You Do. You present application forms to local and distant merchants (stores, flea market sellers, mail order companies, Internet web sites, etc.) seeking to accept credit cards in their business. When you do this work from home you may be called an ISO—Independent Sales Organization. You receive a commission on each merchant account application that is accepted by the bank offering its services. With new businesses coming into being every day, finding potential customers is easy. Some local travel is required in this business because you are expected to inspect the premises the business occupies. You will also meet face-to-face with the applicant because some give and take is needed while the application forms are being filled out. As an ISO you can represent one or more banks or processing firms.

How to Find Clients. Run small classified ads in local newspapers and magazines offering to get merchant status for businesses needing it. You will be swamped with requests.

Money Required to Start. You'll need $500 to $800 for ads in newspapers and magazines, and on the Internet. Other than your ad cost, your personal telephone is acceptable at the start for your business calls. So you need not invest in a business phone. And, as you travel to your clients, no office is needed other than a small space in your home for doing paperwork.

Earnings Potential. $1,000 to $2,500 per week, depending on how productive you are. The lower amount is for an average producer; the larger amount is for an aggressive worker.

Time to First Earnings. It will take at least three weeks for you to get your first income check from this business. This is because you must contact potential merchants, help them fill out their application, and then have it approved by the bank. But once you're up and running, you should have a steady income.

Equipment Needed. Desk, phone, typewriter, fax, PC. A fax is almost a necessity in this business.

QUICK CASH FROM TRASH

Name of Business. Trash and Debris Removal from Vacated Homes and Apartments

What You Do. Remove trash and other debris from apartments and homes after people move out. You will also cart off used furniture, discarded clothing, excess kitchen utensils, ancient TVs, etc. These items will be delivered by yourself or your helpers to an accepted dump site. Or if some of the items are in reusable condition you can deliver them to a recognized charity or a used-furniture store. The store will pay you for the items it buys and you keep all the money. As an alternative, you may wish to sell reusable items at a flea-market, a backyard garage sale, or in any other way you can generate income from the items. During your work you will concentrate on personal items instead of discarded building materials and similar debris. Why? Because personal items have a much higher resale value. The apartment house or homeowner pays you a removal fee with the understanding that you have full freedom to junk, sell, or recycle every item you remove from the apartment or home.

You are paid in advance in cash, by certified check, or money order. Why? Because once the trash is removed you can't return it to the home if a personal check bounces or the apartment or home owner changes his/her mind!

How to Find Clients. Direct mail to apartment house owners and to real estate brokers in your area handling the rental of, and sale of, apartments and homes. Small classified ads in local real estate magazines and in the real estate section of your local newspaper. Internet classifieds to people in your area who are considering moving or subletting their apartments or homes. Place flyers in real estate offices and apartment house rental offices covering your services.

Money Required to Start. You can start this business for as little as $300 to pay for local ads. At the start you can use your car to haul trash and debris to a reseller or dump. Once your business improves you can rent a truck on a daily basis to transport trash and debris. As your income rises you can devote more of it to advertising and promotion.

Earnings Potential. You can earn from $25,000 to $100,000+ in this business. Much depends on the apartment rental and home sales activity in your area. In larger urban areas you have a greater earnings potential. Sparsely populated rural areas offer a lower earnings potential because fewer people move or sell their homes.

Time to First Earnings. You can start earning money within one week after you place your first ads in local newspapers, on bulletin boards in local stores, making mailings to local real estate agents, and placing small classified ads on the internet.

Equipment Needed. Desk, phone, typewriter, PC, fax.

Real-Life Cash from Trash Earnings

Here's a real-life example of what you can earn in this cash from trash business that's needed everywhere in the developed world where individuals sell their homes or move from one apartment to another one. You may—we'll say—have a job to:

1. **Remove trash** from a 5-bedroom, 3-bath house that a person sold and is moving elsewhere, leaving furniture,

clothing, TVs, books, and other personal items behind. This often happens when people are starting a new life elsewhere.

2. **You look over the pile of "stuff"** and estimate that it will take four workers one day to remove the contents of the house and transport it to a suitable dump site in your area.

3. **Your estimate of the cost** for this day's work is $1,700, based on these costs: four day laborers @ $100 per day = $400; one 30-cubic yard roll-off container at $300 per day, including drop-off and pickup with delivery of the contents to the dump site. Your total cost = $400 + $300 = $700, giving you a gross profit of $1,700 – $700 = $1,000 before your advertising, phone, and travel costs.

4. **You request cash payment** because once the trash is removed you can't return it to the home seller if the check you're given bounces.

5. **Your "overhead" costs**—ads, travel, phone—are low, not more than $300. So your total profit is $1,000 – $300 = $700 for the day's work.

6. **If you sell some of the items collected,** as most cash-for-trash people do, your profit can even be higher—often more than the $1,700 total price for this job!

7. **And your first job will often come from** inserting a free 3 × 5-inch typed card on local bulletin boards in drug stores, supermarkets, all-night convenience stores, etc.!

Now here are 19 more go-out profitable home businesses for you. Look them over and see which ones appeal to you. If you have any questions about any of them, just give me a call. I'll be glad to give you my opinions about them.

Business	What You Do	How to Find Clients	Money Required to Start	Annual Earnings Potential	Time to First Earnings	Equipment Needed
Gardening and lawn cutting	Care for gardens and lawns locally	Ads in local papers and Yellow Pages	$200 to $800	$6,000 to $40,000	2 to 4 weeks	Desk, phone, typewriter
Air conditioning installation and repair	Fix and/or install air conditioning units	Ads in local papers and Yellow Pages	$300 to $900	$10,000 to $60,000	2 to 4 weeks	Desk, phone, typewriter, fax, PC
Clean, repair blinds and shades	Clean blinds and shades; repair	Ads in local papers and Yellow Pages	$200 to $600	$5,000 to $45,000	2 to 4 weeks	Desk, phone, typewriter, fax
Organize and install closets in homes	Organize and/or install closets for busy people	Ads in magazines and newspapers	$300 to $800	$6,000 to $40,000	3 to 6 weeks	Desk, phone, typewriter, fax, PC
Advise on and sell cosmetics in others' homes	Advise and supply women with the cosmetics they need	Ads in local papers and magazines	$200 to $500	$5,000 to $52,000	2 to 4 weeks	Desk, phone, typewriter, fax
Stop roof and other home leaks	Find, and stop, leaks of various types in homes	Ads in local papers, Yellow Pages	$600 to $900	$8,000 to $30,000	6 to 12 weeks	Desk, phone, typewriter
Recycle waste that is valuable in your area	Collect and sell waste that's needed in your area	Contact waste-generating firms by mail, phone	$200 to $400	$12,000 to $150,000	6 to 8 weeks	Desk, phone, typewriter, fax, PC
Roving disc jockey for local events	Play music for dances, weddings, parties, etc.	Ads in newspapers and magazines	$600 to $900	$6,000 to $30,000	2 weeks	Desk, phone, typewriter, fax
Run class reunions for high schools, colleges	Arrange class reunions for schools in your area	Contact local schools, class presidents by mail, phone	$300 to $600	$18,000 to $60,000	12 to 18 weeks	Desk, phone, typewriter, fax, PC
Design and install home and commercial walkways	Design and install walkways	Ads in local papers and Yellow Pages	$300 to $900	$12,000 to $40,000	2 to 4 weeks	Desk, phone, typewriter, fax

Business	What You Do	How to Find Clients	Money Required to Start	Annual Earnings Potential	Time to First Earnings	Equipment Needed
Arrange faster payoff of home mortgages	Put home owners in touch with mortgage firms	Ads in local papers and magazines	$200 to $800	$20,000 to $100,000	3 to 6 weeks	Desk, phone, typewriter, fax, PC
Give specialized courses in high-technology topics	Present information on special topics	Ads in high-tech magazines	$300 to $900	$30,000 to $150,000+	6 to 8 weeks	Desk, phone, typewriter, fax, PC
Delivery of news-papers in your area	Deliver daily and weekly newspapers	Work with papers to obtain their subscriber lists	$200 to $600	$5,000 to $50,000	2 to 4 weeks	Desk, phone, typewriter, fax
Run income tax preparation service	Prepare tax returns for individuals and businesses	Ads in local papers and magazines	$300 to $900	$12,000 to $75,000	4 to 8 weeks	Desk, phone, typewriter, fax, PC
Kitchen counter installation and repair	Install and/or repair countertops in kitchens	Ads in local papers, magazines, *Yellow Pages*	$400 to $900	$5,000 to $60,000	8 to 12 weeks	Desk, phone, typewriter, fax, PC
Collect, sell firewood	Find, get, and sell firewood to homes	Ads in local papers, magazines, religious newsletters	$300 to $600	$5,000 to $25,000	12 to 15 weeks	Desk, phone, typewriter
Real estate appraisal	Appraise local real estate for buyers and sellers	Ads in local papers and magazines	$400 to $900	$12,000 to $60,000	8 to 15 weeks	Desk, phone, typewriter, fax, PC
Stock market advice for investors	Advise people on which stocks to buy and sell	Ads in papers and direct mail to prospects	$300 to $900	$10,000 to $100,000	8 to 12 weeks	Desk, phone, typewriter, fax, PC
Auto windshield damage repair	Fix stone and tree damage to auto windshields	Ads in local papers, magazines, *Yellow Pages*	$300 to $900	$6,000 to $30,000	3 to 4 weeks	Desk, phone, typewriter, fax

CHAPTER 7

THE 26 MOST POPULAR "PEOPLE" HOME BUSINESSES

In a "PEOPLE" HOME BUSINESS you deal directly—one-on-one—with people, either in your home or outside it. You can't be a loner and be successful in a people home business Why? Because you *must* deal with people to earn the income and profit you seek.

People Can Make You a Millionaire

If you enjoy talking to people, working with them, and doing deals, you can become a millionaire in your own home business. But you must like people. If you are shy, feel superior to others, or don't like meeting new people, then you're a loner. Pick a home business that's more mail, telephone, fax, e-mail, or Internet based. You'll be happier, you'll earn more money, and your customers will send you more orders with checks and money orders in them.

But if you enjoy meeting people, pressing the flesh, and mixing with groups, then a people home business is for you! You'll have more fun in your business, your income will be larger, and your customers will be happier. That means they'll put more money into your bank account.

When you deal with lots of people in your home business it usually means that you'll have to leave your home for business deals. While there are some home businesses where lots of people come to your home, they are usually the exception. What's more, having lots of people come to your home can lead to questions from neighbors. When you go out into a people home business you'll usually be doing business in your customer's office, site, or factory. So you're provided with the space, light, heat, etc. that's needed free of any charge. This keeps operating costs low.

Most of us are born either "social" people or "nonsocial." While it's possible to change from nonsocial to social, the transition takes time. And it may never be complete. So take my advice for your home business:

> Start a home business that's most comfortable to you. If you like people, start a people home business. But if you're a loner, stick to a one-person non-people business. You'll be much happier and you'll earn a lot more money.

In my own home business—newsletter and book publishing—I've made millions being half social, half loner. This fits me best and the payoff is far greater than I ever dreamed it would be. There's really no way you can beat the combination of enjoying what you're doing and serving your customers well. You'll have enough problems in business without adding another in the form of an unhappy business owner!

With the increasing use of the Internet, it is possible to be "social" while still working alone. How? By putting your business on a web site and on many of the free classified ad sites. On the Internet you can "talk" to people, sell to them, and arrange for delivery without ever speaking to anyone. So you can either be social, or nonsocial, depending on your likes and dislikes.

WIDELY NEEDED WORLDWIDE BUSINESS

Name of Business. Centralized Home-Operated Travel Service

What You Do. Provide tickets and reservations for all types of travel on airlines, cruise ships, trains, buses, etc. for business, pleasure, or vacation. Other travel-related services you can provide include auto-rental reservations, hotel accommodations, vacation packages, cruise planning, etc. If you use the plan I suggest you will need only one telephone at home (your personal phone will do). You will work with a centralized travel service using a toll-free phone number to call in your customer's travel needs. There is no need for you to have any equipment other than your phone, a pencil, and a few pieces of paper! No computers, no fax machines, no printers. These features distinguish the Centralized Home-Operated Travel Service from the Home-Based Travel Agent, covered later in this chapter. As a Home-Based Travel Agent you do need a computer, do need a fax, do need to cut tickets yourself. By contrast, as a Centralized Home-Operated Travel Service owner using the plan I suggest, you work with a highly reputable and widely recognized central travel service that:

1. Sets you up as an Independent Travel Agent working from your home or business office.
2. Provides a 24-hour toll-free reservation service, 7 days a week.
3. Pays you up to 50/50 commissions split without you having to use any equipment other than your home telephone—no computer, no fax.
4. Can furnish First Class upgrades, along with large savings on the cost of hotels, resorts, car rentals, theme parks, and vacation packages.
5. Allows you to access state-of-the-art computer systems which others operate for you to find the lowest fares to thousands of destinations throughout the world.
6 Gives you free hands-on advice from Certified Travel Consultants so you can offer the best fares, routes, and accommodations to your clients.

For a nominal one-time fee you can get started in just hours after you receive your starter kit. All you need do is connect— via the phone—travel-needy customers with the centralized system. Your commissions can soon recover your one-time fee. Since you communicate with your travel supplier via a toll-free phone number, your only other expense is that of finding your customers via low-cost ads.

How to Find Clients. You can start with your relatives, friends, and business associates who need travel services, which gives them the lowest fare, discounts on hotels, etc. Next, you can send a one-page letter to local companies, schools, colleges, churches, synagogues, mosques, associations (Rotary, American Legion, Veterans of Foreign Wars, etc.), clubs, and similar groups offering low-cost travel. Such a letter could bring a strong response to your home business. You could even become a Centralized Mail Order Travel Provider, doing all your business by mail or a combination of mail and toll-free phone. Clients can also be found by running short classified ads such as:

> DO YOU WANT TO SAVE ON TRAVEL COSTS? You can! Call (222) 123-4567 day or night for full details.

Or

> SLASH YOUR TRAVEL COSTS. We'll show you how— for business or vacation. Call (222) 123-4567 day or night.

You can also run classified ads on the Internet where they can be seen by thousands. Such promotion can bring in customers from far beyond your local area.

Money Required to Start. Besides your one-time startup fee, which is $495 at this writing, you will have about $600 for letterheads and promotion—direct mail and classified ads.

Earnings Potential. You can earn from $5,000 to $36,000 a year part-time in this business. Much depends on how active you want to be and on how many clients you find. If you really want to earn more you can easily do so by establishing contacts with large groups of people in organizations in your area.

Time to First Earnings. Your first earnings should arrive four to six weeks after you start your business, though they may arrive sooner.

Equipment Needed. You'll need a desk, phone, and note paper. As your business expands, you may want to keep records of your customers and sales on a PC with a fax/Internet connection. For full data on this centralized service, write IWS, Inc. PO Box 186, Merrick NY 11566 and ask for the *Travel Service Data.*

A BUSINESS NEEDED EVERYWHERE

Name of Business. Personal Computer Maintenance

What You Do. You keep personal computers (PCs) going in businesses of all sizes. To do this you visit offices, stores, factories, and other facilities of your clients either on a regular or an emergency basis. So this is a go-out type home business because you will do few repair jobs in your own home. Almost all your repairs will be done on-site, where the computer is installed. To succeed in this business you must, of course, know PCs backwards and forwards. But you do not need a license or other technical qualifications, other than the usual local business permit. And since PCs have few moving parts your work will usually be confined to replacing circuit boards and other simple tasks. Some people in this great business find that most of their work is confined to cleaning keyboards, monitor screens, and printer typing elements. Even so, their pay is good and they can come and go as they please, without having to punch a time clock or take grief from a nasty boss.

How to Find Clients. Classified ads in business magazines and papers and on the Internet can give you good results. Also consider placing ads in school papers and religious publications.

Money Required to Start. You can get started with $600 in this business. This amount will cover your early classified ads, plus your letterhead and other miscellaneous expenses.

Earnings Potential. Your earnings can range from a low of $12,000 a year to a high of $100,000 a year. The more clients you have, the higher your earnings. And large clients will pay you higher fees for repairing their PC equipment.

Time to First Earnings. It will take at least three weeks before you get your first paycheck in this business. If you start with smaller clients they will usually pay you sooner than larger companies where several signatures may be required before your check is cut.

Equipment Needed. Desk, phone, fax, typewriter, PC.

Real-Life Success Story

Jimmy started his PC maintenance company in the basement of his home. To get word around about his new service, he personally hand-delivered flyers that he ran off on his printer. Early jobs that came to him were mostly for cleaning PCs, disk drives, and printers. On each job he was careful to see that he met the head of the computer department in the firm. Soon he had a whole new string of friends in the local computer field. Doing his work carefully led to new clients. Within six months Jimmy had more work than he could handle. So he started hiring freelance PC maintenance people. Today his PC business is booming. And he still runs it from his basement because the overhead is so low!

GET TO KNOW LOTS ABOUT BUSINESSES

Name of Business. Business Plan Preparation Service

What You Do. You prepare business plans for businesses, seeking funding for startup, expansion, or acquisition of other firms. To prepare a business plan you use information supplied to you by the firm seeking the funding. You blend this into a standard format covering topics that include: The Business (what the business does); The Market (who buys what the business offers); The Competition (who else is in the business and what they offer, compared to this business); The Management (available to run the business so it meets its projected financial results); The Numbers (what revenues and profits the business expects over the next three years). You can buy computer programs that will print out a complete business plan once you input the needed information. So there's really no writing involved. You're paid a fee for preparing a business plan. This fee can range up to $5,000 for a comprehensive plan.

How to Find Clients. Advertise in local newspapers and industrial magazines; do direct mailings to local companies; attend venture capital meetings where owners of startup companies gather to explore ways to get money. Run ads on the Internet promoting your business plan service. You'll be amazed at the number of interested people who ask you for help.

Money Required to Start. You'll need $250 to $600 to start your business, assuming that you already own a computer. If you don't have a PC you can write your first business plan in longhand, have it typed by a secretary at the company for whom you're doing the work, and use the fee you receive as payment for your PC to use for future jobs.

Earnings Potential. You can earn from $10,000 to $100,000 a year preparing business plans for companies. Higher earnings can be yours if you hire others to handle some of the workload of preparing business plans. You then concentrate on selling your services.

Time to First Earnings. It will take at least one month to earn your first income from preparing business plans. You'll need this long to find a client and do the work. Your fees will range from a low of $500 to a high of $5,000, depending on the length of the plan, how much work you must do, and similar factors.

Equipment Needed. Desk, telephone, fax, typewriter, or access to a typist. As noted, a PC is a definite asset but it is not a necessity at the start. IWS-25 *The Business Plan Kit* listed at the back of this book provides much helpful information on preparing a business plan to raise money for any business in the form of a loan or venture capital. In today's financial world, few business loans are made without a business plan being submitted to a lender. And no venture capital is advanced to a startup firm without a detailed business plan being presented to the venture capitalist.

SUPPLY A SERVICE EVERY BUSINESS NEEDS

Name of Business. Office Services

What You Do. You provide a variety of office services for small firms that do not need, or cannot afford, full time staff in their offices. Typical services you can offer include typing, telephone answering, fax receipt, etc. You will bill either on a monthly retainer fee basis or on a per-item basis. Or you can use a combination of the two methods if this would work better. And if the firm requires PC services—such as mailing list preparation, data base entry, or spreadsheets—you can provide these as part of your overall service. You'll find that conventional office services often take on a minor role when PC services are needed by your client firm. Why? Because the demand for PC services continues to grow as you offer more to a small firm. A typewriter will almost disappear from your work area because you'll do many of the needed jobs on the PC. Still, though, your work is one of office services, not computer consulting!

How to Find Clients. Run small classified ads in local newspapers and business publications. Your ad might say:

> ALL OFFICE SERVICES AT ONE LOW PRICE. For details call (222) 123-4567, day or night.

Or

> NEED A LOW COST OFFICE STAFF? We're it—for you. Call (222) 123-4567 for full information.

Your ads should bring you several clients and you should ask for an advance on your monthly retainer. This will help your cash flow.

Money Required to Start. You'll need $700 to start your business, assuming you already have a typewriter or can rent one. Your biggest startup cost will be your ads to get your first clients.

Earnings Potential. You can earn from $15,000 to $100,000 a year in this business. Much depends on how many clients you're able to get and what services you offer them. You can charge a higher fee for PC services than for normal office services. Check competing firms listed in your *Yellow Pages* for local prices. Then prepare price schedules so you offer more and better services for less money!

Time to First Earnings. It will take three to four weeks for your first earnings because you will have to find your clients via classified ads or the Internet. But once you have your first client, others will quickly join your customer list.

Equipment Needed. Desk, telephone, typewriter, PC, fax.

SUPPLY MONEY FOR REAL ESTATE VENTURES

Name of Business. Second Mortgage Loan Broker

What You Do. You find sources of second (and third, fourth, fifth, etc.) mortgages for people and firms seeking such loans. You are paid a commission by the borrower *after* the loan funds are obtained—*not* before. Where you are required to have a license for such work you can (1) apply for the license if it does not require an examination (this is true of certain states); (2) work with a licensed real estate broker or attorney whose license will cover your activities. In these circumstances you are acting as an independent contractor for the licensed person and you will not be involved in the handling of paperwork on the transaction. But you are entitled to your fee for finding the lender and bringing the borrower and lender together. Further, the experience you gain in doing such work will count when you apply for a license of your own at a later date. We strongly recommend that you obtain your license, if you want to make the second mortgage business a steady source of income in your own home business.

How to Find Clients. Small classified ads in local papers can produce many clients. You can run the same ad in local real estate magazines and newspapers, and on the Internet, and get good results. Remember: You must keep the information about your service before the public. Only then will you have a steady flow of new clients whose business will generate sizable fees for you.

Money Required to Start. You'll need $600 to cover your first classified ads plus printing of your letterhead. Once you start to earn fees from your work you can extend your ads to a larger number of papers around the country.

Earnings Potential. You will be paid a fee of 5 percent of the first million dollars in second mortgages you place, 4 percent of the second million dollars, 3 percent of the third million dollars, etc. This fee schedule is called the Lehman Formula. It is only suggestive—it is not necessary that you follow the exact number. Thus, you can reduce the percentage, if you wish. We do not recommend increasing the percentage. Typically, you can earn between $12,000 and $100,000 a year in this business depending on how many second mortgages you place. Most people combine the second mortgage business with another one because it does not require your full time to process the loan applications you receive.

Time to First Earnings. It will take close to one month before you receive your first earnings from this business. Why? Because it takes time to place your ad, find a lender, and close the deal. Ads which pull well include:

> SECOND MORTGAGES AVAILABLE. Call (222) 123-4567 day or night.

Or

> GET JUNIOR MORTGAGES QUICKLY. Call (222) 123-4567 day or night.

Equipment Needed. Desk, telephone, typewriter, PC (if you're actively placing loans).

A useful reference book on this business is *How to Be a Second Mortgage Loan Broker* by Richard Brisky described at the back of this book. It gives you great ideas on getting started in this profitable business.

Real-Life Success Story

Tim J., an unemployed blue-collar worker came to me for advice on what to do to get a decent job. "I've always liked real estate," Tim told me. I asked him which aspect of real estate he liked best. "Financing," was the reply. Since the state Tim lives in is known for lots of "junior financing"(2nds, 3rds, etc.) I suggested to Tim that he might look into becoming a second mortgage loan broker. He did and he liked what he saw. In just a few weeks Tim hooked up with a lender looking to fund junior mortgages in Tim's area. Within days Tim ran a few ads and had clients calling him day and night at home. His first loan (using the lender's funds, *not* his own) earned Tim a fee of $8,000. With no overhead except a few phone calls and a little gas for his car, the fee was almost all pure profit. Today Tim is the biggest second mortgage loan broker in his area and his income continues to rise. Yet he still works out of his low-overhead home!

Tim works as a freelancer under the license of the mortgage broker with whom he's associated. So he does not need a license of his own. This is a common arrangement that can save you the time and expense of getting a license. But if you eventually want to get your own license, the experience you get as a freelancer will count toward your license requirements—meaning you're not wasting your time while you're earning money!

GET INTO THE BEST HOMES IN YOUR AREA

Name of Business. Carpet and Drape Cleaning Service

What You Do. Clean carpets and drapes in place using equipment which you lease. Your customers will be home owners at the start. Once you get enough experience you can expand to cleaning carpets and drapes in hotels, offices, motels, and similar commercial locations. To reduce your startup cost you will lease the cleaning equipment you need. You will need an auto to travel to your job sites. This vehicle can be borrowed at the start, or leased, if you don't own one. While the work is mostly manual labor, you will be getting a lot of beneficial exercise and you probably won't have a weight problem! As you develop satisfied customers you may even work into a route-type situation where you clean carpets and drapes on a set schedule in an agreed-on sequence. Then you will have a predictable monthly income from your business.

How to Find Clients. Local ads in newspapers and community magazines pull well for this business. To get customers in wealthier areas you can either mail or hand-distribute flyers telling people about your great services and how dependable you are.

Money Required to Start. Using direct mail, small ads in newspapers, and hand-distributed flyers, you should be able to start your business for $300 to $500. Once you're established you'll take ads in local *Yellow Pages* because these can bring in lots of business. The cost of these ads will come out of the proceeds of your business.

Earnings Potential. Alone, you can earn $50,000 a year in this business. With a crew of cleaners, your earnings can rise to $150,000 a year, if you have lots of accounts, some of which are commercial.

Time to First Earnings. If you adopt a unique name for your business and dress in any eye-catching uniform (such as pure white coveralls), you can snare your first customer within one week after you start. Since you will charge on the basis of payment on completion of each job, you could have several hundred dollars in hand by the end of your first week.

Equipment Needed. Desk, phone, cleaning machine (which can be leased), auto (which can be borrowed or leased), PC once you have more than 10 accounts.

Real-Life Success Story

A young marine engineer friend of mine decided to stop going to sea when his first child was on the way. So he looked around for a new occupation he could run out of his home. While writing checks to pay family bills he noticed that his wife had spent a large sum to have their carpets cleaned. Yet the carpets seemed just as soiled as before. "I could do a better job—and at a lower cost," he said to himself. Quickly taking some local ads and dressing in his white boiler suit, he made over $1,000 his first weekend, working out of his home. Today he serves hundreds of homes, hotels, motels, and offices from home. And he added drape cleaning, expanding his income even more!

HELP PEOPLE GET MONEY THAT NEVER NEED BE REPAID

Name of Business. Get Grants for Needy Causes

What You Do. You prepare short (one-page) grant proposals for people and organizations for a fee. Once your one-page proposal is approved by the person seeking the grant (called a *grantee*), you send it to a selected list of organizations making grants (called *grantors*). You will charge a standardized proposal preparation fee, which can run from $150 to $5,000, depending on the amount of work you must do to prepare the proposal and the size of the grant sought. The larger fees occur only where a multi-million dollar grant is being sought. Thus, your average fee will be in the $250 range. If your grant proposal is successful you may receive an additional payment of up to 10 percent of the amount of the grant. Again, this fee depends on the amount of work you must do and the dollar amount of the grant. You will negotiate the fee for each job you take on.

How to Find Clients. Run classified ads in newspaper and magazines read by people and organizations seeking grants. Typical responsive media include those serving religious, social, and health interests. Your ads might say:

> GET GRANTS SOONER. We prepare your one page proposal and submit it. Call (222) 123-4567 for full details and prices.

Or

> HAVING TROUBLE GETTING GRANTS? We can help you. Call (222) 123-4567 for full details.

You can also advertise on the Internet to attract clients nationally. Response to your Internet ads can be strong because thousands of grant seekers can see your ad.

Money Required to Start. You can get started for $500, because your major expense will be low-cost classified ads.

Earnings Potential. You can earn from $12,000 to $75,000 a year in this business preparing short proposals. If you find a big grant your earnings can soar to $100,000, on up, if you share in the proceeds of the grant on a percentage basis.

Time to First Earnings. It will take one month before you get your first earnings in this business. Why? Because you must find clients. At the start this can take seven weeks. But once you have a few clients you will find others coming to you, based on recommendations from your earlier clients.

Equipment Needed. Desk, telephone, typewriter. Later, a PC and fax will be helpful. The K-18 *Phone-in/Mail-in Grants Kit* listed at the back of this book can give you much information on getting started quickly in business.

Real-Life Success Story

A woman in an area where there are many defense business layoffs, because of the end of the Cold War, decided to help displaced engineers and scientists. So she found a nonprofit group to help train engineers and scientists to go into their own peace-related business. Applying to the federal government, she received a $500,000 grant, with a promise of more grant money in the future if the organization succeeded in helping out-of-work technical and scientific people. Her organization is booming and now has help from local industries and governments. Grants are allowing her to help others while she builds her own successful business.

Another Approach to Raising Money for Worthwhile Causes

In this approach you raise money for a variety of unusual but needed causes. Some are so unusual you may never have heard of them. Here's a real-life approach to earning money by raising money for unusual worthwhile causes. You can raise the money (1) for others, as a fund raiser, or (2) for your own organization, which you will operate using the funds you raise. As a fund raiser you'll be paid a percentage of the money you raise—usually 5% to 10%, even when some of the money is pledged—that is, people will pay it off over a period of time. In your own organization serving unusual and worthwhile causes, you'll use the money raised to pay your expenses and those of your organization. Unusual activities and organizations for which you can raise money—which may be taxable or non-taxable, include those that:

- **Care for stray animals,** giving them shelter until they're adopted
- **Operate an agency** to prevent child abuse through training
- **Provide help** for the disabled—both children and adults
- **Run local boys' and girls' clubs** to provide a place for children to relax
- **Set up, and run,** youth's athletic associations in your area
- **Establish** a senior's center to help elderly people cope better
- **Teach reading to people** who are impaired in this skill
- **Give help to AIDS victims** who have problems with normal living
- **Find, and provide, shelter** for the homeless year-round
- **Conduct an introduction service** for widows and widowers
- **Start a health group** for people afflicted with certain diseases
- **Train youth** (boys and girls) for success in their lives
- **Have talented people** give music and arts festivals
- **Care for the ill** by establishing a place they can go to recover
- **Select child-care providers** for working mothers and fathers
- **Offer guidance to families** to improve their lives and relationships

There you have 16 services you can raise money for. There are thousands of others you can offer to raise needed funds for today. Almost all seem to have an intense cash need! To raise public money, take these easy steps to build your fortune while helping others:

1. **Decide** what type of group you want to run—profit making or nonprofit
2. **Pick a name** for your business—it should reflect your mission
3. **Get free publicity** for your work by sending out news releases to local newspapers, magazines, TV, and radio stations
4. **Ask people in your area** for donations to continue your help to the needy people, animals, or others you serve
5. **Use part of the money** for your cause and part for management expenses—salaries, rent, etc. Your salary comes from the money you raise. Some groups use as little as 5% of the money raised for the cause; others use 85%. The balance goes for management expenses and fund raising. You can lead a good life helping others while you help yourself to a stable and sizable income being useful to society.

A BUSINESS FULL OF ADVENTURE FOR YOU

Name of Business. Home-Based Travel Agent

What You Do. Arrange travel tickets, hotel reservations, rental auto assignments, and other travel requirements for people and groups in your area. Recent studies show that travel and tourism is the world's largest industry. Some 127 million people work in travel and tourism—one in every 15 people on the globe! More than 6 percent (6.1 to be exact) of the world's gross national product is produced by travel. Further, travel is growing 23 percent faster than the world's economy. What all of this means is that there are enormous opportunities for you in a home-based travel business. And by selling travel to people in your area you can give them personal service that will allow you to overcome any local competition. You can even organize groups and either travel free with the group or collect the regular travel agent commission due you for putting the group together. And you can squeeze by at the start without your own computer. Then, when your sales are larger, you can get your own PC. Home-based travel agents do well in rural areas which do not have any local travel services. Further, you can draw from a large surrounding area, increasing the size of your market.

My firm, IWS, Inc., is associated with a worldwide travel agency which, for an enrollment fee of $495, will set you up as a Centralized Home-Operated Travel Service, as described at the start of this chapter. You receive comprehensive training by mail, phone, and fax. Within a few hours of receiving your starter kit you can book all kinds of business and leisure travel at generous discounts using a toll-free phone number. Your commissions are quickly paid to you. This program differs from being a Home-Based Travel Agent because with the Centralized Home-Operated Travel Service you do not need a computer, do not need a fax, do not need a printer. All these functions are carried out by centralized equipment operated by knowledgeable people. Thus, all you need is your home telephone. To get started in this excellent program, send $495 to IWS, Inc., PO Box 186, Merrick NY 11566-0186. The program is available from IWS only through this address.

How to Find Clients. Advertise in local papers, religious journals, magazines, and on the Internet.

Money Required to Start. You'll need $200 to $800 to get started in this wonderful business.

Earnings Potential. You can earn from $5,000 to $100,000 or more per year in your home-based travel agency. Much depends on how much advertising you do and how strongly you promote your business among your friends and local residents.

Time to First Earnings. It will take six to eight weeks before you get your first earnings in this business. But once you're established, you'll have a steady source of income from your bookings and reservations.

Equipment Needed. Desk, phone, typewriter, fax, PC.

MAKE MONEY HELPING OTHERS OUT OF DEBT

Name of Business. Money Charge-Off Broker

What You Do. You buy and sell money charge-offs offered by banks and other lenders. For example, one of my readers bought $31.5 million in credit card charges for 3¢ on the dollar. He turned around and sold the charge-offs for 4¢ on the dollar. His gross profit was $ \$31,500,000 \times \$0.01 =$ \$315,000. He had the help of three other brokers. So his share of the gross profit A $\$315,000/4 = \$78,750$. From this he deducted his expenses: associated with the deal. These amounted to \$2,000; his profit was \$76,750! You can work this approach with many other types of charge-offs, such as auto paper, appliance paper, boat paper, etc. All you do is buy low and sell high! The whole key is to have your buyers and sellers lined up in advance.

How to Find Clients. Contact banks, savings and loan associations, credit unions, and other issuers of credit cards by mail telling them you're interested in buying their charge-offs. Your letter might say:

Your Letterhead
Dear _____:
We buy credit card charge-offs at competitive prices. Our service is fast, confidential, and accurate. You will have your funds within three days after assigning your charge-offs to us. For more information about our services, please call me at (222) 123-4567 or write me at the above address.
Very truly yours,

Money Required to Start. You can start this business for \$200 to \$400. For a fast start at contacting banks, order the IWS-1 *Business Capital Sources* directory listed at the back of this book. You can then send the above letter to selected banks and other credit card issuers. How do you know if they'll have charge-offs? They all do!

Time to First Earnings. It will take six to eight weeks for you to get your first pay check in this business. The reason for the delay is the time it takes to cultivate buyers and sellers. For a fast start, use the *Portfolio Brokering Kit* listed at the back of this book.

Earnings Potential. You can earn from \$25,000 to \$250,000 per year in this business, depending on how actively you pursue charge-off buyers and sellers.

Equipment Needed. Desk, phone, typewriter, fax, PC. You can find the names of credit card issuers in any large public library.

Here are 17 additional home businesses.

Name of Business	What You Do	How to Find Clients	Money Required to Start	Annual Earnings Potential	Time to First Income	Equipment Needed
Installing and caring for plants in offices	Install and care for office plants	Direct mail and calls to, and on, businesses	$400 to $800	$6,000 to $30,000	8 to 10 weeks	Desk, phone, typewriter, PC
Vinyl repair in homes and offices	Repair vinyl covered items in homes, offices	Classified ads in papers and Yellow Pages	$300 to $900	$5,000 to $18,000	6 to 8 weeks	Desk, phone, typewriter
Real estate surveys	Survey properties	Ads in papers, Yellow Pages; contact real estate brokers	$200 to $700	$8,000 to $36,000	12 to 14 weeks	Desk, phone, typewriter, fax, PC
Bridal and wedding photography	Photograph brides and weddings	Ads in papers, Yellow Pages	$200 to $900	$12,000 to $40,000	8 to 10 weeks	Desk, phone, typewriter, fax, PC
Commodities market investment advice	Advise people on what commodities to buy to make money	Ads in papers; direct mail to prospects	$300 to $900	$10,000 to $100,000	6 to 8 weeks	Desk, phone, typewriter, fax, PC
Agency for senior care attendants	Supply people to care for homebound senior citizens	Ads in local papers; flyers to social agencies	$200 to $400	$6,000 to $35,000	8 to 10 weeks	Desk, phone, typewriter, fax
Present medical supplies to doctors, dentists	Hand-deliver new medicines, devices, to MDs, DDSs	Contact medical, dental suppliers	$300 to $800	$10,000 to $50,000	10 to 12 weeks	Desk, phone, typewriter, fax, PC
Specialized book publishing	Publish books on selected subjects	Ads in papers, magazines	$300 to $900	$6,000 to $100,000+	8 to 16 weeks	Desk, phone, typewriter, fax, PC
Teach public speaking to business people	Show business people how to speak well in public	Ads in business papers, magazines	$600 to $900	$6,000 to $80,000+	12 to 14 weeks	Desk, phone, typewriter
Business broker*	Arrange sale or purchase of a business	Ads in local papers, magazines	$300 to $800	$6,000 to $80,000	10 to 12 weeks	Desk, phone, typewriter, fax, PC

Name of Business	What You Do	How to Find Clients	Money Required to Start	Annual Earnings Potential	Time to First Income	Equipment Needed
Franchisor of business ideas*	Get people to buy a franchise for a business	Contact people with ideas to franchise by running ads; franchise your ideas	$200 to $800	$10,000 to $100,000+	8 to 10 weeks	Desk, phone, typewriter, fax PC
Lease broker for small and large business equipment*	Get leases needed by businesses	Small ads in papers, magazines	$300 to $800	$8,000 to $60,000	6 to 8 weeks	Desk, phone, typewriter, fax, PC
Foreclosure locator and advisor*	Find foreclosure real estate for people	Ads in papers, magazines	$200 to $600	$6,000 to $20,000	4 to 6 weeks	Desk, phone, typewriter, fax, PC
Run school for manners for teenagers	Teach teenagers good manners	Ads in local and school papers	$400 to $800	$12,000 to $50,000	8 to 12 weeks	Desk, phone, typewriter, fax PC
Credit repair consultant*	Correct any errors in, and improve credit reports for people	Ads in papers, magazines	$200 to $900	$10,000 to $60,000	6 to 8 weeks	Desk, phone, typewriter, fax, PC
Mortgage cash-out broker*	Get cash for people holding a mortgage	Ads in papers, magazines	$300 to $800	$12,000 to $100,000+	4 to 6 weeks	Desk, phone, typewriter, fax, PC
Raise money for health professionals	Get loans and equipment financing for health professionals (MDs, DDSs, etc.)	Ads in papers, magazines, direct mail to MDs, DDSs	$200 to $800	$8,000 to $75,000	6 to 8 weeks	Desk, phone typewriter, fax, PC

*See the back of this book for useful, informative books and/or kits on this business.

CHAPTER 8

THE 26 MOST PRIVATE "NON-PEOPLE" HOME BUSINESSES

SOME PEOPLE ENJOY WORKING alone—and only alone. They don't want any help from people in the same office with them. We call such an arrangement a "non-people" business because it is made up only of yourself.

You'll have some people outside your home with whom you'll do some work—such as ordering supplies, having printing done, mailing letters or packages, etc. But you see these people for only a few moments. You do not WORK with them for hours at a time.

In a non-people business you have peace and quiet—except when the phone rings—as it will! And when you don't want the phone to ring you can just put it on busy. I don't recommend that you do this. But some of my friends who have their own home businesses tell me they do it regularly—just to have time to work. Better yet, use an answering machine that answers on the first ring. You won't miss any calls!

A non-people business can be just as profitable as a people business. For instance, importing (a great non-people business) can make you a millionaire. And you'd never have to leave your home. You'll make friends by postal mail, e-mail, the Internet, or fax all over the world. Yet they'll seldom even call you, preferring to use postal mail, e-mail, or fax.

Learn to "Ventilate Your Schedule"

In a non-people firm you'll be by yourself for hours on end. This may become confining. So you must learn how to ventilate your schedule—that is, get out of the house and into a different atmosphere. Some people do this by:

* Walking or jogging
* Going to a restaurant
* Touring the local shopping area
* Taking a drive in the country

The main point here is to get away for a few minutes so you refresh yourself. Your business will prosper when you return because you'll be full of vim and vigor to get more done. Without some kind of schedule break every day or every week, your competitive edge will dull. Ventilate your schedule and you'll enjoy your business and life more than you ever thought you would!

See the Advantages of Your Non-People Business

When you're in a non-people business you have many advantages. These include peace and quiet, small (or no) payroll, minimum personnel problems, reduced opportunities for fraud by employees, etc. But another major advantage that's seldom recognized is this:

> You can switch from a non-people business to a people business (if you wish) much more readily than you can from a people business to a non-people business! This means you have great flexibility in planning your life and your income. No salaried job will ever offer you these advantages!

And—if you wish—you can start your non-people business in your spare time. Then, after it builds to the income level you seek, you can operate it full time. This feature is pointed out in different parts of this book. Now let's put you into one or more great non-people businesses.

Good Non-People Businesses

There are hundreds of good non-people businesses Typical of these are businesses such as:

- Writing books, articles, plays, stories
- Doing craft work—sewing, woodworking, jewelry
- Processing forms for large firms
- Typing or doing word-processing
- Designing software programs for special applications
- Computer programming for local small- and medium-size firms
- Internet web page design and servicing

In any of these and similar businesses, you're working with paper, a computer program, or craft materials. These don't talk back to you, don't destroy your peace and quiet. You can work all day and well into the night without a single interruption. And your work shows that you enjoy your solitude. Why? Because it is either perfect or nearly perfect! So your customers are happy and show it by buying more from you.

AN IDEAL HOME BUSINESS FOR WOMEN

Name of Business. Sale of Patterns for Sewing

What You Do. Sell, principally by mail, patterns for sewing stuffed dolls, animals, toys, and other figures for children's play or for decorative elements in home or office. These patterns are drawn or printed on lightweight paper and are easy to ship by mail. You can start a whole line of children's or decorative figures. With such a line you can build repeat business from your mailing list. Such patterns are anti-recessionary— that is, during bad times people tend to spend more time at home because they don't have the money to go out. So they buy patterns to help them make toys and other figures at low cost—again to save money. Thus, while other business people are crying the blues about depressed sales, you can be rushing around your home office trying to fill the hundreds of orders rolling into your mailbox every day. And your postage costs will be low because all you are sending is lightweight paper!

How to Find Clients. Small classified ads in hobby, children's, and home decorating magazines, and on the Internet can bring both inquiries and sales. Typical ads might include offers such as:

> PATTERNS FOR STUFFED ANIMALS. Low-cost toys safe for all children. Full list free. ABC Patterns, 123 Main St., Anytown 00000.

Or

> DECORATE YOUR HOME AT LOW COST. Unusual patterns for low-cost stuffed figures. Free list. ABC Patterns, 123 Main St., Anytown 00000.

Money Required to Start. You can start a pattern business for $300 to $600.

Earnings Potential. You can earn from $5,000 to $100,000 a year in this business. The more original your pattern the higher—in general—will be your earnings.

Time to First Earnings. It will take 8 to 12 weeks for your first earnings in this business because it takes time for people to become aware of your products.

Equipment Needed. Desk, phone, typewriter, fax, PC.

Real-Life Success Story

A handicapped woman started her own imprinting business in a spare bedroom in her home. She ran the business by herself, getting orders from firms wanting imprinted pens, pencils, and coffee cups. Contacting suppliers, she farmed out the work so she didn't have manufacturing in her home—just orders and delivery. Within ten years her business was grossing more than one million dollars a year. Today this "handicapped" woman is independent and free of those who wouldn't even consider her as a potential job candidate. And today her nine workers wouldn't think of leaving her. They enjoy their work too much!

HELP THE GOVERNMENT HELP OTHERS

Name of Business. Small Business Administration (SBA) Loan Getter for Business

What You Do. Help businesses get loans for a variety of purposes —startup, expansion, machinery, equipment, advertising, employee training, etc.—from, or guaranteed by, the SBA. You help the firm fill out the loan application by typing in the requested data. (Most firms will be happy to send someone to your home to give you the information because this maintains privacy and prevents employees from learning that the firm is applying for a loan.) Once the application is completed and signed you send it to your local SBA office for processing. If there are any questions about the application you answer them on the telephone. You do *not* have to appear at an SBA office to earn your fee for your work. All your work is done by mail or phone. The reference material in Figure 8-1 is helpful for getting information on a variety of SBA loans. You can also call or write your local SBA office for free information on the loan currently being offered, or guaranteed, by the SBA.

How to Find Clients. Run small classified ads in local business newspapers and magazines. Typical ads might say:

GET GOVERNMENT LOANS FOR BUSINESS. We show you how and where. Free information. Call (222) 123-4567.

Or

NEED AN SBA LOAN FOR YOUR BUSINESS? We can help you get it. Free information. Call (222) 123-4567.

"Could You Use $50,000; $100,000; $250,000 Or More For Your Business?"

Each year Your Federal Government provides over $3 Billion to New and Existing Businesses!

Get Your Share . . .

Small to large loans are being given out every day. Each year the SBA provides over $3 Billion worth of assistance to existing and potential small businesses in the form of: Grants; Direct Loans; Guaranteed Loans; Management Training and Counseling. You are probably qualified! All you need to know is the right way to go about getting your share.

Simple, Easy, Direct!

The only reason you are not getting your share of this Small Business Administration assistance is because you have not properly applied for it. Unfortunately you cannot just sit and wait for the SBA to ask you if you need any loans today! First, you need to know the type of assistance that is available and then, exactly how to properly apply for it.

Loan Applications

In order to receive your SBA Guaranteed Business Loan it is necessary for you to be familiar with the instructions on completing SBA loan applications. This is all completely covered in the "SBA LOANS AND PROGRAMS" video.

Get In Business . . . Stay In Business!

The mission of the SBA government agency, simply put, is to help people get into business and to stay in business. The video reveals SBA Guidelines and business size standards, plus programs which offer management training, counseling and financial assistance.

SBA Programs Popular

A recent Arthur Anderson & Co. survey of CEO's of California's small and mid-sized companies revealed that 75% had utilized programs of the SBA in the conduct of their business, making them the most popular source of assistance offered by the state and federal governments. Yet, for all their popularity, it is unlikely that few business executives are aware of the vast array of SBA programs available to them.

SBA Source Booklet

This SBA booklet comes with your video and lists ALL SBA Programs, Loan Procedures, Publications and District and Regional Offices. Also included are sample SBA loan Applications.

Figure 8-1

SBA GUARANTEED Business Loans
"Your Guide to SBA Loans and Programs" is a one-of-a-kind Video that provides a GOLD MINE of essential information on SBA programs. It reveals detailed step-by-step instructions on applying for an SBA GUARANTEED BUSINESS LOAN.

Specific Programs
Your Video Guide covers specific programs offering Business Development Assistance; Federal Government Procurement Assistance; Management Training and Counseling; Handicapped Assistance Loans; Loans for Small Business; Veterans' Loans; Surety Bond Guarantees plus much more.

FREE GIANT DIRECTORY
400 Private Investment companies which are licensed by the SBA to make loans and investments in new and existing small businesses are included in a Directory offered as a FREE BONUS. The Directory lists names, addresses, phone numbers, investment policies and persons to contact. It is a must for anyone searching for private funding.

_____ YES, send me the new business video "Your Guide to SBA Loans and Programs." Enclosed is $49.95 (plus $4 shipping and handling, total $53.95). Include the free bonuses.

Name

Address

City, State, Zip

Mail Today to: IWS, Inc.
24 Canterbury Rd.
Rockville Centre, NY 11570
Call 516-766-5850 to order by credit card.

Figure 8-1 (continued)

Money Required to Start. You can get this business started for $200 to $500.

Earnings Potential. $12,000 to $100,000 per year. Your earnings will be higher in areas having a large number of firms seeking business financing.

Time to First Earnings. It will take six to eight weeks for your first income to be received from this business because it requires several weeks for firms to contact you from your ads.

Equipment Needed. Desk, phone, typewriter, fax, PC. The kit K-21 *Small Business Loan Program* described at the back of this book is a helpful reference for understanding the many SBA loans and guarantees you can use for yourself or others.

AN INTERNATIONAL HOME BUSINESS

Name of Business. Importing to Your Own Country

What You Do. You import products or services into your own country from other countries. The items you choose to import have unique features which make them competitive with products in your country. Or your import may be the only such items or services available anywhere in the world. For successful importing you must:

1. Find a suitable product or service
2. Negotiate a price
3. Have the item transported to you
4. Get the item through customs
5. Sell it in your own country

You can earn large amounts of money importing suitable products or services. The key is in choosing items for which there is a strong demand. And if you can arrange a sale prior to placing your order with your overseas supplier, you can use the order as collateral for a loan to finance your imports. When you import, your profit comes from the sale of each unit instead of the commission you typically earn when exporting.

How to Find Clients. You match an available product or service with an existing need in your own market You do this by contacting by postal mail, e-mail, fax, and phone potential buyers of your imports. Best results are obtained when you work with a product or service line you know well. Then you'll find it easy to contact potential buyers of your imports.

Money Required to Start. If you can sell before you import, your costs are confined to air mail, fax, or phone bills. So you should be able to start your business for $300 to $600. We do not recommend that you import without first having sold your import!

Earnings Potential. Your income can range from a low of $10,000 per year with just a few imports to over $100,000 per year with a full line of imports. Successful importers have a domestic market for their imports *before* they place an order. This way they avoid getting stuck with a garage full of digital watches no one wants!

Time to First Earnings. It will typically take two to three months before you receive your first import earnings. The reason for this is that you must find a buyer for what you import. And it will often take longer to find a suitable buyer than it will to find attractive imports!

Equipment Needed. Desk, phone, fax, PC.

Real-Life Import Business Tips

Importing is the opposite of exporting. When we import, we buy products from overseas firms and sell these products in our own country. As an importer, you hope to find a unique product which will have a large sale in your own country.

BEWARE OF IMPORT TRAPS

Many beginners think that importing is the simplest way to riches known to man or woman. "All you have to do is find a good product and then sell it," they say. That's basically true. But take it from Ty Hicks, who has done plenty importing from throughout the world, that:

- Finding a good product isn't always easy
- Controlling product quality can be a real problem
- Import regulations can be troublesome
- Selling the product in your own country can be the biggest job of all

Now, good friend, don't call me a negative thinker—that I'm not! But I do want to warn you of the day-to-day problems of importing before you rush off to buy some foreign products. If you listen to me and follow my advice, you may be able to beat my present record with imports. What's more, it won't cost you anything to listen!

"And what's your record?" you ask. Just this: Working less than three hours a week on the import business, I've been able to find and import products which are currently achieving sales of more than $250,000 per year—$254,300 during the year of this writing. Now if I can do that in less than three hours a week, think of what you can in 40 hours a week!

ANYBODY CAN MAKE MONEY IN IMPORTING

"Sure, Ty," you say. "*You* can make sales of a quarter of a million dollars per year in importing. But can *everyone* do the same?" Positively—I reply—if they try. However, you can't just sit back and expect the profits to fall from heaven. But I guarantee you this:

> If you follow my suggestions (altering them to suit local conditions), read, and use, the books and other guides I recommend, you can hit the BIG MONEY importing.

To show you that you can easily hit the big money in importing, I'd like to give you a few quick examples of real living people, just like yourself, who hit the big money in importing without:

- Investing large sums of money
- Working long hours

- Selling door-to-door
- Having any special skills or training

Seeing how these "people in the street" made the big time will, I hope, encourage you to do more to build your own success.

DISABLED PERSON WORKS AT HOME AND PROSPERS

Sam T. was injured in an industrial accident and confined to his home. Time hung heavily on his hands because, before his accident, Sam had been a busy and active person. So Sam began to look around for something to do at home that would keep him busy, and possibly increase his income, because his disability payments were small.

Sam was a tropical fish hobbyist. One day, a friend asked Sam if he knew where a rare South American fish could be obtained. Sam didn't know, but he promised to try to find out. This promise led Sam on a two-month mail and phone hunt without turning up one source. "I'd pay anything for such a fish," the friend said when Sam told him of the blanks he'd drawn.

This remark set Sam to thinking. If his friend would pay "anything" (i.e., a high price) for such a fish, would other tropical fish hobbyists do the same? Sam did some quick market research by calling a number of fish hobbyists on the phone. To his surprise, eight out of ten, or 80 percent, said they'd be delighted to pay whatever the going price was just to be able to get such a rare fish. And several suggested other species of fish they'd gladly pay high prices for. The combination of the remark and his research put Sam into the imported tropical fish business.

It didn't take Sam long to take the action needed to convert his market information into money, namely by:

1. Writing up a list of the fish people wanted
2. Contacting by postal mail, e-mail, or fax overseas suppliers of tropical fish
3. Obtaining by postal mail, e-mail, or fax a price list of the fish wanted
4. Negotiating by postal mail, e-mail, or fax prices on quantity purchases

5. Working out by postal mail, e-mail, or fax suitable ways to ship purchased live fish by air freight (the fish are sealed in plastic bags of sea or fresh water)

6. Advertising his service in suitable hobby magazines and on the Internet

Sam's importing business expanded from zero to $5,000 a month in a few months. Fish hobbyists, he found, wanted rare fish of all kinds and were willing to pay high prices to get what they wanted. Since the fish were light and easy to handle, Sam had no shipping problems. Not one fish failed to reach its buyer in a healthy condition.

Today, Sam has a prosperous import business booming for him. Being an invalid, he is delighted that he can conduct his entire business by postal mail, e-mail, fax, Internet, and phone from his home. Sam has never had to leave his home to do a single thing for a customer.

WIDOW MAKES BIG IMPORT PROFITS

When Beverly L.'s husband passed on, he left only a few hundred dollars behind him. Beverly was shocked by her loss and frightened by the prospects of supporting herself. But Beverly, like most people, had more courage, creativity, and energy than she either realized or gave herself credit for.

A chance remark by a friend got Bev to thinking. "If I were you, Bev," this friend said, "I'd take this chance to go into business for myself, instead of looking for a job with some big firm." But like most of us, Bev couldn't take action on her dreams immediately. So Bev took a job in a greeting-card store to earn a few dollars to tide her over. Taking this job was the best decision Bev ever made because it put her into the importing business.

At the store, Bev soon noticed that big, expensive greeting and condolence cards of all types were "in." Since there's an enormous profit on a single sheet of paper printed on two sides and folded only twice, and sold at $5 or more, Bev decided to investigate such cards further.

What Bev quickly learned was that fancy, expensive greeting cards:

- Could be printed cheaply overseas
- Were easy to import by air freight
- Are fast becoming status symbols
- Move quickly in the right stores
- Sell faster when printed in four colors

With these facts in hand, Bev checked out several European printers having offices in the United States. Within a few days, she was given cost estimates by the printers for various numbers of cards.

Using her card-shop experience, Bev made some sales estimates of the number of cards that could be sold by the store in which she worked. She also made some estimates of the number of cards she could sell by mail order to greeting-card stores throughout the United States.

Using these estimates as a guide, Bev placed her first card order using $300 she had borrowed from a friend. Within a few weeks after receiving the cards Bev sold them out for a total of $2,750, more than nine times the cost.

Today, Bev's imported greeting cards are selling at a rate of more than $3 million per year.

Why Importing Can Be So Profitable

Any business has two basic types of costs in operation—fixed and variable. A fixed cost is a cost that goes on and on, for one year or longer, whether you sell a penny's worth of product or not. Typical fixed costs are:

- Rent for office, factory, or other quarters
- Insurance for firm
- Management salaries
- Part of the firm's electric and telephone bills

Fixed costs are also called *overhead* costs.

The other type of cost, the *variable* cost, is sometimes also called an *out-of-pocket*, or *oop* cost. Typical oop costs are:

- Materials
- Freight

- Production labor
- Packing
- Postage

The main feature of a variable cost is that you pay it only when you make a product which you plan to sell.

"Now why are we looking at these costs?" you ask. Because they contain the key to why importing can be profitable. This key is:

The lower the fixed costs (or overhead) in any business, the higher (in general) the profit the business can earn.

In importing, if you can operate from your own home as many people do, your fixed costs are essentially zero. Hence, all your costs are variable, *you don't spend until you're ready to sell!* So your profit on each sale can be enormous because you don't have any:

- Factory
- Large machines
- Big production payroll
- Interest payments on mortgages for business properties

Know the Numbers in Import Profits

"What kind of profit are you talking about?" you ask. I'm talking about a profit of up to 65 cents on $1.00, or 65 percent before taxes. Compare that with the usual profit of 10 cents on $ 1.00, or 10 percent before taxes, which the typical manufacturing firm earns. Now you see what I mean about the high profits you can earn in importing. These high profits mean:

- You'll get a bigger return for your time
- You can start in importing with an investment of less than $200. Your wealth will grow faster than in almost any other business

And if you should make a mistake, which I certainly hope you will not, the money you could lose is small. This is particularly true when you compare the potential losses in importing with the potential losses in almost any other business, such as manufacturing.

So you see, importing can be highly profitable, provided you know what you're doing. And the key to knowing what you're doing is your next step toward great wealth.

Have a Market Before You Buy

Importing comprises three basic steps:

1. Finding your product
2. Getting your product
3. Selling your product

The first two steps are relatively easy. You don't have to look too far to find your product. And you'll soon learn how to get it into your home warehouse. What separates the men/women from the boys/girls is:

SELLING YOUR PRODUCT!

You can import the most beautiful items in the world, but if you can't sell them, you've wasted your time and your money. So that's why I say:

> Have a market for every import BEFORE you buy it. Never order an import until you know how many units you can sell, and at what price.

To find out how many units of a given product you can sell, you'll have to do some market research. Though this may frighten some people, market research is really easy to do, particularly if you are planning to sell a small number of higher priced items—such as 1,000 units at

$25 each. But if you're planning to try to sell one million items at $1 each, your market survey and research can be a big job. To take the scare out of market research just think of it as finding out how many people might buy a certain item!

Recognize right here and now that:

The low-priced, mass-circulation fad-type item is more subject to public whim than the higher-priced more useful item. Hence, you'll usually have more trouble making market estimates for fad-type items.

Pick the "Ideal" Import

The ideal import for you will usually be:

1. Strong—not fragile
2. Light—not heavy
3. Safe—not dangerous
4. Cheap—not costly
5. Shippable by air freight
6. Quickly available
7. Unique—not easily duplicated
8. Solely available to you
9. Smaller than competing items
10. Simpler to use than other products

Now *no* import you will find will ever possess *all* these desirable features. But you must be able to compare prospective imports, one with the other, to see which is the most desirable. Also you must be able to judge probable troubles any import might give you.

Since it's difficult for anyone—and particularly myself to remember all the above factors, I've devised an import rating and profile table for any import. This rating a profile table allows you to score—on a numbers basis—any import that interests you.

Score Your Imports

Unless you can score an import on the basis of the above or some similar factors, your information about it is meager and uncertain. To score your import, copy the import profile table shown in Figure 8-2 on a sheet of paper.

Product Import Profile

Import Characteristics	Characteristics Score
1. Strength or durability	0 1 2 3 4 5 6 7 8 9 10
2. Weight	0 1 2 3 4 5 6 7 8 9 10
3. Safety	0 1 2 3 4 5 6 7 8 9 10
4. Cost	0 1 2 3 4 5 6 7 8 9 10
5. Shipping method	0 1 2 3 4 5 6 7 8 9 10
6. Availability schedule	0 1 2 3 4 5 6 7 8 9 10
7. Uniqueness	0 1 2 3 4 5 6 7 8 9 10
8. Exclusiveness	0 1 2 3 4 5 6 7 8 9 10
9. Overall size	0 1 2 3 4 5 6 7 8 9 10
10. Simplicity of use	0 1 2 3 4 5 6 7 8 9 10
Total Score	

Figure 8-2

Using Your Import Profile Table: Let's say you're thinking of importing cuckoo clocks from Germany. You know the type of clock I mean—it's small, has weights suspended by thin brass chains, and a miniature white cuckoo who comes out of his house every half hour to sing his little song. As soon as you get all the facts on the clock, you sit down to analyze its import profile. Here's the first way you can do this. Later I'll give you another way.

You'll notice that each characteristic listed in Figure 8-2 is scored between 0 and 10. Thus, if the weight of an import were ideal from a shipping and mailing standpoint, you'd score the weight as 10, or perfect. But if the weight was "terrible" from a shipping standpoint (that is, the product is excessively heavy), you would score it 1 or 2 in Figure 8-2. My own import experience indicates that prospective import items which score less than a total of 60 points on Figure 8-2 are questionable buys for most importers.

Develop Your Import Product Judgment

"But how can I use the import profile when I don't know anything about the business?" you ask, in a worried tone. You *can* use the import profile by just using your good, common-sense judgment. It's really very easy.

To score a particular characteristic of any prospective import, just pick that number, between 0 and 10, which best represents—*in your opinion*—the rating you would give this characteristic. Give a perfect rating a score of 10; a bad rating 0. Do this for all ten characteristics and then add up the ratings to find your total score.

This import profile has many uses, and it can put money into your pocket. But one beautiful aspect of it is that the profile is self-correcting. By that, I mean that a slight error in judging one characteristic will usually be made up by an error in the other direction for another characteristic. So you really can't go too far off when you use the import profile in Figure 8-2.

Where to Find Profitable Imports

To make importing as profitable as possible for the time you invest, you:

- Should pick products quickly
- Make fast market surveys
- Develop import profiles rapidly
- Test the market speedily
- Move into full-scale sales fast

You can find profitable imports faster if you know something about the publications and Internet sites that can help you.

To find suitable imports quickly, I suggest that you read the monthly newsletter *International Wealth Success* every month. This useful publication regularly lists imports available, as well as:

- Sources of 100 percent financing for businesses
- Real estate opportunities
- Numerous capital sources
- Mail-order lenders
- Compensating-balance loan sources
- Finder's fee opportunities
- Financial broker deals
- Consulting opportunities

The Internet has a number of sites listing imports available. You can find them by going to the main site of the country from which you want to import. Such sites list a variety of imports you can consider for your home-based business.

Decide How to Sell Your Import

There are a number of ways you can sell an import. They include:

- Mail order and direct mail
- Sales to retailers
- Catalog houses
- Wholesale
- Internet listing

Mail Order Sales Probably the most profitable way to sell your imports is by mail order. Why? Because you can get a higher price for a specialty item offered direct to your customers through the mail.

But to sell any item by mail order you must know what you're doing. Earlier chapters in this book give you many hints on mail sales. But if you're new to both importing and mail order I suggest that you get yourself some specialized training in both fields. So check the local schools in your area for suitable courses. You'll find the K-2 *Starting Millionaire Program* and K-4 *Mail-Order Riches Program*, both available at $99.50 each from IWS Inc., P.O. Box 186, Merrick, N.Y. 11566, excellent self-study courses for giving you the data you need to get started in importing and mail order.*

Retail Sales You can sell imports to retailers—that is, large and small stores of all kinds—best by local calls in person. While you might dislike personal selling of this kind, you may be able to sell more units than by direct mail or mail order. So with a big payday in view, you can get out and sell hard!

You can also sell to *retailers* by direct mail and mail order, but:

- Sales take longer
- Number of units ordered may be smaller
- You are uncertain of the results
- Reorders take longer

So I recommend that you use direct mail and mail order for selling to retailers only as a secondary way of moving your imports—unless you decide that you want to make sales to retailers your main source of income.

Catalog House Sales Catalog houses are familiar to most of us. The catalog house prepares a neatly printed annual or holiday catalog, or both, for distribution to prospective direct-mail and mail-order buyers. Today, most of these catalogs are printed in four colors and handsomely illustrated.

To make a hit with catalog houses, do what I've been doing in my import business. That is, build your fortune quick by being sure to:

> Offer every catalog house as large a discount as you can, and larger than his or her other suppliers offer him or her.

---

*See the back of this book for details on subscribing.

This means that you'll probably have to start offering a discount of at least 45 percent—that is $4.50 off on an item having a list or selling price of $10. Thus, the catalog house will pay you $10.00 minus $4.50 = $5.50 for the item. From this $5.50 you must pay your:

- Cost of the item
- Freight cost
- Advertising cost
- Packaging cost
- Other costs

Lastly, of course, you must have something left over for profit. Earning a profit on our labor is the name of this game of importing!

To be able to offer the biggest discount to catalog houses:

- Buy items as cheaply as possible
- Price items as high as possible
- Seek large orders from every catalog house
- Limit the number of free samples you give away
- Keep all your operating costs as low as possible

You can make big money selling imports to catalog houses. But you have to use your head, as I've shown you above.

Sales to Wholesalers Wholesale sales of imports can relieve you of many headaches—if you can find a few real "gunslinger" wholesalers. And what's a gunslinger wholesaler? He or she is an all-out, gung-ho salesperson who really moves imports. He or she sells your imports to stores, catalog houses, mail-order firms, and others seeking imports.

Typical wholesalers I know operate from cheap office buildings. Their "furniture" is made of cast-off fruit and vegetable crates or even cardboard boxes. Yet they make huge profits on imports because their:

- Expenses are low
- Turnover is large
- Items move in and out fast

To summarize, the best way to sell your import is to:

Select the major method of sale such as retail, mail order, and the like for your import, then promote it in other markets also.

You can make a big, quick fortune in importing if you take my advice at the start and then:

- Improve your methods
- Keep searching for larger sales
- Think success at all times

An Internet listing of your imports for sale can bring you additional business. Put your offers on your own home page or on a mall. You'll be pleased with the results if you have unique products to offer.

Improve Your Methods

The only constant in life is change. Recognize that fact and resolve that the changes in your life will be for the better, that is, the changes will be:

- Improvements
- Positive—not negative
- Helpful to people
- Good for yourself
- Beneficial to business

To run your import business more profitably, you should have a copy of *How to Prepare and Process Export Import Documents, A Fully Illustrated Guide*. This 8 ½ × 11 inch book, designed to lie flat when open, gives you more than 300 pages of the forms and documents you need to be a successful importer or exporter. Available at $25 from IWS Inc., P.O. Box 186, Merrick, N.Y. 11566, it will soon become your day-to-day operating bible.

Know When to Order Your Imports

If you're importing Christmas decorations, you don't place your order in November for this year's holidays. "That's obvious," you say. Perhaps it is to you. But too many novice importers have done just that and been stuck with unsalable items for a year or more. The time to order Christmas items is in the *previous* May.

As a general guide, consider using the Hicks Rule for Imports (HRI):

> Order seven months in advance for repetitive holidays, five months in advance for repetitive seasons.

You may, as you advance your own business, want to change these rules. Fine! I've never "written" a golden word yet. But the rule will serve as a starting point in developing your import planning. And when doing your import planning, just remember the other Hicks rule:

> In business it always takes you longer and costs you more than you figure it will!

COMBINE COMPUTERS AND INFORMATION

Name of Business. Computer Bulletin Board

What You Do. Put up, on a computer bulletin board, information useful to people interested in a specific subject area. Thus, your bulletin board might cover business opportunities, export-import leads, items for sale in a specific industrial category, real estate opportunities, etc. People with a computer access your bulletin board for a fee and pull down the information they seek. Today there are thousands of bulletin boards earning a profit for their owners. You, too, can be a bulletin board owner. You just have to isolate an area of information that people need and put it up on your board. Then you publicize it among interested people. Give them a free trial run and then charge them for any additional accessing of your bulletin board. You are paid either by check or money order. Or, if you get a credit card merchant account (IWS can help you get one), you can allow your customers to charge by credit card.

How to Find Clients. Run small classified ads in newspapers and magazines devoted to the subject you're covering. Run similar ads on the Internet. People will call or e-mail you to learn how to access your bulletin board. Thus your ads might say:

DO MODEL SHIPS TURN YOU ON? If so, you should check our computer bulletin board for listings of models available from collectors. Call (222) 123-4567.

Or

DO YOU SEEK BUSINESS OPPORTUNITIES? If so, check our bulletin board listing thousands of desirable opportunities nationwide. Call (222) 123-4567.

Money Required to Start. You can start this business for $300 to $600, depending on the publications in which you take ads.

Earnings Potential. Your earnings can range from $10,000 to $100,000 (and up) per year, depending on the subject(s) of your board and the number of customers you can *develop*.

Time to First Earnings. It will take 8 to 12 weeks build to a suitable client list and income stream from your bulletin board.

Equipment Needed. Desk, phone, typewriter, fax, modem, PC.

SPECIAL NOTE: You can get much of the same bulletin-board results with your own web site on the Internet. The difference? On the Internet you "open" your business to millions of prospects. Thus, a recently opened computer game sales web site is getting 8,000 "hits" (visits) a day! And these inquiries come from all over the world. If these games were offered on a bulletin board (some 10,000 games!), it's likely that many fewer visits would occur.

You can get started free of charge on the Internet if you have your offer put up on a mall. Once you see what kind of response you get to your home business offers on a mall, you can decide if you should invest in your own home page on the Internet. (As a reminder, a mall is an Internet grouping of pages which offers a number of products, much like a shopping mall offers a number of different stores with different products in each.)

BUILD AN INCOME SERVING OTHERS

Name of Business. Run an Investment Club

What You Do. Run a club that invests in selected items for the benefit of the club members. The items you invest in can range from stocks and bonds, real estate, antiques, autos, oil tankers, to any of thousands of other items. Most investment clubs invest in only one class of item such as stocks or bonds, real estate, etc. People become club members to pool their resources and get expert advice on the class of assets they're buying. You run the club from your home and receive a fee for your work. And you can also invest with other club members to build a future profit for yourself. Since you need not spend more than a few minutes each day on the club's business, you can take on a number of clubs and become their manager. Each club will pay you a management fee, thus increasing your total income.

How to Find Clients. Run small classified ads in newspapers and magazines read by potential club members and on Internet sites accessed by potential members. Thus, typical ads might read:

JOIN THE ABC INVESTMENT CLUB and earn more from your investments in stocks and bonds. Call (222) 123-4567.

Or

INTERESTED IN REAL ESTATE INVESTING? Join the best real estate investment club around! Call (222) 123-4567.

Money Required to Start. You will need $400 to $800 to start an investment club, not counting the funds used for the investment. At the start, your investment fund will come from members. So it will not be necessary for you to put up any investment money.

Earnings Potential Your earnings will vary with the number of clubs you manage. With just one club your earnings can range from $5,000 to $20,000 per year. With five clubs your earnings may range from $25,000 to $100,000 or more per year, depending on club size and the number of members.

Time to First Earnings. It will take 8 to 12 weeks before you're generating income from this business.

Equipment Needed. Desk, phone, typewriter, fax, PC, modem.

Help People Get Credit Cards

Name of Business. Getting People Secured Credit Cards by Mail, Phone, and the Internet

What You Do. You show people how and where to get secured credit cards by mail, phone, and the Internet. A secured credit card is one that is backed by a deposit in a savings account in the bank issuing the card. The typical deposit required is a minimum of $300. Against this minimum the bank will allow the card holder to charge 50 percent ($150) to 75 percent ($225) of the deposit. You help people obtain a secured credit card by (1) showing them which banks issue such cards, (2) helping them fill out the application for the card, (3) sending in the application to the bank after it is satisfactorily completed. You can typically charge $100 or more for your services to each applicant. Why would an applicant be willing to pay you a fee? Because most of the applicants for secured credit cards have a poor credit rating and past credit problems. Getting a secured card is a step forward for them because most of these people have been turned down for unsecured cards. Further, if they pay their secured bills promptly they have an excellent chance of being issued an unsecured card at a later date.

How to Find Clients. Run small classified ads in local papers, on the Internet, and in shopper-type papers. These ads can say:

> GET A CREDIT CARD FAST! We show you how. All
> major cards. Call (222) 123-4567.

Or

> NEED A MAJOR CREDIT CARD? We show you how to
> get your own card, regardless of past credit. Call (222)
> 123-4567.

Money Required to Start. You'll need $300 to $600 to start this
business.

Earnings Potential. You can earn $10,000 to $75,000 year in
this business. Much depends on how actively you advertise
and how many customers you process.

Time to First Earnings. It will take four to six weeks to obtain
your first income check from this business.

Equipment Needed. Desk, phone, typewriter, fax, PC.

The book, *The Insider's Guide to Bankcards with No Credit Check,*
described at the back of this book is a helpful guide to banks
offering secured credit cards. It will help you give the best
service to your clients.

FILL INFORMATION NEEDS FOR A FEE

Name of Business. Back Issue Magazine Sales

What You Do. Sell, principally by mail and Internet, back
issues of magazines which people need for various uses. You
are actually a middle person between the back-issue buyer
and the supplier of back issues. Your profit comes from the
difference in price you pay for the back issue and what you
charge the buyer for the same issue. Thus if you pay $2.50
for a back issue of a magazine, you might charge the buyer
$6.00, giving you a gross profit of $6.00 − $2.50 = $3.50. The
buyer is willing to pay you more because you give personal
attention and fast service to the unique needs of the buyer.
As time passes you can develop a list of loyal customers who
depend on you for their back issue needs. Once a customer
buys a back issue of a magazine, he or she generally comes

back for more. And you can encourage sales by making regular mailings of information on back issues to your customers.

How to Find Clients. Run small classified ads in local papers and hobby journals, and on the Internet, offering to supply back issues of any magazine. Such ads might say:

> NEED A MAGAZINE BACK ISSUE? We supply all back issues quickly, at low cost. Call (222) 123-4567.

> SEARCHING FOR A BACK ISSUE OF A MAGAZINE? We have them all, at low cost. Call (222) 123-4567 now.

Money Required to Start. You can start this business for $300 to $700, depending on where you advertise, and how many ads you run.

Earnings Potential. You can earn from $5,000 to $100,000 a year in this business, depending on how many customers you acquire and the types of back issues they seek.

Time to First Earnings. You can begin earning income from this business in four to six weeks after you start.

Equipment Needed. Desk, phone, typewriter, fax, PC.

ONE OF THE BEST HOME BUSINESSES FOR A WRITER OR A WRITER'S MANAGER

Name of Business. Publish a Helpful Newsletter at Home .

What You Do. Write, or have others write, a helpful newsletter for a specific group of people needing specialized help. Thus, you might write a newsletter for real estate investors, for stock-market speculators, for a branch of high-technology you know well, for female home-workers, for beginning wealth builders (similar to *International Wealth Success*), etc. If a subject is of interest, it is almost certain that a newsletter will be started to serve this field of interest. You could be one of the many people who make their fortune in newsletters—if you choose an active field of interest for your publication.

To understand what I mean about making your fortune in newsletter publishing, let's take a quick look at the "numbers" of this business. For example, a *consumer-type newsletter* (one that's sold to the general public) might be priced at $95 per year for a 12-issue subscription. Get 1,000 subscribers and your income will be 1,000 × $95 = $95,000 per year. With 2,000 subscribers (an easy number to reach with a consumer-type newsletter that helps people), your income will be $190,000 per year—all from the comfort of your home without having to meet people.

To show you what you can do from home with a consumer-type newsletter (or any other type), here's a letter from a reader who writes: "Using many of Ty's ideas, we established a new alternative life-style publication. Eight months ago we took in $200 for the month. Last month we grossed over $5,000 from our home, and this month will be even better.... We can see $2 million a year coming up—all from a home start using Ty's ideas!"

Business newsletters serve any number of information needs in industrial, commercial, and institutional activities. Subscription prices for business newsletters often range from $395 per year to as high as $2,500 per year. With these prices, your number of subscribers can range from 400 to 1,000. Thus, with 500 subscribers at $395 per year, your income will be 500 × $395 = $197,500 per year. Not bad for serving just 500 customers! One famous newsletter publisher started his first business newsletter at home with $1,000 in capital. Today, some 24 years later, his newsletters reached $310 million in sales! All from a home start with just $1,000.

How to Find Clients. Almost every newsletter is sold by direct-mail letters sent to prospects. Some promotion is done on the Internet; some by telemarketing; some by fax marketing. But for most newsletters, at least 80 percent of its subscribers are obtained from letters sent to prospects. You never have to sell face-to-face—almost all your selling will be done via the printed word in a direct-mail letter. If you decide to use telemarketing you will hire an outbound telemarketing firm to do both the calling and selling for you. They will be paid a commission on each sale they make for your newsletter.

Money Required to Start. You'll need $600 to $900 to get started. Money can be saved in your mailing costs by using Third Class instead of First Class Mail. If the subject of your newsletter is of key interest to your prospects, the class of mail you use to sell to them is unimportant. They'll send you money either way!

Earnings Potential. You can easily earn $50,000 to $500,000 a year in this business from home. Beyond the top number you'll probably have to get an outside office for your staff.

Time to First Earnings. It will take six to eight weeks for you to get your first subscriber. But once this happens, your subscriber base should build rapidly to the number you seek.

Equipment Needed. Desk, phone, PC, fax, typewriter.

On the next page, you'll find 18 more Private "Non-People" Businesses.

Name of Business	What You Do	How to Find Clients	Money Required to Start	Annual Earnings Potential	Time to First Income	Equipment Needed
Write greeting card verses	Compose verses for greeting cards	Contact greeting card firms for their needs	$100 to $300	$5,000 to $50,000	4 to 6 weeks	Desk, phone, typewriter, PC
Geese raising, sales	Raise geese for sale	Advertise in papers, magazines	$300 to $700	$8,000 to $35,000	3 to 6 months	Desk, phone, typewriter, fax, PC
Sell how-to videos on various subjects for adults, children	Collect, and sell, top-level how-to videos by mail	Ads in national papers and magazines	$300 to $900	$8,000 to $60,000+	12 to 16 weeks	Desk, phone, typewriter, fax, PC
Collect and sell posters of various types	Specialize in posters people want to collect	Ads in fan magazines, booths at trade shows	$600 to $900	$6,000 to $75,000	8 to 12 weeks	Desk, phone, typewriter, fax, PC
Translate documents for businesses	Translate letters and other written items	Ads in local *Yellow Pages*, newspapers	$300 to $800	$6,000 to $50,000	3 to 6 months	Desk, phone, typewriter, fax, PC
Give pension advice and guidance	Advise people on pension alternatives	Ads in local newspapers and magazines	$300 to $700	$5,000 to $30,000	3 to 7 months	Desk, phone, typewriter, fax, PC
Stuttering correction	Help people rid themselves of stuttering	Ads in local religious papers, newspapers	$300 to $600	$6,000 to $24,000	4 to 6 weeks	Desk, phone, typewriter
Run cents-off coupon exchange agency	Provide place for people to swap cents-off coupons	Ads in local papers, magazines, newspapers	$400 to $800	$20,000 to $100,000+	8 to 12 weeks	Desk, phone, typewriter, fax, PC
Handwriting analysis for business and individuals	Analyze handwritten items for character traits	Ads in business magazines and newspapers	$400 to $900	$6,000 to $75,000	8 to 12 weeks	Desk, phone, typewriter, fax, PC

Name of Business	What You Do	How to Find Clients	Money Required to Start	Annual Earnings Potential	Time to First Income	Equipment Needed
Fund raising by mail for charities	Get people to contribute to charitable causes	Direct mail to potential clients to offer your services	$500 to $900	$8,000 to $80,000	10 to 12 weeks	Desk, phone, typewriter, fax, PC
Instruction-manual writing	Write instruction manuals	Send writing resume to firms needing manuals	$200 to $600	$6,000 to $35,000	8 to 10 weeks	Desk, phone, typewriter, fax, PC
Hand-knitted goods making	Knit gloves, sweaters, etc.	Ads in papers, letters to stores offering items	$200 to $500	$5,000 to $30,000	6 to 12 weeks	Desk, phone, typewriter, fax, PC
Teach parenting to expecting parents	Show people how to be good parents	Ads in parenting papers, magazines	$400 to $900	$12,000 to $48,000	6 to 8 weeks	Desk, phone, typewriter, fax, PC
Necktie cleaning and alteration	Clean and narrow or widen ties	Ads in magazines and business newspapers	$400 to $900	$6,000 to $35,000	6 to 12 weeks	Desk, phone, typewriter, fax, PC
Mitten making, repair, and sales	Make special mittens for people	Ads in papers and magazines, mail to stores	$300 to $800	$5,000 to $25,000	8 to 12 weeks	Desk, phone, typewriter, fax, PC
Help people eliminate language accents	Show people how to speak without an accent	Ads in papers read by immigrants	$600 to $900	$8,000 to $30,000	8 to 12 weeks	Desk, phone, typewriter
Personal advice by mail or phone	Advise people on personal matters by phone or mail	Ads in papers and magazines; religious publications	$300 to $800	$6,000 to $40,000	8 to 12 weeks	Desk, phone, typewriter, fax, PC
Ostrich raising, breeding, feather sale	Raise, breed ostriches	Advertise in industry papers, magazines	$500 to $900	$5,000 to $100,000	16 to 24 weeks	Desk, phone, typewriter, fax, PC

CHAPTER 9

50 UNUSUAL HOME BUSINESSES THAT CAN MAKE YOU HAPPY AND WEALTHY

YOU MUST BE HAPPY in your home business! Why? Because if you're not happy with what you're doing, your success will be limited. Your cash flow will be less than you'd like. This will make you unhappy.

Being happy in a business you run from your home is based on choosing the right business for you! Earning money at home is nice—no matter what business you're in. But when your business goes on, year after year, it won't be much fun if you don't like what you're doing. So, for long-range success, you *must* choose a home business that gives you pleasure and joy. You'll do a better job, your customers will be happier, and your cash flow will be large. All of these pluses are certain to make you happy—and wealthy! And that—after all—is the whole purpose of going into your own home business. We must all keep our goal in mind at all times.

Check Out Unusual Businesses

If you look into unusual businesses—as you'll do in this chapter—you may find one or more that are ideal for *you*. Once you've looked over several appealing businesses you can choose which one you'd like to make your main source of income. And—if you'd like—you can choose a second business to increase your income from spare-time work.

The whole key is to find a business for you. Any old business won't do. What I want to give you in this chapter is a business that will make *you* wealthy at home doing something you really enjoy!

In these unusual businesses we ignore—for the moment—whether they're go-out or stay-at-home types. Why? Because if a business attracts you there is the chance that you'll change your view of staying at home or going out.

So let's take a fast look at these unusual business—I'm sure that one or more will interest you. And if you have any questions about the business you can call me day or night—and I'll tell you all I know!

SELL INFORMATION BY MAIL, PHONE, AND INTERNET

Name of Business. Sell Useful Information by Mail, Phone, TV, Radio, and Internet

What You Do. Obtain information in suitable form (such as a book, newsletter, report, etc.), and sell it to people needing what you offer. You can sell via direct mail by sending letters to prospects, have telephone sales people call prospects and sell directly, advertise in suitable publications (magazines, newspapers, newsletters) the availability of your information and sell directly (called direct marketing), or run ads on the Internet in classified columns and on home pages to sell the information you have. Radio and TV ads are also good for some types of information.

How to Find Clients. Almost all information has a specific market. Thus, medical information goes to doctors, nurses, hospital managers, etc. Plumbing information will go to plumbers; electrical information to electricians. So your information defines your market. You can use direct mail, classified and space ads, telemarketing, Internet, radio and video ads to reach your prospects. Probably the best way to sell information is by direct-mail letters to prospects. Next, classified and space ads in publications serving your prospects can bring strong sales. Internet, radio, phone, and TV ads can also be used. But you must be careful to focus on prospects—not suspects. Only prospects buy—suspects just look and don't buy! As your sales increase you can broaden your advertising.

Money Required to Start. You can get into the information selling business very cheaply. All you need is a few buyers to get a steady stream of cash rolling into your business. To find such buyers will take $600 to $900 for startup capital. Once your income flow starts, it will continue if you contact your buyers by mail, phone, Internet. Satisfied buyers will continue to send money to you daily to buy your information. Put out a catalog once you get six or more information products. A catalog will sell strongly because it stays around longer than other types of promotion.

Earnings Potential. Part-time you can earn $5,000 to $50,000 a year selling information to people seeking it. Full-time you can earn $50,000 to $250,000 a year from home in this great business.

Time to First Earnings. It will take four to six weeks to make your first sale in the information business. But once you make your first sale, the cash will continue to roll in. Then all you need do is expand your list of products supplying information to sell to your customers and prospects. The more prospects you can find, the greater your sales.

Equipment Needed. Phone, desk, fax, PC, modem, and printer. At the start, a typewriter will help.

Here are seven information business you can run from home. Look these over and see if any of them interest you as a way to build your future wealth.

Type of Business	What You Do	How to Find Customers	Money Required to Start	Annual Earnings Potential	Time to Start	Equipment Needed
Newsletter publishing and sales	Publish helpful newsletter(s)	Direct mail, classified ads	$600	$1 million	6 weeks	Desk, PC, fax, phone
How-to nonfiction book sales	Sell how-to books (and possibly write them too)	Direct mail, classified ads, space ads	$600	$60,000	4 weeks	Desk, PC, fax, phone
Sales of short reports on helpful topics	Sell reports to people and companies	Direct mail, classified ads, space ads	$600	$60,000	4 weeks	Desk, PC, fax, phone
CD-ROM sales	Sell CD-ROMs to people who seek specialized information or entertainment	Direct mail, classified ads, space ads	$600	$300,000	8 weeks	Desk, PC, fax, phone
How-to videos	Sell how-to videos to people and companies	Direct mail, classified ads, space ads	$600	$300,000	8 weeks	Desk, PC, fax, phone
Tape-recorded information	Sell audiotapes to people and companies	Direct mail, classified ads, space ads	$800	$100,000	6 weeks	Desk, PC, fax, phone
Write success materials	Help people succeed in life	Direct mail, classified ads, space ads	$500	$1 million+	12 weeks	Desk, PC, fax, phone

Use Today's Newest Way to Sell Your Information

The newest way to sell information is on the Internet. A great "community" of people who log onto (view) the Internet talk to one another, buy and sell, swap views and opinions, and do many types of business on the Internet. Some 100 million viewers around the world can potentially see your ads on the Internet. Today, thousands of products are being sold on the Internet.

Fortunes are being made on the Internet. You can tie into this flood of money—and you don't need a computer to get started! It isn't even necessary that you be computer literate, as they say. But if you do want to get online yourself, you can borrow time on a friend's computer or use a computer at a local quick-copy shop. To tap into the money avalanche on the Internet:

1. **Decide** what products you want to sell on the Internet. Items that sell well on the Internet include books, tools, perfumes, toys, sports clothing, newsletters, self-study courses, etc. As a general guide, any product that sells well by mail order will—in general—sell well on the Internet.
2. **Name your business** and get a home page on the World Wide Web. You do this by contacting a web-site provider. You'll find them listed in any large-city *Yellow Pages* under "Web Site Design." Some designers will put you up on a "mall" (a web site with several different products advertised on it—just like a shopping mall with many stores).
3. **Promote your Web site** in all your mailings and all your ads which you run outside the web. Do this in magazines, newspapers, on the radio and TV. This will help your sales.
4. **Be ready** and able to accept credit-card orders. On the Internet, almost everyone orders by credit card. If you can't yet accept credit-card orders because you don't have a merchant account, ask your Internet provider to take these orders for you. Most providers can give you credit-card service for a small fee for each charge.
5. **Develop** a catalog of your products. Do this by adding Internet pages describing your products. Prospects can

print any page of your catalog from their computer and study it at their leisure. And your catalog should increase your sales markedly.

6. **Look for sites** where you can run free Internet ads for your products and catalog. Running these free ads will increase the traffic (called "hits" or lookers) at your site. And the more lookers—in general—the more sales for you.

7. **Follow up Internet sales** with information sheets or catalogs you mail to customers. Why? Because even though the Internet is the wave of the future, people still enjoy getting mail about the products that interest them for either business or personal use.

8. **Continue expanding your sales** to build your fortune in the hottest new ad medium to come along in years! People are making millions on the Internet. So too might you. All it takes is a line of good products promoted on the right site!

TALK AND GROW RICH

Name of Business. Lecturer on Subjects You Know

What You Do. Conduct public lectures on subjects you know well. These subjects could be in any number of fields such as business, hobbies, religion, personal relations, sports, etc. You give your lectures—which can run from one hour to two hours—in a public meeting place such as a hotel, motel, conference center, etc. Attendees pay a fee either personally or through the company. In some instances, there is no attendance fee. Instead, you, as lecturer, rely on back-of-the-room sales of books, tapes, kits, calculators, computer software, and other material. Your costs for the lecture—travel, room rental, materials that are sold, etc.—come from your back-of-the-room sales. What you have left is your profit.

How to Find Clients. Classified and space ads in newspapers and magazines. Ads on the Internet can also bring lots of attendees.

Money Required to Start. $300 to $900.

Earnings Potential. $12,000 to $100,000+ per year can be earned as a lecturer. The higher earnings levels are achieved by lecturers serving the needs of the general public, especially in the business area.

Time to First Earnings. Six to eight weeks.

Equipment Needed. Desk, phone, typewriter, fax, PC.

SPECIAL NOTE: Your author is an active lecturer in several areas of small business—real estate, business finance, import-export, and a number of others. These lectures (more often called seminars) are conducted in both the United States and Europe. Based on long experience in this field, I can tell you that:

* Lecturing can be fun and highly profitable
* Lecturing has no age barriers—you can lecture into your nineties
* Lecturing can help you sell other products to your audience

So consider lecturing for your home business. It could be your ticket to financial independence!

HELP PEOPLE GET AN EDUCATION

Name of Business. Scholarship Consulting

What You Do. You advise students on the availability of scholarships of various types in schools throughout the country. In the United States alone, some $75 billion a year is available in scholarships, grants, and student aid to pupils in colleges, universities, and high school. Bringing this money to the attention of students can be profitable for both you and the student. You will usually work with a computerized data base containing information on the scholarships available in a given area or at a specific school. You are paid by the student or his or her parents for the information you provide. Information on various data bases you can work with can be found in your *Yellow Pages* or your local library.

How to Find Clients. Advertise the availability of your scholarship services in local newspapers, school papers, and magazines. Post your ads on the Internet also because there is worldwide interest in scholarships.

Money Required to Start. $300 to $900.

Earnings Potential. $6,000 to $100,000+ per year is possible in this field. Higher earnings are achieved by people who work with large numbers of students.

Time to First Earnings. Three to six weeks.

Equipment Needed. Desk, phone, typewriter, fax, PC.

SUPPLY MONEY DATA FOR MONEY

Name of Business. Money Watch Advice

What You Do. Watch money rates and availability for companies in all types of businesses. Thus, you will watch for the availability of loans in a given field—for example, real estate. And you will report to your client companies each month which lenders are making real estate loans and at what interest rates. Your report can be either mailed (postal or e-mail) or faxed to your clients. They will pay you a monthly fee for the information you provide. You find the data you need by scanning magazines and newspapers printing information on loans, money rates, exchange rates, and other financial numbers. All these data can be obtained free of charge in your local public library where there are free newspapers, magazines, and books.

How to Find Clients. Send direct mail ads to potential client firms. Take small classified ads in business newspapers and magazines. Run classified ads on the Internet.

Money Required to Start. $300 to $900.

Earnings Potential. You can earn $5,000 to $100,000+ in this business each year. Your higher earnings will come when you develop a large number of clients.

Time to First Earnings. It will take 8 to 12 weeks for your first earnings check to arrive.

Equipment Needed. Desk, phone, typewriter, fax, PC.

HELP PEOPLE GET SMALL LOANS

Name of Business. Get SBA "Micro" Loans for Small Businesses

What You Do. Get small loans—as little as $600—for very small businesses. Typical "very small businesses" include home-based businesses run by a homemaker to earn extra income. The largest loan offered by the Small Business Administration (SBA) in its micro loan program is $25,000. In working on the micro loan program you will be dealing either directly with the borrower and the SBA, or a local nonprofit agency and the borrower. Your fee will be paid by the borrower *after the loan is obtained*—not before. With very small loans, in the under $1,000 category, you will charge a negotiated fee which might be $50 or $75. This may not seem like a large fee but such loans are approved quickly. So you can go from one borrower to another in a matter of hours.

How to Find Clients. Run classified ads in Loans Available sections of newspapers and business magazines; encourage word-of-mouth among local business and crafts people. Put ads on Internet pages—many will run such ads free of charge for you.

Money Required to Start. $200 to $400.

Earnings Potential. $4,000 to $50,000 per year.

Time to First Earnings. One to two weeks.

Equipment Needed. Desk, phone, typewriter, fax, PC.

SELL BEFORE YOU PAY

Name of Business. Sell On-Consignment Type Products

What You Do. Sell—usually by direct mail/mail order, and on the Internet—products you can obtain without putting up any money in advance. Typical of such products are professional books, paints, auto parts, etc. You may be given a 90-, 180-, or 270-day grace period by your supplier before you have to pay for the products you ordered. So you get to work and sell what you have on hand before you have to pay for it. If you're good at telephone sales, you might even use this method to move your inventory into the hands of your customers. This is an ideal no-capital way to wealth success operating from your own home. More details are given in the example that follows the *Equipment Needed* section of this entry.

How to Find Clients. Direct mail/mail order to prospects. Telemarketing to buyers of the product(s) you have available. Internet sales for both domestic and international sales of your inventory.

Money Required to Start. $300 to $900.

Earnings Potential. $5,000 to $100,000 per year.

Time to First Earnings. Four to six weeks.

Equipment Needed. Desk, phone, typewriter, fax, PC.

Real-Life Example of a No-Capital Way to Wealth Success

Morton P. called me one Sunday evening to ask for money and success advice. "Ty," he said, "I'll summarize my problems as quickly as possible. I:

1. Have no cash
2. Am a poor credit risk
3. Never ran a business
4. Hate to work for others
5. Often lose my temper
6. Sometimes feel lazy
7. Am over forty

"What," Morton wailed, "can I do to get rich fast?" "Anything you want to do, Morton," I replied. "You just have to figure:

1. What you want to do in life
2. When you want to reach your goal
3. Who can help you
4. How to achieve your wealth goal

"The first three steps are the easiest, Morton. It's the fourth step that can give you problems. But let me give you a thought." That is:

When you are low on cash and you want to start a business, seek a no-capital type of set up where you invest only your time, energy, and skill.

So if you're in a situation similar to Morton's, take these steps:

1. Decide what you want to do
2. Check to see if a no-cash deal is possible
3. Investigate other arrangements
4. Apply *thinking power* to your situation
5. Go ahead with the deal

Now, "What kinds of businesses can be started with *no* cash?" you ask. Thousands, I reply. And here's the main characteristic of each such business:

You can obtain the main commodity, i.e., the item you sell or service, of the business without making any investment until after you've sold the commodity.

The usual way business people refer to such an arrangement is by saying that you obtain the item you sell "on consignment." This means that the maker or supplier of the item is giving you 100 percent financing because *you don't put up a cent to get the item into your place of business.*

Now I'm sure you may be frowning a trifle as you read this because you have a number of key questions. Since I believe I know what most of these questions are, I'll present them below in concise question-and-answer form.

Q.   Why would any product maker or manufacturer give me 100 percent financing?
A.   Because he or she wants to sell his or her product or service.

Q.   How long can I keep the item before selling, without paying for it?

A. This varies with the item. Usually, though, you can send it back if you don't sell the item in one year.

Q. Must I lay out any cash to obtain the item I want to sell?
A. No, if you overlook the postage or phone bill for the order you place.

Q. My place of business, and some of the items in it, is damaged by fire. Who pays for the damaged items?
A. The maker of the items—*not you!*

Q. What businesses offer on-consignment arrangements for their products?
A. Here are a few you should look over to see if the consignment arrangement applies in your area:

1. Medical and technical books
2. Paints and painting supplies
3. Auto repair parts
4. Certain real estate properties
5. Some mail-order items

Besides these there are hundreds of other items you can obtain without putting up a cent.

Q. Are there any other on-consignment type arrangements I might use?
A. Yes, some firms offer 180-, 210-, 270-, 300-, 330- and 360-day on-consignment deals. While these are not quite the same as "forever," they do allow you to go into business quickly and with minimum investment.

Morton P. decided to sell medical books as the way to a quick fortune because he could get the books on consignment without putting up a dime. Then all he had to do was to find enough buyers to move a large enough number of copies to give him the income he sought. There's another secret of this method, namely:

With a long allowable payoff time you should seek to sell as many units as possible to bring in a large sum of money with which you can work—such as by putting the money into other investments—until you have to pay for the items you sold.

Morton P. used thinking power again to find a way to sell medical books against the competition. He came up with two great ideas:

1. Sell at a big discount
2. Give his customers a longer time to pay

Using these ideas, Morton soon had zooming sales of medical books to local doctors, nurses, hospitals, medical schools, and libraries. Today Morton is the biggest medical-book dealer in his area and his income is over $200,000 a year. Yet he started without a cent and built his fortune using good ideas and hard work.

USE THE PAST TO MAKE MONEY NOW

Name of Business. Sell Historical Items to Companies

What You Do. You find historical items related to a company and sell these to the firm by mail, Internet, or phone. Typical historical items you might find and sell include old advertisements (as described in the example at the end of this entry), company histories in the form of a book or magazine article, photos of early leaders of the firm, etc. Many firms are careless about historical matters. So when they're approached with some genuine items they will usually snap them up quickly at a good price. You will often be able to obtain many times your purchase price for the items you offer to firms.

How to Find Clients. Contact by mail (postal or e-mail), phone, or fax the firm associated with the historical item. When the firm is old, you may have to do some research in your local library to find its current name. There are a number of reference works on company names that will be helpful to you.

Money Required to Start. $300 to $900. To save startup funds, you can take an option to buy an item for a small amount of earnest money—say $10. Then, if a firm wants to buy the item you can use its advance down payment to pay for the item.

Earnings Potential. $5,000 to $100,000+ per year.

Time to First Earnings. Six to eight weeks.

Equipment Needed. Desk, phone, typewriter, fax, PC.

Real-Life Example of Selling Old Ads

Bill M. enjoys reading out-of-date, back-issue magazines. Once, when he was extremely short of money, Bill decided to think over his cash problem while lying on the grass alongside a beautiful lake in northern Michigan. Since it was a warm, sunny summer day, Bill relaxed quickly after lying down on the grass.

As he lay there, trying to think of ways to obtain quick cash, the idea of trying to earn money from his reading hobby kept repeating itself to him. Suddenly he thought of the amusing ads which appeared in magazines published in 1895, 1900, 1910, and so on. Perhaps, Bill thought to himself, the firms which ran those ads would be interested in having copies of them. Bill followed through on the idea and soon was:

- Collecting hundreds of old magazines
- Making a photocopy of old ads
- Sending the ad photocopy to the advertising manager of the company which ran the ad
- Charging $5 for one photocopy, and $50 for the page on which the ad originally appeared

Today Bill has a highly profitable mail order business, which he runs in his spare time and which nets him at least $100,000 a year. Why is such a simple idea profitable? Because:

- All firms are interested in their old ads
- A price of $5, or even $50, is a small amount for any firm to pay
- Most firms will order hundreds of extra copies of ads, increasing the profit potential

- Companies pay their bills quickly
- There is hardly any overhead and very little labor expense in this business

HELP PEOPLE TEST THEMSELVES

Name of Business. Develop Specialized Tests

What You Do. Work up mental tests (and physical ones also) for individuals and companies wanting to evaluate their skills in a particular subject or activity. Typical mental tests might evaluate a person's knowledge of such subjects as international trade, accounting, purchasing, etc. Physical tests might evaluate a person's throwing, kicking, running, or jogging abilities. You will sell the tests by mail order/direct mail to both individuals and firms. Each test will have the correct answers so the person taking the test can score himself or herself.

How to Find Clients. Direct mail to individuals and companies offering the tests for sale in single or bulk copies. Promote your tests on the Internet also. See example below.

Money Required to Start. $300 to $900.

Earnings Potential. $12,000 to $100,000+ per year.

Time to First Earnings. Three to four months.

Equipment Needed. Desk, phone, typewriter, fax, PC.

Real-Life Example of Specialized Test Sales

Clem L. wanted to sell tests which would help people check their knowledge. And his dream was to sell the tests by mail order/direct mail. "Who'd ever buy a mail order test?" you ask. Thousands of executives, business men and women, and similar people here and abroad do.

Clem's dream was to sell 500,000 tests per year for $1 each. This would turn his dream into $500,000 per year. "Could it be done?" you ask. Certainly! In fact, with a little help, Clem L. was able to double his dream in three years. Here's how.

BUILD YOUR INCOME FAST

Clem's dream was to sell tests that any executive business-man or business woman could use to:

- Check his or her business know-how
- Help update his or her business information
- Use as a guide to courses he or she should take in a college or business school
- Otherwise update his or her general knowledge

Clem believed he could sell these tests both to companies and individuals. The advantages of selling to companies, as Clem saw them, were:

- Companies buy in large lots
- A firm pays fast
- There are few bad debts
- Repeat business is always possible
- The test business could easily be expanded
- International sales are possible

But there were also advantages in selling to individuals, namely:

- People would tell others about the tests
- Some people would show the tests to their firm, possibly increasing sales
- The tests would help many people

TAKE ACTION TODAY FOR RESULTS TOMORROW

Clem took action immediately because:

- He believed in his idea
- By acting he was moving forward
- It would be easy to correct errors
- He would soon know if his idea was salable

To get moving on the proving of his idea, Clem:

- Prepared one sample page of a typical test
- Obtained a list of company names and addresses free from his local library

- Wrote a simple letter describing his test and the prices he was charging
- Addressed envelopes to the company training director, using the library list
- Had his letter and sample test printed
- Mailed the letter and sample to 100 firms

The response to Clem's mailing was enormous. Thirty-one companies ordered tests, forcing Clem to finish writing his first test, for which he had only one sample page. (That's a return of 31/100, or 31 percent. Most mail order operators can get rich on a 3 percent return.) Then good luck stepped in. Several of the companies which *didn't* order tests on the first mailing wrote to:

- Ask Clem to edit similar tests which they had been using
- Prepare specialized tests for them
- Print their tests
- Correct their tests

So, in a matter of just days, Clem's idea expanded from a single business of selling tests by mail order to several other profitable, related businesses—all because good luck stepped in when Clem was ready! Today Clem has a booming business here and abroad selling all sorts of testing services to firms and individuals. At this writing his sales are more than $1 million a year and they're still growing. That's not bad in three years!

GET LOANS FOR BUSINESSES

Name of Business. Loan Brokerage

What You Do. Operate a loan-getting service for individuals, businesses, and real estate operators using loan correspondents to increase your productivity. A loan brokerage is somewhat different from a person operating as a financial broker in that the brokerage concentrates solely on loans. The financial broker offers somewhat wider services and requires a wider background of experience. In a loan brokerage, your loan correspondents act as independent contractors. So you do not have payroll of any kind. And needed office services can be contracted out. Since loan applicants rarely visit a loan brokerage office, you can easily operate from home using postal mail, e-mail, phone, and fax. Further, lenders usually visit potential borrowers, if they visit anyone at all. Hence, you can run your business from the privacy of your home and no one need know where your communications originate from.

How to Find Clients. Small classified ads in local and national papers and magazines can bring in hundreds of customers, especially individuals. And if you specialize in credit card debt consolidation you can have more customers than you ever dreamed of. The credit card debt consolidation loan is the most needed loan for individuals today. Ads on the Internet will help you get national clients for your loan brokerage and debt consolidation business.

Money Required to Start. $300 to $600 will get you started.

Earnings Potential. $12,000 to $100,000+ per year depending on how many clients you seek and service and the amount of their loans.

Time to First Earnings. Two to three weeks.

Equipment Needed. Desk, phone, typewriter, fax, PC. To convince potential clients and loan correspondents of your credibility, you'll need a business plan. A concise business plan follows on page 212.

Picking a Name for Your Brokerage

To give this sample business plan greater meaning for you, we use the name "ABC Loan Brokerage" throughout the plan. Please recognize that the "ABC Loan Brokerage" mentioned throughout the plan is a generic name. You will substitute your own favorite name. Typical choices you might want to consider include:

- International Loan Finders
- Loan Finders International
- Metropolitan Loan Agency

- Universal Funding Sources
- Spectrum Loan Services
- Loans Unlimited
- Friendly Loan Services
- Capital Money Agency
- Nationwide Credit Services
- Debt Consolidation Agency
- Loan Arrangers International
- National Loan Sources Group
- First Security Loans
- Equity Money Agency
- Professional Loan Brokerage
- Your Name Loan Services
- Best Loan Agency
- Coastal Financial Services
- Worldwide Loan Brokerage
- Low-Cost Loan Services
- Business Financing Group
- Capital Services Agency
- Money Help for All
- New Money Agency Group

Concise Business Plan for Loan Brokerage

THE BUSINESS

ABC Loan Brokerage will service three major types of clients: (1) those seeking personal loans of various types, (2) those seeking business loans of all kinds, and (3) those seeking real estate loans of any type. Specific loan types under each category are as follows:

PERSONAL LOANS
- Debt consolidation
- Medical and dental
- Home repair and renovation
- Vacation
- Education

- Auto and van purchase
- Boat and private aircraft purchase
- Emergencies of all types
- Any other valid personal need

BUSINESS LOANS
- Expansion of an existing business
- Machinery, equipment, and tools
- Acquisition of other businesses
- Employee training
- Advertising, publicity, community relations
- Purchase of real estate for business use
- Auto, truck, earth-moving vehicle purchase
- Any other valid business need

REAL ESTATE LOANS
- Home mortgage
- Home equity loans
- Second mortgages
- Other junior mortgages
- Property improvement
- Land development
- Property down payment
- Any other valid real estate need

ABC Loan Brokerage will not charge prospective borrowers any front or advance payments for obtaining a loan for them. However, it will follow the generally accepted Lehman formula in its fee structure for loans obtained through its efforts. Thus, the fees for loans obtained for borrowers will be:

Up to $1 million loan	5 percent of the loan amount
$1,000,001 to $2 million	4 percent of the loan amount
$2,000,001 to $3 million	3 percent of the loan amount
$3,000,001 to $4 million	2 percent of the loan amount
$4,000,001 to $5 million	1 percent of the loan amount
Over $5 million	Negotiated

Where the ABC Loan Brokerage incurs expenses for its client-borrowers, the client will be charged for such direct costs on a non-reimbursable basis if the loan sought is not obtained. If the loan sought is obtained, these costs will be deducted from the fee paid to the ABC Brokerage by the client. Typical direct expenses which will be charged to the client are those directly related to the loan being sought and include:

- Postage
- Telephone and fax
- Approved travel
- Appraisal fees, if required by lender
- Any other client-approved charges

The client will be given a written agreement covering the expected fees, if any, that ABC Loan Brokerage expects to incur. The returnable and nonreturnable aspects of the fees will be detailed in this written agreement. Further, ABC Loan Brokerage will provide the client with an estimate of the probable total amount of these fees. Thus, the client will have an opportunity to either accept or reject proposed fees before starting to work with ABC Loan Brokerage.

LOAN PACKAGING

Where a lender requires a loan package prior to approving a loan, the client will be expected to provide a suitable package to ABC Loan Brokerage for submission to the lender. If the client is unable, or unwilling, to prepare such a loan package, ABC Loan Brokerage can offer to do so at an agreed-on fee to be paid by the client. The agreement covering the preparation of the loan package will be in writing and signed by both the client and ABC Loan Brokerage. Progress payments will be made to ABC Loan Brokerage by the client in four steps: One-fourth on signing the agreement; one-fourth on one-third completion of the package; one-fourth on two-thirds completion; one fourth on final completion of the loan package. This fee will not be refundable from the loan proceeds because preparation of a loan package can require many hours of time on the part of ABC Loan Brokerage.

AREA OF OPERATION

ABC Loan Brokerage will operate internationally. At the start of the business, however, it is expected to operate within the domestic borders of the United States. As the business grows, the operations of ABC Loan Brokerage will be extended to Europe, Asia, and other parts of the world. Local offices will be opened in various countries as the need arises for on-site representation. A local representative of ABC Loan Brokerage will be paid on a commission basis for loans he or she closes successfully.

OFFICE FACILITIES

At the start, ABC Loan Brokerage will operate out of the home of _____, its founder. Since loan applicants seldom visit a loan brokerage in person, the business can be successfully carried out as proposed. And, as the business expands, additional loan correspondents, working on commission, will also use their homes as their headquarters. This will reduce the overhead of the business and raise profits on each successful deal. Loan correspondents will be classified as Independent Contractors to ABC Loan Brokerage and will: (1) carry their own insurance, (2) pay their own travel expenses, (3) pay local and federal taxes associated with their income. The founder, _____, expects ABC Loan Brokerage to have three (3) Loan Correspondents within six months of starting up, and six (6) within the first year of startup. Additional Loan Correspondents will be added as needed.

At the start, a variety of office services will be performed by outside vendors. Such services can include:

- Photocopying
- Computer data entry
- Fax and phone services
- Telephone answering
- Internet advertising
- Any other needed services

THE MARKET

There is an enormous market need for loan brokers throughout the world. Almost every person and business needs a loan at some time. Most people, and businesses, need several loans during their existence. ABC Loan Brokerage is being set up to serve these needs in an efficient, ethical, and profitable manner.

ABC Loan Brokerage will never charge advance fees of any kind to any prospective borrower. However, ABC Loan Brokerage will contract with prospective borrowers to reimburse ABC Loan Brokerage for direct out-of-pocket expenses associated with a given loan, as detailed above. As seen by ABC Loan Brokerage, the market for assisting people and firms in obtaining needed loans is:

Individuals People seeking loans for a variety personal needs. At present, the largest need appears to be debt consolidation loans to pay off outstanding credit card obligations. There are literally billions of outstanding credit card debts that individuals wish to consolidate into one loan to reduce their monthly payment and save on interest costs. ABC Loan Brokerage plans to specialize in credit card debt reduction because it is a most promising area that is constantly growing as more people obtain credit cards and then proceed to "max out" on each new card they obtain. The market is growing so rapidly that ABC Loan Brokerage could almost specialize in this field alone and build an enormous worldwide business. Further, no other loan brokerage appears to be working in this area of the business.

Companies Businesses of all types need loans for active business use. Larger fees can be earned serving companies of all types because their loans—in general—are bigger than those sought by individuals. The market for business loans is in the multi-billions, weekly. Hence, ABC Loan Brokerage has enormous potential in the business field. At the start, ABC Loan Brokerage will offer its service to local businesses because it is easier to contact such people at lower cost. As business expands, distant firms will be contacted if the local area has a limited number of businesses seeking loans. As Loan Correspondents are put under contract, ABC Loan Brokerage will direct them to specialize in businesses with which they are familiar. Thus, ABC Loan Brokerage will be able to develop skills in handling loans for businesses in a variety of fields, including:

* Textiles and fabrics
* Engineering and architecture
* Construction and contracting
* Electrical supply and construction
* Retail establishments of many types
* Auto dealerships
* Publishing and printing
* Real estate and development
* Food and food services
* Trucking and shipping
* Any other business needing funding

Real Estate Real estate is the largest borrowed-money business in the world. So it offers enormous opportunity to the ABC Loan Brokerage for fees of many different amounts. Clients can vary from individuals seeking a simple first mortgage for a starter home to the largest corporation needing a mortgage for a new factory or production facility. And once a person or firm acquires a property, there are endless possibilities for additional real estate loans of all types—such as home equity loans, second mortgage property improvement loans, etc. ABC Loan Brokerage will offer a wide variety of loans to this enormous market. It is expected that a significant portion of ABC's fee income will be derived from real estate loans because these are often the easiest to fund because the property is the underlying collateral for the loan.

ADVERTISING AND PROMOTION

ABC Loan Brokerage will promote its services with small classified ads in local papers and magazines. As the business grows this ad coverage will be expanded to national newspapers and magazines, and the Internet. Typical of the starter ads are:

CONSOLIDATE YOUR DEBTS. We show you how, get you the funding. Call (222) 123-4567 any time.

Or

DO YOU NEED A BUSINESS LOAN? We can help get it quickly, at low cost. Call (222) 123-4567.

ABC Loan Brokerage will also promote word-of-mouth advertising because it has been found that loan recipients are happy to recommend their loan source to others. This will be done by rendering continuous high-quality service to every customer. Such service almost always produces a satisfied customer who is glad to tell his or her friend about the excellent service received. Word-of-mouth recommendations grow in numbers as more loans are obtained for clients.

Space ads will be run as the business grows. The ads will appear in national newspapers and magazine: Typical media considered for such ads will include:

Wall Street Journal
New York Times
Los Angeles Times
Forbes Magazine
Time Magazine
Barron's
Income Opportunities Magazine
Money Making Opportunities Magazine
Spare Time Magazine
International Wealth Success
Other suitable publications

Such space ads are expected to produce a strong response from individuals and businesses needing loans for a variety of purposes. One fee from a large loan can pay for numerous ads in several publications.

Publicity will be sought when the business opens. News releases announcing the formation of the ABC Loan Brokerage will be mailed to local and national publications. This will produce free publicity for the brokerage and should generate some inquiries which will lead to customers who need loans. Fee income will follow.

ABC Loan Brokerage expects to actively pursue opportunities in the market as they develop. With individuals and businesses constantly seeking larger and larger loans or lines of credit, the Brokerage sees a steady growth ahead. Its financial projections reflect this expected growth produced by careful marketing of its services.

The Management At the start of business, ABC Loan Brokerage expects to have one full-time employee and two part-time employees. Data on the education and business experience of each are given below:

Enter here the educational and business qualification of the principals of the ABC Loan Brokerage.

Financial Projections ABC Loan Brokerage is expected to grow each year of its existence. A summary of its financial projections is given below.

Year Number	1	2	3
Fee Income	$100,000	350,000	900,000
Salaries, Benefits	$ 50,000	200,000	600,000
Office Expenses	$ 25,000	90,000	200,000
Profit before Taxes	$ 25,000	60,000	100,000

Full details of expected expenses will be provided to anyone seeking them. However, the above projections are indicative of the expected growth of the business during its first three years.

MAKE MONEY FROM BANKING

Name of Business. Banking Information Agency

What You Do. You provide printed information about banks of all types—domestic, international, local, and out-of-town to individuals and companies. Data you provide might include current rates for Certificates Deposit (CDs), types of loans made, savings account rates, capital, etc. With the many bank failures and the various scams in recent years, people and firms are concerned about choosing a bank. You can provide helpful information to answer various questions. Your printed data can be in the form of reports, a newsletter, or special communications. You charge an annual fee for this information to subscribers—usually business firms. Individuals will buy special reports from you on a one-at-a-time basis. You will obtain information about the banks you survey from public documents issued by banks, from directories available in any large public library, and from annual reports issued by the bank. Your job is to distill this information into an understandable report that's useful to the people and firms you send it to.

How to Find Clients. Classified ads in local papers and magazines will get you customers in your area. National publications will bring customers from wider areas. And classified ads in business publications will bring inquiries from companies. Follow-up direct mail can convert these inquiries to customers. Internet ads will bring inquiries from potential customers worldwide.

Money Required to Start. You'll need $300 to $900 to get started in this business.

Earnings Potential. You can earn $12,000 to $100,000+ a year in this business. The higher earnings level will occur after you've acquired some business subscribers for your reports.

Time to First Earnings. It will take up to three to four months before your first income check arrives. The reason for this is that it will take you time to assemble the data you need and to find subscribers to and buyers of your reports.

Equipment Needed. Desk, phone, typewriter, fax, PC.

Here are 41 more unusual home businesses for you.

Name of Business	What You Do	How to Find Clients	Money Required to Start	Annual Earnings Potential	Time to First Income	Equipment Needed
Have your pet perform on television	Train your pet so it can be a TV performer	Contact TV stations and show producers	$300 to $600	$10,000 to $100,000+	3 to 6 months	Desk, phone, typewriter, fax, pet
Operate 900 numbers to sell items	Use an answering machine to sell to callers	Advertise your 900 number in local media	$600 to $800	$12,000 to $75,000+	4 to 6 weeks	Desk, phone, typewriter, PC
Conduct special exercise classes	Run exercise classes for people with health problems	Run classified ads in local media	$300 to $600	$5,000 to $40,000	6 to 8 weeks	Desk, phone, typewriter
Run a mini goat farm	Raise, breed small goats for cheese, milk, litter	Advertise goat products for sale	$200 to $800	$10,000 to $60,000	12 to 18 weeks	Desk, phone, rented land
Teach the game of billiards	Show people how to be good billiard players	Ads in local media and at billiard rooms	$300 to $600	$6,000 to $25,000	4 to 6 weeks	Desk, phone, typewriter
Run wine tasting parties	Teach people the difference in wines	Ads in local media and club publications	$200 to $600	$4,000 to $36,000	6 to 8 weeks	Desk, phone typewriter, fax, PC
Teach computer literacy in one weekend	Give people a crash course in personal computer use	Ads in local and national publications	$300 to $900	$12,000 to $75,000	3 to 4 weeks	Desk, phone, typewriter, fax, PC
Sell, service, teach people notebook computers	Get people and notebook computers together; keep them running	Ads in local and national media	$200 to $900	$10,000 to $80,000+	6 to 8 weeks	Desk, phone, typewriter, fax, PC

Name of Business	What You Do	How to Find Clients	Money Required to Start	Annual Earnings Potential	Time to First Income	Equipment Needed
Show people how to reduce excess papers in their lives	Demonstrate how people can unclutter their lives	Ads in local, national media	$200 to $600	$8,000 to $24,000	4 to 6 weeks	Desk, phone, typewriter, fax, PC
Teach magic to people who want to learn it	Show people how to perform tricks	Ads in local, national media	$200 to $800	$6,000 to $20,000	3 to 4 weeks	Desk, phone, typewriter
Run luggage rental agency for travelers	Rent out other people's travel luggage for a fee	Ads in travel and local papers and magazines	$600 to $900	$6,000 to $18,000	12 to 16 weeks	Desk, phone, typewriter, fax, PC
Review book manuscripts for a fee	Read technical or scientific book proposals and manuscripts and write an evaluation	Mail resume and letter to book publishers	$200 to $400	$3,000 to $18,000	8 to 12 weeks	Desk, phone, typewriter, fax, PC
Teach people how to win at blackjack	Show people the basics of blackjack and how to win	Ads in local, national media	$300 to $600	$5,000 to $25,000	3 to 6 weeks	Desk, phone, typewriter
Show people how to develop better conversational skills	Teach people how to start, and carry on, a good conversation	Ads in local, national media	$400 to $800	$6,000 to $24,000	2 to 4 weeks	Desk, phone, typewriter
Show restaurant workers how to earn extra tips	Train waiters and waitresses how to serve better and earn larger tips	Ads in restaurant publications	$200 to $800	$12,000 to $60,000	3 to 6 weeks	Desk, phone, typewriter, fax, PC
Teach people how to enjoy and understand classical music	Explain music to people who want to enjoy it more	Ads in local publications	$200 to $800	$6,000 to $18,000	4 to 8 weeks	Desk, phone, typewriter

Name of Business	What You Do	How to Find Clients	Money Required to Start	Annual Earnings Potential	Time to First Income	Equipment Needed
Show people how to read faster	Teach speed reading	Ads in local papers, *Yellow Pages*	$400 to $900	$12,000 to $35,000	8 to 12 weeks	Desk, phone, typewriter, fax, PC
Picture framing for people, firms	Frame photos, paintings, sketches	Ads in local papers, *Yellow Pages*	$400 to $900	$4,000 to $25,000	4 to 6 weeks	Desk, phone, typewriter, fax
Holiday ornament making	Make ornaments for Christmas, 4th of July, etc.	Ads in media serving retailers	$330 to $800	$3,000 to $15,000	6 to 12 weeks	Desk, phone, typewriter
Record and compact disc sale, exchange	Supply records or CDs to people seeking the unusual	Ads in music media	$400 to $800	$4,000 to $50,000	6 to 8 weeks	Desk, phone, typewriter, fax, PC
Collection and sale of sea shells	Make sea shells available to serious collectors	Ads in hobby publications	$300 to $900	$3,000 to $18,000	4 to 6 weeks	Desk, phone, typewriter, fax, PC
Roller skate/blade repair and customizing	Repair worn skates; customize skates for serious skaters	Ads in skating publications	$400 to $800	$6,000 to $30,000	6 to 8 weeks	Desk, phone, typewriter, fax, PC
Give advice on how to enter, and win, contests	Show people how to win contests, either in person or in print	Ads in contest publications	$400 to $900	$5,000 to $75,000	6 to 8 weeks	Desk, phone, typewriter, fax, PC
Run art shows in local parks	Conduct shows for artists in local facilities	Ads in art journals, newspapers	$300 to $600	$3,000 to $24,000	4 to 6 weeks	Desk, phone, typewriter, fax, PC
Design and make fancy aprons	Sew aprons with customized designs for people, firms	Ads in papers, magazines	$300 to $800	$4,000 to $25,000	8 to 10 weeks	Desk, phone, typewriter, fax, PC

Name of Business	What You Do	How to Find Clients	Money Required to Start	Annual Earnings Potential	Time to First Income	Equipment Needed
Make photo buttons for people, firms	Snap photos, mount on buttons	Ads in recreational media	$400 to $800	$3,000 to $12,000	2 to 3 weeks	Desk, phone, typewriter
Design and make silk flowers	Make flowers for retail sale	Ads in local and retail publications	$300 to $600	$4,000 to $18,000	4 to 8 weeks	Desk, phone, typewriter
Make, collect, sell teddy bears	Supply teddy bears to people who love them	Ads in local and hobby papers, magazines	$400 to $800	$3,000 to $45,000	6 to 8 weeks	Desk, phone, typewriter, fax, PC
Sell secondhand toys, games	Supply used toys to people seeking them	Ads in papers and magazines	$300 to $600	$5,000 to $30,000	6 to 8 weeks	Desk, phone, typewriter
Chimney sweep service	Clean chimneys in your area	Classified ads in local papers, magazines	$300 to $600	$5,000 to $20,000	6 to 8 weeks	Desk, phone, typewriter
Write letters for people who hate to	Write letters for all kinds of people	Classified ads in personal columns of papers	$300 to $500	$3,000 to $12,000	8 to 10 weeks	Desk, phone, typewriter
Sketch or paint people or pets	Prepare special portraits	Small space ads in local papers, magazines	$600 to $900	$8,000 to $25,000	8 to 10 weeks	Desk, phone, typewriter
Bicycle repair and service	Fix broken or worn bicycles	Ads in hobby and sport magazines, newspapers	$500 to $900	$6,000 to $35,000	6 to 8 weeks	Desk, phone, typewriter, tools
Window washing service	Wash windows in homes and businesses	Ads in local papers, business publications	$300 to $600	$12,000 to $36,000	4 to 6 weeks	Desk, phone, typewriter, fax
T-shirt design and printing service	Design, print special T-shirts for people, organizations	Ads in local and national media	$600 to $900	$8,000 to $30,000	2 to 4 weeks	Desk, phone, typewriter, fax, PC
Give personalized boat operation instructions	Show people how to run a boat safely	Ads in boating papers, magazines	$400 to $900	$6,000 to $30,000	12 to 16 weeks	Desk, phone, typewriter

Name of Business	What You Do	How to Find Clients	Money Required to Start	Annual Earnings Potential	Time to First Income	Equipment Needed
Conduct flea markets in your area	Provide space for people to sell low-priced items	Ads in local papers	$200 to $800	$6,000 to $150,000+	8 to 12 weeks	Desk, phone, typewriter, fax
Provide security services for local organizations	Hire, and supply, security guards for club, churches, stores, factories	Ads in local business, religious, educational papers	$300 to $900	$5,000 to $100,000+	12 to 16 weeks	Desk, phone, typewriter, fax, PC
Provide striping service for industry	Paint floors, parking lots with stripes	Ads in local business papers, magazines	$400 to $900	$12,000 to $100,000+	12 to 16 weeks	Desk, phone, typewriter, fax, PC
Coach local athletic teams	Show kids and/or adults how to win at sports	Contact local sports leagues; ads in papers, magazines	$200 to $400	$8,000 to $30,000	6 to 8 weeks	Desk, phone, typewriter
Run lecture agency for speakers	Get speaking assignments for experts	Ads in industry papers, magazines	$300 to $600	$12,000 to $100,000+	8 to 12 weeks	Desk, phone, typewriter, fax, PC

CHAPTER 10

QUICK TIPS FOR STARTING AND PROSPERING IN THE HOME BUSINESS OF YOUR CHOICE

TO BE SUCCESSFUL in your own home business you must run it in accordance with all local regulations (if any) governing such businesses. The best way to find out if any regulations exist for home businesses is to contact your County Clerk. Look in your local phone book at the front or back Government pages for the Clerk's phone number.

Call, or write, the County Clerk and ask if local home businesses must conform to any particular laws. In some communities there are no local laws covering home businesses. In other communities there are simple laws that say—in effect—you can't run a factory in a tenth floor apartment. We all know that. But the law still states no factories in apartment houses!

Why Rules Exist

Communities which control home businesses seek to prevent:

- Large crowds from gathering in residential areas
- Smoke, noise, and pollution in residential areas
- Large trucks from entering areas with lots of children playing in the streets

So the community is not against the business. Instead it is against the side effects the business may create—heat, street traffic from pick ups or deliveries, noise, smoke, pollution, etc.

All the businesses we recommend to you in this book are pollution free, don't attract large crowds to your home, and can be run using the mail, phone, Internet, and a fax. So you can start your business without worrying about breaking any laws. But you still must contact your County Clerk to be certain you do comply with whatever regulations may exist.

Get Right—Taxwise

I hope you have to pay lots and lots of taxes in your own home business! Why? Because the more taxes you pay the more money you're putting in the bank every day. Don't moan and groan about having to pay taxes. We all must pay what's due the Government. Just pay on time and go out and earn more money!

Contact your local Internal Revenue office and ask them to send you their free booklets on small businesses. They're excellent and tell you—step by step—what you have to do to get started right—taxwise. Further, the booklets have many helpful ideas on setting up your business bank account, deductions to which you're entitled, payroll taxes, etc. If you have a personal computer, you can download from the Internet many IRS tax forms and booklets. Doing this can save you time in getting started.

You should also have the advice of a qualified accountant. But to be sure the accountant understands your business, you should know something about the tax laws that apply to your business. The Internal Revenue Service booklets will help you gain the knowledge you need.

Your accountant will help you with any state or local taxes to which your business may be subject. Here again, you can get free information on how to comply with the various laws. Be sure to watch for any sales taxes in you area. And look for any small business tax simplification offered. Many states offer an easy form for small businesses that will save you time, energy, and money. Be sure to use such forms. For example, if the sales taxes on your business are less than $2,000 a year, some states will allow you to file and pay these taxes once a year instead of quarterly. Using these provisions of the law will save you time and energy.

Taxes may seem to be a bore. But they really aren't. They're a cost of doing business. And once you get into the rhythm of paying taxes you'll never even feel the pain. Now let's get down to the enjoyable chore of running your own home business. We'll give you lots of tips and examples of how to get the most from every hour you devote to your business. And that, after all, is why you're about to start (or take over) a great home business that will make you rich!

How to Pick a Good Name for Your Business

Have you ever tried to pick a name for a business. Or for a division of a business? If you have, you know that getting a good name isn't easy! And a good name can—in my opinion—make the difference between great success and only fair success. Since I want you to be a great success, I'd like to give you some ideas for naming your business or for helping others name a business if you work for them as a financial broker-finder-business broker. You can often earn big fees helping others pick a good name.

Most beginners, when picking a business name, settle for the obvious—such as any of the following:

- A combination of partners' names—thus Jo-Ann Clothes, owned by John and Ann Doe
- Use of a street or city name—thus Evergreen Cleaners, on Evergreen Street
- Use of the last name of the owner—thus Smith Farms, owned by the Smith family

This approach to naming your business is good, and works for many people. But there are other approaches you might want to consider, such as:

- Putting what you do in the name—thus Pumps, Inc., for a pump company
- Picking a name which complements your business thus Money Unlimited for a lender. (On a recent trip I saw a second-hand store called Nearly New, Inc., which sells second-hand items of many types. Isn't Nearly New sweeter than Second-Hand?)
- Creating a name from what you do—thus Ideas, Inc., from International Distribution Engineering and Services

Should you say what you plan to do in your company name? Such as Jones Mail Order? Or should you widen your field of business beyond mail order by calling your firm Jones Enterprises? I vote for the second name because under its banner you can do anything that is legal in your area. But under the mail-order name your activities are somewhat limited. Of course, you can do other kinds of business under the mail-order name but you may puzzle people! And a key principle in any business is: Try not to confuse your customers. It only wastes time.

Should your firm name be long or short? Well, take your pick! A long name can be impressive, but you can make the life of typists and secretaries answering the phone difficult. If you want a long name, try to have nice sounding initials—like IWS, IBM, GE, etc.! That way you get the best of both worlds—an impressive name with short initials.

Lastly, try to pick a positive name—such as International Wealth Success, Think Rich Associates, etc. You might as well keep people happy when they're dealing with you!

When you register your business or form a corporation, you may find that your state prevents you from using certain words in the name of your company. Thus, one state prohibits use of the following words in the names of corporations:

Acceptance	Guaranty
Annuity	Indemnity
Assurance	Insurance
Bank	Investment
Benefit	Lawyer
Board of Trade	Loan
Bond	Mortgage
Casualty	Savings
Chamber of Commerce	State Police
Doctor or Dr.	Surety
Endowment	Title
Fidelity	Trust
Finance	Underwriter

Note that this list of restrictions is only for corporations and only for one state! Your state may have different rules and laws. So check it out with your attorney and state.

Some states also restrict use of certain other words such as: Architect, Blind, College, Co-operative, Council Court, Engineer, Federal, Financing, Handicapped, Hospital, Insurance, Labor, Mason, National, Olympic, Reserve, Surveying, U.S., etc. Again—check it out!

Which Is Better, a Post Office Box or Street Address?

People in their own home mail-order/direct-mail business often argue the advantages/disadvantages of doing business from a street address versus a post office box number. People who like street addresses say that, with a street address, your customers:

1. Trust you, the businessperson, more
2. Think you will be easier to track down—if necessary
3. Feel safer when ordering
4. Will order faster

But the box number people seem to have just as many arguments on their side, including these:

1. Some of the largest firms in the world run their business from a P.O. box number
2. A firm using a box number in the United States must give full information to the post office
3. Most direct-mail/mail-order firms in business today are honest and dependable
4. With a box you can collect your mail any time of the day or night—from the post offices

We've run our business very successfully from a post office box number for more than 30 years. Using the box number has not seemed to discourage our customers. And with the box number we can get mail seven days a week meaning that we can give faster service to our customers keeping them happier and less likely to complain!

Studies by various mail-order/direct-mail experts seem to indicate that you can run your mail business from a box number and do as well as from a street address if you have a good product. What these experts are indirectly saying is that people will order a good item no matter what the address it's sold from!

What we and other successful mail operators like about the box number is that you can get your mail several days a week from the box. This speeds up your mail inflow and the shipping of products. The post office services the boxes seven days a week, meaning that there is less lost time in getting an order and sending out products.

Get to Know the Numbers of Your Home Business

Every BWB (Beginning Wealth Builder) gets involved with numbers sooner or later! Why? Because business is a matter of numbers. And if you are building a fortune you will do it in a business of some kind. Let's look at some of the numbers of your fortune:

$1,000,000 = one million dollars = one million items
    sold at $1 each, or
= 1,000 items at $1,000 each, or
= 100,000 items at $10 each, or
= 500,000 items at $2 each

Find a way to sell any of the above numbers at the prices given and you will have taken in $1 million. You should keep—we think—at least 15 percent of that, or $150,000 as your own profit for yourself if you run your business carefully.

In income real estate, such as apartment houses or stores, your rental income can really build up as you get more units, such as:

$300 per month per unit = $3,600 per year per unit, and
10 units @ $300/mo ea = $36,000/yr for you
100 units @ 300/mo ea = $360,000/yr for you
500 units @ $300/mo ea = $1,800,000/yr for you
1,000 units @ $300/mo ea = $3,600,000/yr for you
5,000 units @ $300/mo ea = $18,000,000/yr for you

And remember that today a rent of $300 per unit per month is low! Or,

100 units @ $450/mo ea = $540,000/yr for you
1,000 units @ $450/mo ea = $5,400,000/yr for you
100 units @ $600/mo ea = $720,000/yr for you
1,000 units @ $600/mo ea = $7,200,000/yr for you

And it's relatively easy for you to get 100, or 1,000 units of rental real estate in just a few years—starting with little or no cash!

How much should employees make for you? That depends on the business you are in, or will be in. But let's look at some numbers for you:

In most businesses, each worker will earn money for you. The amount the worker earns will depend on many things, but here are some numbers that might help you:

At $ 10,000 per worker per yr, 2 workers earn you $20,000
At $15,000 per worker per yr, 2 workers earn you $30,000
At $25,000 per worker per yr, 2 workers earn you $50,000
At $50,000 per worker per yr, 2 workers earn you $100,000

The most important area for numbers for your own home business is in that of borrowed money—or Other People's Money (OPM). You'll probably have to borrow money if you want to expand your business to its full earning capability. And OPM has all sorts of numbers attached to it, including: interest rate charged, term of loan (number of years for which your loan will run), month semiannual or annual payments on the loan, and the amount you can borrow, based on your income, credit history, and ability to repay.

While all of this may seem frightening, OPM can be a powerful force in the success of your own home business. Here are a number of examples of how people started their own home business with OPM—Other People's Money. And we're more convinced than ever that you can become a millionaire by going the OPM road to your great wealth. Why? Here are a few good reasons:

In just 12 years, there were 143,000 new millionaires made in the United States! Most used OPM to build this wealth.

As proof that you can hit it big on borrowed money we'd like to tell you about a few people who've hit it big recently—using borrowed money to start. Here they are:

- Two brothers in their twenties borrowed $10,000 and bought a restaurant. Now they have a whole restaurant chain, an aviation flight training school, and an employment firm for executives!
- Two young partners borrowed $25,000 to start an investment firm. In just five years, both become multi-millionaires from their borrowed money income which they earned from investments, including real estate. Today they have a travel agency, a residential development firm, and movies.

- A young woman who needed money to launch a line of greeting cards couldn't get a loan. So she got credit instead (which is just as good as a loan) from an attorney, a printer, and a used-auto dealer. In just three years she built a firm doing several millions in business cards, clothes, gifts, and even a cartoon strip.
- A young salesman borrowed $1,000 and went into the insurance business. He has sold over $50 million in insurance since then—in just 12 years—and is now a millionaire. Sure he works hard—but he loves it!

Now these four millionaire fortunes were made in the last five years. This was a time of these conditions—which some people say will "kill" you:

- High income taxes
- Strong competition from other businesses
- Tight money and high interest rates
- Many changes in the political and business scenes

So you see, it *can* be done! Sure, you must work hard, but you will find—after you make your first million—that you get as much fun from your business as you do from your money. So you will probably keep working—just for the fun of it!

Now what did each of these BWBs have? They have a number of factors going for them. We think you have the same. That's why we believe you *can* hit the big money soon. Here's what these BWBs had in their favor:

- A strong desire to help others while earning money
- The push of borrowed money to keep them moving ahead
- Belief in themselves that they could hit it big
- A willingness to work long hours—if necessary

These successful BWBs hit the big money fast. That's what we want *you* to do. We don't want to see you working 30 years to get rich if you can do it in 3 years. That's why we try to give you *speed methods* for making money. They work for others and we believe they can work for you if you work with them! Some of the speed methods that have helped our readers include:

- Zero-cash takeovers of real estate and business
- Mail-order/direct-marketing riches methods
- Unique borrowing methods that get you loans
- Getting money for your ideas
- "Paper" business methods that make big money
- Exporting wealth ways
- Option methods for making real estate millions

All these methods *do, can,* and *are* working! You can make them work for you in your own home business. Why not try now and see? You may be delighted, surprised, and rich! And since mail order/direct marketing is one of the best home businesses for you to start, let's see how you can find a unique market for your home mail order business using OPM.

Find a Unique Market for Your Home Mail Order Products

Mail-order/direct-marketing millions are still possible! Almost every year a new mail-order promoter will come to market with an unusual product and hit the big money. Why isn't this you—if mail order is "your" business? It *can* be *you* if you get the right start in this great business. And you need not be a genius to hit it big!

Decide early if you want to sell a lot of items at a low price or a few at a high price. Then pick your product to sell. Today we see the greatest mail-order/direct-marketing successes by BWBs who will sell a few items at a high price to industrial firms, large companies, etc.

For example, one firm we know of is doing great in mail-order sales of management books and newsletters to hospitals. From what this firm has found, hospital managers are almost the "forgotten people" of the business world. So when some firm sends them mailings on items for sale the results are great! Why? Because few other firms are sending information on these products and there is very little competition! This is a basic principle of good mail order/direct marketing!

Now you might not like the hospital market. Fine. Just find yourself another type of market which is not being oversold by too much advertising and direct mail. Then jump in with good products that help people. You will be delighted with the results you get from your ads in such a market. Returns (sales) as high as 50 per 1,000 mailed (5 percent) are sometimes met in such a market. Returns this high can make you a million in a short time in this great business!

So don't give up looking for the "right" product! Our experience is that you can find it and the market and make yourself a bundle. So start today—with the right know-how—now!

And remember this: Of all the businesses you might want to start, mail order/direct marketing is best in the opinion of many people who know what the odds are in starting a business. Why? Because in mail order/direct marketing you can compete with the biggest and outsell them—if you have a good item for sale. You can do better in mail order than in almost any other business you might start—if you know what you're doing. And the K-5 *Mail Order Riches* success kit mentioned at the end of this book can get you started. Knowing what the experts know can put you into a favorable money position!

Why We Recommend Some Mail Order/Direct Marketing for Your Home Business

Many times BWBs don't know exactly why they pick a business to go into. But many times they do pick the right business! Take, for example, those BWBs who want to go into mail order/direct marketing. They're picking the right business, as the following Department of Commerce quote indicates.

MAIL ORDER AND DIRECT SELLING

Direct and mail order sales will continue to expand rapidly. A more affluent and older population, with limited time for shopping at a retail store, will prefer to make purchases in the home. Ease of entry into direct selling should continue to offer enterprising people and companies an opportunity to provide a viable service. The field is expected to remain dominated by large firms using modern sales management and production techniques.

The big secret of hitting the big money in mail order direct marketing is the unique product which not many other people have for sale. The unique or different product or service can make you millions in MO/DM—if you buy the product at a suitable price.

Or, if you can't get products at a suitable price, can you get your supplier to do more work for you at a slightly higher price? Work like drop-shipping, wrapping, or packing of an order, special services to your customers, etc. can save you money while giving better service to your customers. This will reflect favorably on you!

Another key secret to big money in mail order/direct marketing is finding the right customers for your offer. What you want are *prospects,* not suspects! And prospects come in many sizes, colors of skin, views of life, etc. The main thought here is this: Find people who *want* your product or service; you may be able to sell them!

When you think about mail order/direct mail, give some thought to doing things differently while doing them the same! "And what do you mean by that?" you ask. By doing things in many different ways while doing them the same, we mean this:

- Advertise differently from your competition—use different magazines, newspapers, and different kinds of ads. Use the Internet to get a wider audience for your ads

- Try new ideas—the world is ready for new ideas which can help save time, money, energy, tempers, etc.
- Don't try to sell items you "love" because you might find that your loving of the item makes you see the facts less clearly
- Be sure to cover the same fields as your competition does so you get a "free ride" from the promotional effort of your competitor. While competition can help a field grow by calling more attention to it and making folks more aware of you, stay away from nasty name calling, etc.
- Try other forms of ads, such as "stand-up inserts" in the Sunday papers; insertions with the billing statements of other firms, ads on the Internet, e-mail to people seeking information, and product faxes to your customers and inquirers

Yes, there *are* all sorts of ways for people with new ideas to hit the big money in MO/DM. Do you have a new idea which you think can really sell big in the MO/DM field? If you do, then your best chance usually lies in testing the idea to see if it goes. To test, you can:

- Run ads in papers, magazines, on the Internet, etc.
- Get free publicity for your item
- Make a mailing to prospects (not suspects)
- Show the item to mail order houses

Each of these tests will tell you something. If your ads pull strongly, you know you have a hot item; the same goes for your test mailing. And if publicity for your product generates orders, or if mail order/direct marketing houses order your item, then you know that your idea is a winner. Recently, a BWB introduced a new item which sold $176,000 worth of product in its first four months. It took off so fast he couldn't keep up with the orders! His tests were so good he stopped testing and launched a full ad campaign on the basis of his early results. Money poured in!

Another BWB wrote me saying: "Over the past couple of years I have been selling two courses I personally wrote and recorded on audio cassettes. One is "How to Make a Fortune Operating Your Own Mail Order Dating Service," The other is "How to Make Your Fortune with Your Radio Control Hobby." Both courses have been selling well with very little advertising; the majority of my sales are due to publicity press releases and free ads." This is a good example of how free publicity can bring you lots of sales!

Tie Your Home Wealth Future to Growing Companies

What's one secret to fast and steady growth of income in a business? There are—of course—any number of reasons why a business grows fast and pays you more and more: money every year. But one reason some folks don't often recognize is this:

Sell products or a service to businesses that are growing, and you, too, will grow!

Thus, if you have a business selling work gloves (we say) to firms that grow fast, your business will grow fast too! So the key is for you is to:

- Pick a product or service that you can sell to
- Firms which you have figured are growing faster than others, and
- Then make an all-out sales effort to sell these firms by either
- Mail order, direct sales calls, TV or radio ads, the Internet, etc.

The key is in picking what you have to sell and the firms to whom you plan to make these sales. You can of course—try to sell to people. Plenty of BWBs have made their millions selling to people in the street, in their home, on their vacations, etc. But the way you make millions selling to people is by large volume sales, usually at a low price. When you sell to firms you might sell a small number of items but at a much higher price. You can still make millions this way, too

By selling to firms, you get in on their growth. Their success becomes part of your success! And firms pay their bills with checks that don't bounce. Such firms often will come back to buy again and again! So think about tying your success to the success of others! It can really pay off for you!

For example, many of the fastest growing and most successful businesses operating today are computer related. Typical computer-related businesses you can run from home include:

- Mail-order/direct-marketing sales of software for business use
- Mail order/direct marketing sales of computer-game software
- Mail-order/direct-marketing sales of computers and computer equipment (cables, monitors, printers, modems, etc.)

Some of the largest computer companies in the world started at home—Dell in a dormitory room, Gateway in a barn, Apple in a garage, Hewlett-Packard in another garage. The enormous growth of these companies and their great products prove that starting a computer-related business at home can be the smartest step you'll ever take!

Now let's look at other ways that home business entrepreneurs make money—starting with almost no cash at all. You too can use similar methods to build your fortune in your own home business.

Start with $25 and Grow to $2 Million—at Home

Beginning Wealth Builders (BWBs) make money in the most unusual ways. Like the BWB I know of who started an incense business with $25 capital, using the bathtub in his home as an experimental lab. Last year the sales of his ompany passed $2 million. In just eight years he went ɔm nearly a zero-cash start to over $2 million!

When his apartment became too small to house his business this BWB moved to larger quarters. Today he sells his incense through the mail and through 25,000 retail outlets in the United States. Both his products and business smell good!

To get started, this BWB read some rare books on incense and incense making. Then he started on his own, making what he thought the world wanted. His strawberry incense is a big seller in many outlets.

So what does this mean to you? This short, real-life story is full of good news for all BWBs because the story shows:

- It *is* possible to start with very little or no cash
- You *can* teach yourself the beginnings of a business
- Studying—as we've often said—*does* pay off for BWBs
- Know-how that can be turned into real cash *can* be yours
- Books and courses *can* put you on to the road to wealth

But if you would rather have another type of business, consider becoming a "Retirement Consultant" to help firms and people prepare for retirement. Many firms are concerned that their potential retirees be happy and content after they leave their jobs. So these firms hire consultants to:

- Advise upcoming retirees on what's ahead
- Suggest ways to obtain greater happiness in retirement
- Give information on taxes, Social Security, etc.
- Provide information on selling a home, moving, etc.
- Give data on retirement villages, good health areas

Internet marketing of mail-order/direct-marketing type products is producing large sales for many BWBs. The consultant is paid by the company, not the individual. So your fees can be such that you can make a lucrative living by having two or three firms for which you consult. Where will you get information to use to help the retiree? There's plenty in your local library and from the federal government through the Government Printing Office.

One firm we know prepares and prints a retirement review which is sent to those people eligible for retirement in a few years. The retiree's company pays the subscription cost. Since the information is the same for most people, the same book is used widely.

But if consulting and a product-type business don't interest you, then you might wish to try selling high-priced hobby items by mail, Internet, phone, and fax. "There's no nut like a hobby nut," someone once said. And that's true—hobbyists will search for months to buy something special for their hobby. And you can make money catering to hobbyists interested in:

- Hunting, fishing
- Dogs, horses, tropical fish
- Boats, cars, planes
- Model trains, ships, planes

Just get yourself a neat, low-cost catalog, run a few low-priced classified ads to get a mailing list, and send out your catalog. You will be delighted with the business you do in high-priced items for a hobby which people love.

To help guide your thinking in any home business, there are certain rough numbers rules that allow you reach a quick decision. For instance, with hobby catalogs, you will generate a certain number of sales dollars per catalog mailed. The exact dollar amount will rise with the cost of the hobby item. Thus, boat owners tend to spend more than auto owners. But airplane owners spend the most! Here are some additional helpful rules for your home business.

Useful Rules of Thumb for Home Businesses

Here are some useful and interesting business facts you can use to make more money in any business you might pick to make your fortune in—starting today!

- **Working as an executive recruiter?** It usually takes an out-of-work executive one week for each $1,000 of salary to find a job. Thus, an executive earning $50,000 per year will need 50 weeks to find a new job; $75,000, 75 weeks; $100,000, 100 weeks, etc.
- **Looking for income property to build your fortune?** The usual asking price for rental income property (apartment houses, etc.) is five to seven times the annual rent. Thus, if the apartment house you like brings in $100,000 per year in rents, the asking price will be $500,000 to $700,000. Houses in changing neighborhoods usually go for three to five times the annual rent income. Plenty of these are yours for no cash—if you look around enough!
- **If you sell by direct mail,** that is, send out letters selling a product or service, you can expect a return of 2 percent on a good mailing. This means that if you send out 1,000 sales letters, you will make sales with $0.02 \times 1,000 = 20$ letters. Some of your mailings may be better—up to 3 percent, or 30 sales per 1,000. But it is rare that a mailing will go over 3 percent, though some direct-mail people report returns of 6 percent and even 8 percent—at times.
- **Exporting products** to build your fortune? Then do not overlook small countries! The smaller countries need more, pay faster, are easier to deal with, and stay as your customer longer than some of the larger countries (though this is not a criticism of the larger countries—just a fact of business life). So pay attention to small countries everywhere—and particularly in Central and South America today.
- **You can reduce postage costs** by as much as 90 percent—if you use co-op mailings for your products and services. A co-op mailing is one in which your mailing piece is put into a mailing being made by another firm. Thus, your mailing piece might be put into a bill, a package, a catalog, etc. Your mailing piece must not compete with the item that the firm is mailing! Your only cost is a small fee for the insertion, the cost of printing your mailing piece, and a fee to the firm. But if you're paying 50¢ to mail your flyers now, a co-op mailing might cost you only 5¢! Nice savings for you.

- **Licensing deals can make you millions.** What you do is arrange for an overseas firm to use the patents, copyrights, or other protections of a local firm in making, printing, publishing, or selling a product, book, song, etc. You get either a percentage or a flat fee on every item sold. Thus, the percentage might be 1 percent of the selling price of the item; the flat fee might be 10¢ per unit sold. A great paper business for you!

Rules of thumb like these come from thinking—putting the facts about a business through one's mind and coming up with results. You can get many ideas for earning more from your own home business by using a similar technique of thinking. Here are some profitable ideas generated using this easy and fun technique.

11 Bright Ideas for Earning More from Your Home Business

A method of getting ideas that some people use is called "Brainstorming." You—we think—can brainstorm your way to wealth! How? By sitting down with pencil and pad and writing down ideas as they come into your mind. Here are a few that might make you rich:

- *Sell by mail order/direct mail* high-ticket items like autos, planes, boats, houses, etc. Sounds wild? It may just be so wild that it will work! (And does—for many people.)
- *Start a high-priced service* for important business people or firms. Thus, one BWB sells a newsletter to banks at an annual subscription of $3,000. Just 1,000 subscribers will give a $3,000,000 a year income!
- *Get free advertising* for items you want to sell by learning how to write "New Product" releases (it's really easy) and use these releases as mailing pieces for direct mail sales of your item. This can work wonders!
- *Start a "rap" session service* in your area so people can come to a room and complain about what bothers them. At the session people will exchange complaints, ideas, solutions.

Charge $3 (say) per session. Or you might franchise such an idea to others. You can also start such a room on the Internet. Since people everywhere have complaints, you can now get their "beefs" from worldwide sources. Using the Internet you can expand your business to international markets at an extremely low cost!

- *Start a franchise company* that gets a fee for franchising the ideas of others. Your fee will be paid at the time that you get a franchise buyer, but you will also be paid for your expenses as you meet them.
- *Become a "packager"*—that is, a person who prepares loan packages for a fee for business people looking for loans. You might charge anywhere from $100 to several thousand, depending on the package size and complexity. Find people via free ads in the IWS newsletter and local papers.
- *Get the rights* to out-of-print successful books and reissue the books with a new date on them (provided the info is still usable). You can sell such books at a very high price because people know they are no longer available.
- *Become an invention marketer* or inventor helper and help people figure out if their invention is marketable, what it will sell in terms of numbers and dollars, etc. You will be paid a fee by the inventor for this work.
- *Rent income property* and then rent it out at a higher income than you are paying for rent. Thus, if you pay $1,000 a month for a building or part of a building you can rent out at $2,000 a month, you pick up the difference.
- *Learn income-tax procedures* and help people with their tax returns. Specialize in companies and you will have year-round work because firms have tax years ending in any month.
- *Take a course in any subject* that interests you. Then find a way to earn money from the information you got in the course.

The preceding is some simple brainstorming. What ideas do these ideas suggest to you/your firm/your friends. If none, then brainstorm some yourself! Get moving—*ideas build riches!*

You *must* take action to put your ideas into being so yo⁀ start earning a good income in your own home busine⁀ And my job is to get *you* to take action for yourself that⁀

put money into *your* pocket! Here's a plan of action that works for thousands of people thinking of starting their own home business. Start putting this plan to work *now*.

31 Steps to Take to Great Wealth in Your Own Home Business

Do you make every day count? You *should* if you want to make big money in a business of your own! Why? If you don't try to make every day count, you may find that the days slip by, one after another, without your doing much.

Why not take this month and make it, or any other month, *your* month to accomplish great works for your future wealth? It's worth a try. Why? Because even if nothing results, you have "lost" only—at most—31 part days because I'm assuming you are working at some other job while you are taking the actions I think could help you! So here's an action for each of the 31 days you might have in the month you want to try my *Wealth Action Plan*. Remember—it really *could* work for you!

The main point to keep in mind with any action you take is that even the wrong action can give you positive results if you correct the wrong action as soon as you see that there's a better way to do what you are trying to do! Action can put you in the *right* place at the *right* time. No action can leave you out of the big money at the time when other BWBs are getting in on their share of the wealth that is being earned all over the world today in many kinds of businesses. So get to know now what action can do for you by taking some action for the next month—shown as 31 days to cover the longest months in the year. On a sheet of notepaper, just copy numbers from 1 to 31 in a column, or use a calendar—and check off each action as you do it.

There you now have your wealth action plan for the ˑxt 31 days. Get to work on it *now* to make it work for you. ˑ good luck from me to you!

My Wealth Action Plan

Day of the Month	Action I Will Take This Day for My Future Wealth
1	Think about what kind of business I want
2	Seek printed information about the business I want
3	Talk to people in the business I want
4	Look for ads for such businesses for sale
5	Contact people having businesses for sale; get financial data
6	Learn the finances of "my" business
7	Get books, papers, other items on "my" business
8	Read the information I've collected
9	Make—on paper—estimates of income, expenses
10	Vary the estimates to see what happens
11	Imagine myself in the business, facing problems
12	Make a list of how I would solve problems
13	My lucky day—I'll relax and think about vacations
14	My second week—review what I've done so far
15	Visit and really look at one business I like
16	Think about what I saw at the business
17	Decide if I really do like what I saw
18	Get some prices on buying or taking over
19	See if the prices are fair for the business
20	Develop some easy rules of thumb for the business
21	Apply the rules of thumb to the business I saw
22	If the rules work, great! If not, why not?
23	See if I could borrow any money I need
24	Check out ten lenders today—by mail or phone
25	Look for ten more lenders, in case the first decline
26	If refused money, find out why—ask until told why you were declined
27	Relax for a day; I've been working hard
28	Try the next ten lenders, if necessary
29	Get what the lender wants—cosigners, collateral
30	Apply for my loan again, if necessary
31	Get my money to get my business

Once you're ready to start your business you'll probably need some financing. Why? Because few people have enough cash on hand to start their own business—expenses of ordinary living being what they are today.

And I believe you're better off borrowing the money you need to start or expand your business. Since every business in this book can be started for under $1,000, the amount of money you'll borrow is relatively small. Even so, you should understand why there are good reasons for borrowing money for your own home business.

14 Good Reasons for Borrowing Money for Your Home Business

Why borrow money for your future or growing business? Here's a whole raft of good reasons for borrowing money which BWBs have proven useful over the years. Read the reasons now and see how many apply to you. We're sure you will get some good ideas as you read! Good reasons are:

1. *Speed*—you get your money fast—usually in just a few days or weeks. This is much faster than setting up a business to earn the same amount of money as you borrow.
2. *No taxes*—there are *no* taxes of any kind on money you borrow from a lender anywhere.
3. *Much less work* is needed to get a loan than to earn the same amount of money from business. See the example below for full details on this important point.[1]
4. *Help others* by putting their money to work earning interest for them while it provides an income for you and the people you hire. Thus, everyone benefits from money use.
5. *Thousands of money sources* are available to you throughout the world. And most of these sources are seeking to make good loans and want you to borrow from them!
6. *Get more later*—you can often borrow more after getting your first loan from a lender—particularly after you've

---

1 Let's say you borrow $200,000 for business. To get the same amount out of business earning a profit of 15 percent before taxes (which is a typical profit these days), the business would have to sell $1,333,333 worth of goods or services. And you would do a lot more work to sell $1.33 million worth of goods or services than to borrow $200,000 but you'd wind up with the same amount of cash!

made a few payments. And your second, third, fourth, etc. loan may come from the same or from a different lender!

7. *Payoff time can often be extended*—if you want more time to repay your loan. This makes things easier for you, giving you a small payment to make each month.

8. *Loan costs are low,* when you compare the interest cost with the cost of an office or factory in which you would produce the same amount of profit as the loan amount.

9. *Little or no selling is needed*—you can sometimes get a big loan quickly after filling out a few simple papers and sending them into the lender. Often, you need never appear in the lender's office to get your money—it's sent to you in the mail. And some lenders today have their loan application on the Internet. You can download the application to your printer. Once you print out the application, you fill it out (typed!) and e-mail it to the lender.

10. *No fees are required by most lenders*—so it doesn't cost you anything except time and energy to get the business money you seek from the lender.

11. *One hundred percent* financing is possible with loans. Many different deals can be worked out which can give you all the cash you need for your business. In some deals you may even get more money than you need—called *mortgaging out,* or a *windfall.*[2]

12. *Loans carry built-in motivation* for you! Having to work to pay off a loan makes you work harder and faster, helping your business grow stronger, sooner. Thus, borrowed money can help you build your riches faster! The loan makes you more successful!

13. *Loans can be used* in almost any business. Almost every business needs money at some time during its life. And a loan can be its answer and your answer!

14. *Borrowers are welcomed* by the best of lenders! Listen to lenders talk. You'll soon learn that it is not easy to find good

---

2 A builder received $400,000 more than he asked for when he applied for loan. A BWB real estate owner bought a 160-unit income property with no cash down and got a loan for $200,000 more than he needed to take over the property. He used the extra $200,000 windfall in other deals which he wants to start. And when he got this loan his cash assets were rather low.

borrowers! Lenders seek them out everywhere. You can keep a lender happy while you borrow the funds the lender wants to put out into the world of business. So keep a lender happy today—borrow money you need for business!

Learn How to Borrow Money from Commercial Banks

There are 14,000 commercial banks in the United States today. Commercial banks are the banks which lend money to businesspeople for business use. With this many banks around, it should be easy for you to borrow the business money you need—if you apply in the right way. "And what's the 'right' way?" you ask. "Because I've tried and been turned down." Here are the "right" steps for *you* to follow to get *your* business loan from a commercial bank. We call these steps "right" because they have worked for other BWBs and they could work for you!

The right way to apply for a business loan involves a number of businesslike approaches to the problem of raising money. Here they are for your use:

1. Apply at a commercial bank—not all banks are this type. (Use the IWS-1 *Business Capital Sources* book.) A commercial bank usually has the initials N.A. (National Association) after its name.
2. *Fill out* your application neatly—type it, if possible. You'd be amazed at what a difference a neat application makes over a sloppy one!
3. *Know how much money you need.* Never ask the lender to help you figure out what you need! He or she has too many other things to think about.
4. *But leave the amount needed blank* on the application. Why is this? Because the lender might suggest that a smaller or larger loan would be easier to get at this time. Be flexible!
5. *Dress in business clothes* when you visit the bank or have a business letterhead when you send your application in by mail. (If you apply by mail, do enter the amount you need on your application.)

6. *Listen to what the lender tells you,* and learn! You can learn an enormous amount in just a few minutes—if you listen and don't talk!

7. *If one lender turns you down, apply at the next!* Never give up! Keep trying!

Today's Best Quick Money Source for Home-Based BWBs

Do you need money for your home-based business? If you do, there's a great way to get the money you need. This way will save you time and eliminate giving a reason for needing the money. This way is:

1. **Use your credit card line of credit** to get money you need for your home business. You're never asked why you need the money.

2. **Look for lines of credit** on both personal and business credit cards that go to $25,000 per card. A few special cards go to $50,000 per card. But we'll stick with the $25,000 card because they're the most popular.

3. **Get four $25,000-line-of-credit cards** and you have a total line of 4 x $25,000 = $100,000. This is enough for most BWBs to start their own home business, or expand an existing business.

4. **Use the money for your home business** and the interest you pay is deductible on your tax return. However, be sure to check this with your accountant. So, while the interest rate you pay on a credit-card line of credit may be higher than on a conventional loan, the interest you pay is deductible.

Use a Banker's Acceptance to Speed Your Business Loan

Another way to borrow money is with *Banker's Acceptances* (BA). A BA is a promissory note that you give a bank when they lend you money. The bank, in turn, sells this note to a depositor or other person or firm. Let's say the bank lend you $25,000 at 12 percent interest. Then the bank takes your note and "sells" it to a depositor for, say, 119 days @ 10 percent. The bank keeps the difference in interest—2 percent in this case—and gets back its $25,000 which it loaned you. Thus, the bank has its $25,000 back and can lend it to someone else. Bankers often call this the technique of "making money on money."

And how can you get in on banker's acceptances? You'll have to work through your own bank. Further, your need for money must be short-term—say 30, 60, 90, 119 days. Then if you can find someone who'll buy your acceptance from the bank, you're ready to go. Or if your bank can find someone, you're set to go. While the loan is short-term (say 90 days) it can usually be "rolled over or renewed at the end of 89 days for another 90 days. And as long as you keep paying the interest, the bank is usually glad to roll over your note for you. But each time your note is rolled over the interest may change. It may rise or it may fall. So your cost of renting the money can change from time to time.

The smallest amount of money handled by big-city commercial banks dealing in banker's acceptances is $25,000, though some banks won't go below $ 100,000. So you can't usually use the BA for loans in the $5,000 to $10,000 range. To get more info, see your commercial bank today.

How Women Can Get Loans for a Home Business

Probably more women contact me about starting their own home business than men. And many of these women report they have trouble getting loans for a home business. How can women find the funds they need for their own home business? Here are some useful hints that work anywhere:

1. **Build** a good credit rating—this always pays off when you visit a lender
2. **Prepare** careful plans for your business—without cash-flow plans you're lost

3. **Be businesslike** at all times—lenders respect the capable businesswoman
4. **Apply** to as many lenders as you can—the more the better
5. **Be flexible**—if the lender suggests different terms, try to accept them
6. **Learn** to listen more—let the lender do the talking— you'll learn something
7. **Don't** go into long detailed histories, unless you're asked
8. **Concentrate** on business details—skip personalities, unless asked
9. **Line up** some reliable cosigners in advance—a cosigner can mean yes instead of no
10. **Muster** your collateral—in advance. You may not like it, but collateral helps!
11. **Never be afraid** of any lender—he or she wants to help you!
12. **Keep trying**—never give up—the more lenders you apply to, the greater your chances of getting a loan

And men readers, these 12 hints will work equally we for *you!* You, too, can get the business funds you need but you must work at it! Have courage. For, as Mark Twain said, "Courage is resistance to fear, mastery of fear—not absence of fear."

You're Now Ready to Start, and Prosper In, Your Own Home Business

You now have what you need to start your own home business. And I'm sure you'll prosper in that business—if you use the ideas in this book. But to be sure you really do earn money in your own home business, I—Ty Hicks—make this offer to you:

1. I'll be glad to help you in every way I can, either on the telephone or by mail or fax, if you're a 2-year or longer subscriber to my newsletter, *International Wealth Success,* described at the back of this book. The reason I suggest

you be a subscriber is because you'll get hundreds of profitable ideas every year from this monthly newsletter. And it will motivate you to do more for yourself and your business—making *you* more successful!

2. If you have a good idea for a profitable home business, I'll even consider financing it myself, or helping you get the financing you need—if you're a subscriber, as described above. While these services are also available to non-subscribers, I must admit that subscribing can be very helpful in terms of ideas you get from the newsletter.

3. If you want to talk to me personally, I'm as close to you as your own phone. Just pick it up and dial my number. Don't expect me to accept collect calls. If you want free advice as a subscriber (see No. 1, page 253), the phone call is on you! I'll spend as much time as you need and will answer every business question you ask. Remember, also, to be the courteous and businesslike person who identifies himself or herself when first contacting someone for advice. I won't talk to you unless you tell me your name, address, telephone number, and why you're contacting me. Why? Because I can help you more when I have this information. You'd demand the same from me if I were to call you unannounced! So adopt businesslike manners—it will really pay off in higher profits in your own home business.

4. If you write me, please include your phone number. I'll call you with my answers to your questions. Why do I prefer to call? Because when I'm writing letters I'm *not* writing books. And my reading public seems to want more books. I can talk to you a lot faster than I can write you. So have a heart, good friend, and let me help you—my way!

5. Lastly, you *do* have a good friend in Ty Hicks. I *will* talk to you on the phone, no matter how much you might disbelieve what I say. Some people call and say "Oh, I just wanted to see if what you say in your book is really true." Then they hang up, having wasted their time, my time, and the cost of the call. And I'm not a computer in Rocklin, CA, as some people believe! I have a wife, three kids, two cars, a beautiful home, and a great boat. So if you want a good friend who lives, breathes, and will help you, you have it in Ty Hicks! My business phone number is 516-766-5850; my business fax number is 516-766-5919.

PROFIT-BUILDING TOOLS FROM TYLER HICKS'S INTERNATIONAL WEALTH SUCCESS LIBRARY

As THE PUBLISHER of the famous *International Wealth Success* newsletter, Ty Hicks has put together a remarkable library of dynamic books, each geared to help the opportunity-seeking individual—the kind of person who is ready and eager to achieve the financial freedom that comes from being a successful entrepreneur. Financial experts agree that only those who own their own businesses or invest their money wisely can truly control their future wealth. And yet, far too many who start a business or an investment program of their own do not have the kind of information that can make the difference between success and failure.

Here, then, is a list of publications hand-picked by Ty Hicks, written especially to give you, the enterprising wealth builder, the critical edge that belongs solely to those who have the *inside* track. So take advantage of this unique opportunity to order this confidential information. (These books are *not* available in bookstores.) Choose the publications that can help you the most and send the order form with your remittance. Your order will be processed as quickly as possible to expedite your success. (Please note: If, when placing an order, you prefer not to cut out the form, simply photocopy the order page and send in the duplicate.)

IWS-1   *BUSINESS CAPITAL SOURCES.* Lists more than 1,500 lenders of various types—banks, insurance companies, commercial finance firms, factors, leasing firms, overseas lenders, venture capital firms, mortgage companies, and others. $15. 150 pgs.

IWS-2   ***SMALL BUSINESS INVESTMENT COMPANY DIRECTORY AND HAND-BOOK.*** Lists more than 400 small business investment companies that invest in small businesses to help them prosper. Also gives tips on financial management in businesses. $15. 135 pgs.

IWS-3   ***WORLDWIDE RICHES OPPORTUNITIES,*** Vol. 1. Lists more than 2,500 overseas firms seeking products to import. Gives name of product(s) sought, or service(s) sought, and other important data needed by exporters and importers. $25. 283 pgs.

IWS-4   ***WORLDWIDE RICHES OPPORTUNITIES,*** Vol. 2. Lists more than 2,500 overseas firms selling products to import. (Does NOT duplicate Volume 1.) Lists loan sources for some exporters in England. $25. 223 pgs.

IWS-5   ***HOW TO PREPARE AND PROCESS EXPORT-IMPORT DOCUMENTS.*** Gives data and documents for exporters and importers, including licenses, declarations, free-trade zones abroad, bills of lading, custom duty rulings. $25. 170 pgs.

IWS-6   ***SUPPLEMENT TO HOW TO BORROW YOUR WAY TO REAL ESTATE RICHES.*** Using government sources compiled by Ty Hicks, lists numerous mortgage loans and guarantees, loan purposes, amounts, terms, financing charge, types of structures financed, loan-value ratio, special factors. $15. 87 pgs.

IWS-7   ***THE RADICAL NEW ROAD TO WEALTH*** by A. David Silver. Covers criteria for success, raising venture capital, steps in conceiving a new firm, the business plan, how much do you have to give up, economic justification. $15. 128 pgs.

IWS-8   ***60-DAY FULLY FINANCED FORTUNE*** is a short BUSINESS KIT covering what the business is, how it works, naming the business, interest amortization tables, state securities agencies, typical flyer used to advertise, typical applications. $29.50. 136 pgs.

IWS-9   ***CREDITS AND COLLECTION BUSINESS KIT*** is a 2-book kit covering fundamentals of credit, businesses using credits and collection methods, applications for credit, setting credit limits, Fair Credit Reporting Act, collection percentages, etc. Gives 10 small businesses in this field. $29.50. 147 pgs.

IWS-10   ***MIDEAST AND NORTH AFRICAN BANKS AND FINANCIAL INSTITUTIONS.*** Lists more than 350 such organizations. Gives name, address, telephone, and telex number for most. $15. 30 pgs.

IWS-11   ***EXPORT MAIL-ORDER.*** Covers deciding on products to export, finding suppliers, locating overseas firms selling exports, form letters, listing of firms serving as export management companies, shipping orders, and more. $17.50. 50 pgs.

IWS-12   ***PRODUCT EXPORT RICHES OPPORTUNITIES.*** Lists over 1,500 firms offering products for export—includes agricultural, auto, aviation, electronic, computers, energy, food, health care, mining, printing, and robotics. $21.50. 219 pgs.

IWS-13   *DIRECTORY OF HIGH-DISCOUNT MERCHANDISE SOURCES.* Lists more than 1,000 sources of products with full name, address, and telephone number for items such as auto products, swings, stuffed toys, puzzles, oils and lubricants, CB radios, and belt buckles. $17.50. 97 pgs.

IWS-14   *HOW TO FINANCE REAL ESTATE INVESTMENTS* by Roger Johnson. Covers basics, the lending environment, value, maximum financing, rental unit groups, buying mobile home parks, and conversions. $18.50. 265 pgs.

IWS-15   *DIRECTORY OF FREIGHT FORWARDERS AND CUSTOM HOUSE BROKERS.* Lists hundreds of these firms throughout the United States which help in the import-export business. $17.50. 106 pgs.

IWS-16   *CAN YOU AFFORD NOT TO BE A MILLIONAIRE?* by Marc Schlecter. Covers international trade, base of operations, stationery, worksheet, starting an overseas company, metric measures, profit structure. $15. 202 pgs.

IWS-17   *HOW TO FIND HIDDEN WEALTH IN LOCAL REAL ESTATE* by R. H. Jorgensen. Covers financial tips, self-education, how to analyze property for renovation, the successful renovator is a "cheapskate," property management, and getting the rents paid. $17.50. 133 pgs.

IWS-18   *HOW TO CREATE YOUR OWN REAL ESTATE FORTUNE* by Jens Nielsen. Covers investment opportunities in real estate, leveraging, depreciation, remodeling your deal, buy- and lease-back, understanding your financing. $17.50. 117 pgs.

IWS-19   *REAL ESTATE SECOND MORTGAGES* by Ty Hicks. Covers second mortgages, how a second mortgage finder works, naming the business, registering the firm, running ads, expanding the business, and limited partnerships. $17.50. 100 pgs.

IWS-20   *GUIDE TO BUSINESS AND REAL ESTATE LOAN SOURCES.* Lists hundreds of business and real estate lenders, giving their lending data in very brief form. $25. 201 pgs.

IWS-21   *DIRECTORY OF 2,500 ACTIVE REAL ESTATE LENDERS.* Lists 2,500 names and addresses of direct lenders or sources of information on possible lenders for real estate. $25. 197 pgs.

IWS-22   *IDEAS FOR FINDING BUSINESS AND REAL ESTATE CAPITAL TODAY.* Covers raising public money, real estate financing, borrowing methods, government loan sources, and venture money. $24.50. 62 pgs.

IWS-23   *HOW TO BECOME WEALTHY PUBLISHING A NEWSLETTER* by E. J. Mall. Covers who will want your newsletter, planning your newsletter, preparing the first issue, direct mail promotions, keeping the books, building your career. $17.50. 102 pgs.

IWS-24   *NATIONAL DIRECTORY OF MANUFACTURERS' REPRESENTATIVES.* Lists 5,000 mfrs. reps. from all over the United States, both in alphabetical form and state by state; gives markets classifications by SIC. $28.80. 782 pgs., hardcover.

IWS-25   *BUSINESS PLAN KIT.* Shows how to prepare a business plan to raise money for any business. Gives several examples of successful business plans. $29.50. 150 pgs.

IWS-26   ***MONEY RAISER'S DIRECTORY OF BANK CREDIT CARD PROGRAMS.***
         Shows the requirements of each bank listed for obtaining a credit card
         from the bank. Nearly 1,000 card programs at 500 of the largest U.S.
         banks are listed. Gives income requirements, job history, specifications,
         etc. $19.95. 150 pgs.

IWS-27   ***GLOBAL COSIGNERS AND MONEY FINDERS ASSOCIATION.*** Publicize
         your need for a cosigner to get a business or real estate loan. Your
         need is advertised widely under a Code Number so your identity is
         kept confidential. $50.

IWS-28   ***WALL STREET SYNDICATORS.*** Lists 250 active brokerage houses who
         might take your company public. Gives numerous examples of actual,
         recent, and new stock offerings of startup companies. $15. 36 pgs.

IWS-29   ***COMPREHENSIVE LOAN SOURCES FOR BUSINESS AND REAL ESTATE
         LOANS.*** Gives hundreds of lenders' names and addresses and lending
         guidelines for business and real estate loans of many different types.
         $25. 136 pgs., 8½ × 11 in.

IWS-30   ***DIVERSIFIED LOAN SOURCES FOR BUSINESS AND REAL ESTATE
         LOANS.*** Gives hundreds of lenders' names and addresses and lending
         guidelines for business and real estate loans of many different types.
         Does not duplicate IWS-29. $25. 136 pgs., 8½ × 11 in.

IWS-31   ***CREDIT POWER REPORTS.*** Five helpful reports to improve your credit
         rating and credit line. Report No. 1: *How to Get a Visa and/or Mastercard
         Credit Card.* $19.95. 192 pgs., 5 × 8 in. Report No. 2: *How to Increase Your
         Credit Limits, Plus Sophisticated Credit Power Strategies.* $19.95. 208 pgs., 5
         × 8 in. Report No. 3: *How to Repair Your Credit.* $19.95. 256 pgs., 5 × 8 in.
         Report No. 4: *How to Reduce Your Monthly Payments.* $19.95. 192 pgs., 5 ×
         8 in. Report No. 5: *How to Wipe Out Your Debts Without Bankruptcy.* $19.95.
         152 pgs. Each book is also available on a cassette tape which duplicates
         the entire content of the report. The tapes are priced at $19.95 each
         and run 60 minutes. Please specify which tape you want when order-
         ing; the tape title duplicates the report title.

IWS-32   ***GOOD MONTHLY INCOME*** gives you a way to earn money every month
         via mail order selling books and kits to people seeking a business of
         their own. With this plan the money comes to you and you keep a large
         share of it for yourself. $15. 36 pgs., 8½ × 11 in.

IWS-33   ***HOW TO BUY A BUSINESS WITH NO MONEY DOWN*** by Jeryn W.
         Calhoun. Gives step-by-step guidance on how to figure the value of a
         business; negotiating with the seller; no-money-down strategies; doz-
         ens of sample forms to help you buy right; startups vs. existing
         businesses; rules of thumb for pricing a business; understanding the
         P & L statement; making an offer that's right for you; financing the
         business you buy; effective closes when buying; legal considerations
         for you; closing checklist for any business. 110 pgs., 8½ × 11 in., paper-
         back, $19.50; First Class Shipping $4 extra.

IWS-34   ***HOW TO MAKE A FORTUNE AS A LICENSING AGENT*** by Tyler G.
         Hicks. Shows the reader how to earn big fees bringing together one
         company wanting to license its industrial or entertainment products
         and another seeking to use these products. Gives examples of typical

products licensed, agreements covering the license, plus where to find suitable items to license. 66 pgs., 8½ × 11 in., paperback, $15.00; First Class Shipping $4 extra.

IWS-35   *HOW TO RUN A PROFITABLE CHILD-CARE REFERRAL SERVICE* by William Frederick. Gives a comprehensive coverage of this much-needed business in today's working-mother world. Topics include starting your child-care referral center, assessing your community's child-care needs, recruiting child-care providers, marketing your services, day-to-day operations, child-care resource directory, sample letters, forms, and a prewritten news release. $22.95. 64 pgs.

IWS-36   *SUCCESSFUL FINANCING TECHNIQUES FOR BUSINESS AND REAL ESTATE* by Tyler G. Hicks. This comprehensive book covers how, and where, to get loans for any business; getting venture capital today; finding free-money grants; going public to get money that never need be repaid; making big money in your own business; proven money-making results for real estate; mail-order success secrets; building riches in exporting. $24.95. 96 pgs. Includes three bonus items related to the book's topics.

IWS-37   *HOW TO BE A SECOND MORTGAGE LOAN BROKER* by Richard Brisky. Shows the reader how to make money as a second mortgage loan broker. Covers these important topics—why second mortgages; how to get started; starting on a part-time basis; the money broker/finder business; glossary of real estate and mortgage terms; how to get clients; how to handle loan inquiries; advance fees; commissions; loan presentation; think like a lender; what a difference a point makes; the truth in lending law; the Fair Credit Reporting Act; the Equal Credit Opportunity Act; the Fair Debt Collection Practices Act; how to help financially distressed people when you can't get their loan approved; you will learn many things in dealing with lenders; other prime loan projects; other types of loans; mortgage payment tables; it's almost time to get started; second mortgage money sources; 90 pgs., 8½ × 11 in., paperback, $25; First Class Shipping $4 extra.

IWS-38   *HOW TO START AND FINANCE A BUSINESS THAT WORKS FOR YOU* by Tyler G. Hicks. This big book covers turning your wealth-building dreams into reality; making a business of your own work for you; smart ways to get loans for your business or others; building your wealth in exporting; keys to mail-order business success; making riches in real estate like a professional; great ways to get venture capital today; getting the credit you deserve; how to get money that does not need to be repaid. $24.75. 96 pgs. Includes three bonus items related to the book's topics.

IWS-39   *YOU CAN GET THE MONEY! How to Finance Your Small Business Startup or Expansion* by Robert Highman. Big, useful book covers many topics including: how to borrow $90,000 from a stranger in 5 days; earn $15,000 a month buying and selling assets you don't own; invest $500 to raise $329,000 to make $108,000 in one year; go from near-bankruptcy to $117,000 in credit cards; free advertising for your offer in over 100 trade journals; from zero to 100,000 letters per week in mail order; how to increase your business 62% in 2 years; how 100% was borrowed to buy a building for retirement; raise enough money in 17 hours to buy 3 brand new Cadillacs; includes nearly 1,000 lenders, with over 300 microloan lenders; plus much more. $59.50. 348 pgs.

IWS-40   *OPTIONS REPORT* covers real estate options, explaining what an option is, using an option, getting the option, locating properties to option, and how to use options to build your wealth in non-real-estate real estate. $20. 16 pgs., 8½ × 11 in.

NEWSLETTERS

IWSN-1   *INTERNATIONAL WEALTH SUCCESS.* Ty Hicks' monthly newsletter published 12 times a year. This 16-page newsletter covers loan and grant sources, real estate opportunities, business opportunities, import-export, mail order, and a variety of other topics on making money in your own business. Every subscriber can run one free classified advertisement of 40 words, or less, each month, covering business or real estate needs or opportunities. The newsletter has a worldwide circulation, giving readers and advertisers very broad coverage. Started in January 1967, the newsletter has been published continuously since that date. $24.00 per year. 16 pgs. plus additional inserts, 8½ × 11 in., monthly.

IWSN-2   *MONEY WATCH BULLETIN,* a monthly coverage of 100 or more active lenders for real estate and business purposes. The newsletter gives the lender's name, address, telephone number, lending guidelines, loan ranges, and other helpful information. All lender names were obtained within the last week; the data is therefore right up to date. Lenders' names and addresses are also provided on self-stick labels on an occasional basis. Also covers venture capital and grants. $95.00. 20 pgs., 8½ × 11 in., monthly, 12 times per year.

SUCCESS KITS

K-1   *FINANCIAL BROKER/FINDER/BUSINESS BROKER/CONSULTANT SUC-CESS KIT* shows YOU how to start your PRIVATE business as a financial broker/finder/business broker/consultant! As a financial broker YOU find money for firms seeking capital and YOU are paid a fee. As a finder YOU are paid a fee for finding things (real estate, raw materials, money, etc.) for people and firms. As a business broker YOU help in the buying or selling of a business—again for a fee. See how to collect BIG fees. Kit includes typical agreement YOU can use, plus four colorful membership cards (each 8 × 10 in.). Only $99.50. 12 Speed-Read books, 485 pgs., 8½ × 11 in., 4 membership cards.

K-2   *STARTING MILLIONAIRE SUCCESS KIT* shows YOU how to get started in a number of businesses which might make YOU a millionaire sooner than YOU think! Businesses covered in this big kit include mail order, real estate, export-import, limited partnerships, etc. This big kit includes four colorful membership cards (each 8 × 10 in.). These are

NOT the same ones as in the Financial Broker kit. So ORDER your
STARTING MILLIONAIRE KIT now—only $99.50. 12 Speed-Read
books, 361 pgs., 8½ × 11 in., 4 membership cards.

K-3   ***FRANCHISE RICHES SUCCESS KIT*** is the only one of its kind in the
world (we believe). What this big kit does is show YOU how to collect
BIG franchise fees for YOUR business ideas which can help others make
money! So instead of paying to use ideas, people PAY YOU to use YOUR
ideas! Franchising is one of the biggest businesses in the world today.
Why don't YOU get in on the BILLIONS of dollars being grossed in
this business today? Send $99.50 for your FRANCHISE KIT now. 7
Speed-Read books, 876 pgs., 6 × 9 & 8½ × 11 in. & 5 × 8 in.

K-4   ***MAIL-ORDER RICHES SUCCESS KIT*** shows YOU how YOU can make a
million in mail order/direct mail, using the known and proven methods of the experts. This is a kit which is different (we think) from any
other—and BETTER than any other! It gives YOU the experience of
known experts who've made millions in their own mail order businesses,
or who've shown others how to do that. This big kit also includes the
Ty Hicks' book *How I Grossed More Than One Million Dollars in Mail Or-
der/Direct Mail Starting with NO CASH and Less Knowhow.* So send $99.50
TODAY for your MAIL-ORDER SUCCESS KIT. 9 Speed-Read books,
927 pgs., 6 × 9 & 8½ × 11 in.

K-5   ***ZERO CASH SUCCESS TECHNIQUES KIT*** shows YOU how to get started
in YOUR own going business or real estate venture with NO CASH!
Sound impossible? It really IS possible—as thousands of folks have
shown. This big kit, which includes a special book by Ty Hicks on *Zero
Cash Takeovers of Business and Real Estate,* also includes a 58-minute cassette tape by Ty on "Small Business Financing." On this tape, Ty talks to
YOU! See how YOU can get started in YOUR own business without
cash and with few credit checks. To get your ZERO CASH SUCCESS
KIT, send $99.50 NOW. 7 Speed-Read books, 876 pgs., 8½ × 11 in. for
most, 58-minute cassette tape.

K-6   ***REAL ESTATE RICHES SUCCESS KIT*** shows YOU how to make BIG
money in real estate as an income property owner, a mortgage broker, mortgage banker, real estate investment trust operator, mortgage
money broker, raw land speculator, and industrial property owner.
This is a general kit, covering all these aspects of real estate, plus
many, many more. Includes many financing sources for YOUR real
estate fortune. But this big kit also covers how to buy real estate for
the lowest price (down payments of NO CASH can sometimes be set
up), and how to run YOUR real estate for biggest profits. Send $99.50
NOW for your REAL ESTATE SUCCESS KIT. 6 Speed-Read books,
466 pgs., 8½ × 11 in.

K-7   ***BUSINESS BORROWERS COMPLETE SUCCESS KIT*** shows YOU how and
where to BORROW money for any business which interests YOU. See
how to borrow money like the professionals do! Get YOUR loans faster,
easier because YOU know YOUR way around the loan world! This big
kit includes many practice forms so YOU can become an expert in
preparing acceptable loan applications. Also includes hundreds of loan

sources YOU might wish to check for YOUR loans. Send $99.50 NOW for your BUSINESS BORROWERS KIT. 7 Speed-Read books, 596 pgs., 8½ × 11 in.

K-8   *RAISING MONEY FROM GRANTS AND OTHER SOURCES SUCCESS KIT* shows YOU how to GET MONEY THAT DOES NOT HAVE TO BE REPAID if YOU do the task for which the money was advanced. This big kit shows YOU how and where to raise money for a skill YOU have which can help others live a better life. And, as an added feature, this big kit shows YOU how to make a fortune as a fund raiser—that great business in which YOU get paid for collecting money for others or for yourself. This kit shows YOU how you can collect money to fund deals YOU set up. To get your GRANTS KIT, send $99.50 NOW. 7 Speed-Read books, 496 pgs., 8½ × 11 in. for most.

K-9   *FAST FINANCING OF YOUR REAL ESTATE FORTUNE SUCCESS KIT* shows YOU how to raise money for real estate deals. YOU can move ahead faster if YOU can finance your real estate quickly and easily. This is NOT the same kit as the R.E. RICHES KIT listed above. Instead, the FAST FINANCING KIT concentrates on GETTING THE MONEY YOU NEED for YOUR real estate deals. This big kit gives YOU more than 2,500 sources of real estate money all over the U.S. It also shows YOU how to find deals which return BIG income to YOU but are easier to finance than YOU might think! To get started in FAST FINANCING, send $99.50 today. 7 Speed-Read books, 523 pgs., 8½ × 11 in. for most.

K-10   *LOANS BY PHONE KIT* shows YOU how and where to get business, real estate, and personal loans by telephone. With just 32 words and 15 seconds of time YOU can determine if a lender is interested in the loan you seek for yourself or for someone who is your client—if you're working as a loan broker or finder. This kit gives you hundreds of telephone lenders. About half have 800 phone numbers, meaning that your call is free of long-distance charges. Necessary agreement forms are also included. This blockbuster kit has more than 150 pgs. 8½ × 11 in. Send $100 now and get started in one hour.

K-11   *LOANS BY MAIL KIT* shows YOU how and where to get business, real estate, and personal loans for yourself and others by mail. Lists hundreds of lenders who loan by mail. No need to appear in person—just fill out the loan application and send it in by mail. Many of these lenders give unsecured signature loans to qualified applicants. Use this kit to get a loan by mail yourself. Or become a loan broker and use the kit to get started. Unsecured signature loans by mail can go as high as $50,000 and this kit lists such lenders. The kit has more than 150 pgs. 8½ × 11 in. Send $100 now to get started in just a few minutes.

K-12   *REAL ESTATE LOAN GETTERS SERVICE KIT* shows the user how to get real estate loans for either a client or the user. Lists hundreds of active real estate lenders seeking first and junior mortgage loans for a variety of property types. Loan amounts range from a few thousand dollars to many millions, depending on the property, its location, and value. Presents typical application and agreement forms for use in securing real estate loans. *No* license is required to obtain such loans for oneself or others. Kit contains more than 150 pages., 8½ × 11 in. Send $100 now to get started.

K-13   *CASH CREDIT RICHES SYSTEM KIT* shows the user three ways to make money from credit cards: (1) as a merchant account, (2) helping others get credit cards of their choice, and (3) getting loans through lines of credit offered to credit card holders. Some people handling merchant account orders report an income as high as $10,000 a day. While this kit does not, and will not, guarantee such an income level, it *does* show the user how to get started making money from credit cards easily and quickly. The kit has more than 150 pgs., 8½ × 11 in. Send $100 now to get started soon.

K-14   *PROFESSIONAL PRACTICE BUILDERS KIT* shows YOU how to make up to $1,000 a week part time, over $5,000 a week full time, according to the author, Dr. Alan Weisman. What YOU do is show professionals— such as doctors, dentists, architects, accountants, lawyers—how to bring more clients into the office and thereby increase their income. Step-by-step procedure gets you started. Provides forms, sample letters, brochures, and fliers YOU can use to get an income flowing into your bank in less than one week. The kit has more than 150 pgs., 8½ × 11 in. Send $100 now! Start within just a few hours in your local area.

K-15   *VENTURE CAPITAL MILLIONS KITS.* Shows how to raise venture capital for yourself or for others. Gives steps for preparing an Executive Summary, business plan, etc. You can use the kit to earn large fees raising money for new or established firms. $100. 200 pgs.

K-16   *GUARANTEED LOAN MONEY.* Shows how to get loans of all types— unsecured signature, business, real estate, etc.—when your credit is not the strongest. Gives full directions on getting cosigners, comakers, and guarantors. $100. 250 pgs.

K-17   *IMPORT-EXPORT RICHES KIT* shows you how to get rich in import-export in today's product-hungry world. This big kit takes you from your first day in the business to great success. It gives you 5,000 products wanted by overseas firms, the name and address of each firm, procedures for preparing export-import documents, how to correspond in four different languages with complete sentences and letters, names and addresses of freight forwarders you can use, plus much more. Includes more than 6 books of over 1,000 pages of useful information. $99.50.

K-18   *PHONE-IN/MAIL-IN GRANTS KIT.* This concise kit shows the reader how to jump on the grants bandwagon and get small or large money grants quickly and easily. Gives typical grant proposals and shows how to write each so you win the grant you seek. Takes the reader by the hand and shows how to make telephone calls to grantors to find if they're interested in your grant request. You are given the actual words to use in your call and in your proposal. Also includes a list of foundations that might consider your grant application. $100. 200 pgs., 8½ × 11 in.

K-19   *MEGA MONEY METHODS* covers the raising of large amounts of money—multimillions and up—for business and real estate projects of all types. Shows how to prepare loan packages for very large loans, where to get financing for such loans, what fees to charge after the loan is obtained, plus much more. Using this kit, the BWB should be able to prepare effective loan requests for large amounts of money for suitable projects. The kit also gives the user a list of offshore lenders for big projects. $100. 200 pgs., 8½ × 11 in.

K-20   *FORECLOSURES AND OTHER DISTRESSED PROPERTY SALES* shows how and where to make money from foreclosures, trustee sales, IRS sales, bankruptcies, and sheriff sales of real estate. The kit contains six cassette tapes plus a workbook containing many of the forms you need in fore-closure and trustee sales. Addresses of various agencies handling such sales are also given. $51.95. 80 pgs. and 6 cassette tapes, 8½ × 11 in.

K-21   *SMALL BUSINESS LOAN PROGRAM* is designed to obtain loans for small and minority-owned businesses doing work for government agencies, large corporations, hospitals, universities, and similar organizations. The small business loan program pays up to 80 percent on accounts receivable within 48 hours to manufacturers, distributors, janitorial services, building contractors, etc. Startups acceptable. You earn a good commission getting these loans funded, and receive an ongoing pay-ment when the company places future accounts receivable with the lender. $100. 200 pgs., 8½ × 11 in.

K-22   *PHONE-IN MINI-LEASE PROGRAM* helps you earn commissions getting leases for a variety of business equipment—personal computers, copy machines, typewriters, laser printers, telephone systems, office furniture, satellite antennas, store fixtures, etc. You earn direct commissions of 3 percent to 10 percent of the cost of the equipment up to $10,000. You get immediate approval of the lease by phone and the lender finances the equipment for the company needing it. Your commission is paid by the lender directly to you. $100. 150 pgs., 8½ × 11 in.

K-23   *THE FORTUNE BUILDERS PROGRAM KIT* shows you how to get rich in your spare time at home in mail order/direct mail, rental real es-tate, specialized consulting, venture capital, export-import, finder's fees, financial brokerage, projects using 100% financing, and many unusual businesses. You get personal, on-the-phone, step-by-step supervision from IWS on selecting, starting, and getting rich in your own business. And—if you wish—you can visit IWS to get face-to-face help for your new business. This kit will help you get started in any—or all—of these businesses. $300.00. 1000 pgs.

K-24   *MERCHANT ACCOUNT KIT* shows you how and where a new or long-established business can obtain merchant status so it can accept credit card charges for its sales of products or services to customers. This big kit features typical applications for merchant accounts and shows the user how to fill out the forms for maximum chance of success. It gives sources of merchant accounts for all types of businesses—such as store-front, home-based non-swipe, telemarketing, flea-market, garage and tag sale. Many users of this kit have successfully obtained their own merchant account for their business. $100.00. 200 pgs., 8½ × 11 in.

K-25   ***HARD MONEY COMMERCIAL REAL ESTATE LOANS KIT*** has a 4-hour+ video showing exactly how to get these loans. A fully illustrated manual gives you the forms you need, along with the steps to fill them out so you have a better chance of getting the loan you need. Loans range from $300,000 to $20 million+; close in 1–3 weeks; nationwide lending; minimal documentation needed; short-form appraisals accepted; flexible loan structures. You can use this kit to get loans for yourself, or for others, and earn a nice commission on the transaction. $150. Video and 90-page manual.

K-26   ***EXECUTIVE REPRESENTATIVE SALES PLAN KIT*** allows you to sell all IWS products—newsletters, kits, and books by any normal means (mail order, direct mail, telemarketing, Internet, e-mail, or face-to-face)— and earn a commission starting at 40% of the list price ($40 on a $100 list price) and rising to 50% for life after $2,000 in total list-price sales. You do *not* have to carry any inventory, do *not* have to make any shipments, do *not* have to send a bill to your customers. You are supplied camera-ready ads, along with sample classified ads, plus pre-written promotion materials, and an agreement covering your independent contractor status with IWS. A 5-year subscription to the IWS newsletter is given to you when you become an Executive Rep. $120.00.

K-27   ***AUTO AND TRUCK LEASING KIT*** shows you how to work directly with leasing companies to earn a commission on lease customers you bring to them. This big kit gives you a Startup Manual showing you how to work with potential lease customers and the companies who finance auto and truck leases. It gives you typical lease application forms, ads you can run to find potential customers, plus much more. So if you're interested in working—part-time—as a lease referral commission agent, this kit can help you get started. $100. 150 pgs., 8½ × 11 in.

K-28   ***REAL ESTATE INVESTMENT TRUST RICHES KIT*** shows you how to start and prosper in your own Real Estate Investment Trust (REIT). Your REIT can be an equity REIT which owns any kind of real estate from apartment houses to motels; a mortgage REIT in which you lend money from your REIT to real estate investors for their holdings; or a hybrid REIT which combines ownership and mortgage lending. A brokerage house raises money from public or private investors to fund your REIT. This Kit shows you exactly how to get started, where to find a suitable broker, and what types of real estate or mortgages to hold in your REIT. The money raised for your REIT never has to be repaid. 500 pages, 8 1/2 × 11 in. paperback; $100.

Besides his longer books, such as the one you are now holding, Ty Hicks has written a number of books he calls *Slims*—that is, thin books slim enough to fit into a person's back pocket or purse. Each of these *Slims* is 5 × 8 inches in trim size. The titles alone are listed below because they—in general—describe the content of each *Slim*.

S-1   *Build Your Wealth with a Powerful Real Estate Tool—Foreclosures,*
        74 pgs., $12.50.

S-2   *How to Buy Up to Two Properties a Month with No Down Payment,*
        82 pgs., $12.50.

S-3   *Real Estate Can Make You Rich—in Good Times and Bad Times,*
        68 pgs., $12.50.

S-4   *How to Earn a Fast-Fortune Guaranteed Income in a Little-Known Dollar-Rich Business,* 64 pgs., $12.50.

S-5   *100 Ways to Make One Million Dollars Quickly in Real Estate Starting with No Cash,* 78 pgs., $12.50.

S-6   *Secrets of Building Great Riches Fast in a One-Person Business That Is Hassle-Free,* 64 pgs., $12.50.

S-7   *Successful Creative Money Borrowing Techniques for Business,*
        96 pgs., $12.50.

S-8   *Big and Easy Moneymaking Ideas for Finders, Beginning Wealth Builders, and Licensing Agents,* 72 pgs., $12.50.

S-9   *Mail Order/Direct Mail Fast Wealth Success Secrets, Including Building Riches in Import/ Export,* 60 pgs., $12.50.

S-10   *Make a Bundle in Real Estate Using Borrowed Money Techniques,*
        70 pgs., $12.50.

S-11   *Tips for Using OPM and Mortgaging Out to Make Real Estate Millions,*
        74 pgs., $12.50.

S-12   *Sure Steps for Raising Money for Real Estate Wealth Accumulation,*
        66 pgs., $12.50.

S-13   *How to Build Great Real Estate Riches Quickly Using Creative Financing,*
        82 pgs., $12.50.

When ordered in quantities of 4, 8, or 13, the cost of each of the above *Slims* is $10. Thus, 4 *Slims* = $40; 8 *Slims* = $80; 13 *Slims* = $130. For other quantities, the price is $12.50 each, which includes postage and handling. Order by using book numbers (for example—S-1, S-2) instead of titles. To receive a copy of the IWS 48-page catalog, send $5.00 to IWS, Inc., P.O. Box 186, Merrick, NY 11566-0186.

INDEX

267